Music of Japan Today

Music of Japan Today

Edited by

E. Michael Richards and Kazuko Tanosaki

Cambridge Scholars Publishing

Music of Japan Today, Edited by E. Michael Richards and Kazuko Tanosaki

This book first published 2008 by

Cambridge Scholars Publishing

15 Angerton Gardens, Newcastle, NE5 2JA, UK

British Library Cataloguing in Publication Data
A catalogue record for this book is available from the British Library

ISBN (10): 1-84718-562-2, ISBN (13): 9781847185624

TABLE OF CONTENTS

Part I: Composer Lectures and Discussions

Part II: Essays on Contemporary Japanese Music

LIST OF ILLUSTRATIONS

LIST OF TABLES

PREFACE

During our more than twenty-five years performing and organizing events of contemporary Japanese music, we have become indebted to many people and organizations. We are especially grateful to Professor Joji Yuasa, our teacher beginning in 1981 at the University of California, San Diego. When Hamilton College asked us in 1991 to recommend a distinguished Asian artist to present a talk, sponsored by the Mellon Foundation, he accepted our invitation, which proved to be the start of the *Music of Japan Today* symposia. Over the years, Professor Yuasa has generously given his time to us on many occasions, and we have learned much from him.

We began the series of international symposia that form the frame for this book in 1992 (*Music of Japan Today: Tradition and Innovation*), and continued in 1994, 1997, 1999 (*Asian Music in America: A Confluence of Two Worlds*), 2003 and 2007 (*Music of Japan Today*). During this time, we have received a variety of international, national and local support. We are especially grateful to the Embassy of Japan (Washington, DC) and All Nippon Airways, under the auspices of which the 2003 and 2007 symposia were presented, and to the distinguished composers who participated since 1992: Shirotomo Aizawa, Masao Endo, Masao Honma, Toshi Ichiyanagi, Hiroyuki Itoh, Harue Kunieda, Bun-Ching Lam, Masataka Matsuo, Isao Matsushita, Tokuhide Niimi, Akira Nishimura, P.Q. Phan, Toshimitsu Tanaka, Richard Tsang, Hiroyuki Yamamoto, and Joji Yuasa.

Music of Japan Today symposia have received additional support from the Japan-United States Friendship Commission (Washington, DC), the Japan Foundation Tokyo and Japan Foundation NY, the Asian Cultural Council (NY), the Association for Asian Studies (Ann Arbor), the Freer Gallery of the Smithsonian Institution (Washington, DC), the National Cherry Blossom Festival (Washington, DC), the Maryland State Arts Council, an agency funded by the State of Maryland and the National Endowment for the Arts, the Japan Commerce Association of Washington DC, the Shimadzu Corporation, the Selmer Corporation, and the Syracuse Society for New Music.

We would like to express our thanks to the University of Maryland, Baltimore County and Hamilton College for their financial support, and also to Freeman A. Hrabowski, III, president of UMBC; Arthur Johnson, provost of UMBC; Sheldon K. Caplis, vice president, Institutional Advancement UMBC; John Jeffries, dean of the College of Arts, Humanities, and Social Sciences UMBC; Thomas Moore, director of arts and culture, Institutional Advancement UMBC; Eugene Tobin, president of Hamilton College; Bobby Fong, dean of Hamilton College; and the Class of 1940 Cultural Endowment Fund at Hamilton College.

In the Department of Music at UMBC, we extend our heartfelt appreciation to Linda Dusman, Chair, who has selflessly supported and encouraged our work. We also thank our many colleagues and staff members of the music departments at UMBC and Hamilton College for their artistic and organizational contributions. Finally, we offer special thanks to the hundreds of students who have participated in the six symposia – we hope that the spirit of artistic cooperation, scholarly investigation, and cross-cultural understanding that they experienced will remain in their lives.

With regard to this book, we thank European American Music, Schott Music Japan, Mannheim Musikverlag, Chester Music Limited, and C.F. Peters Corporation for permission to reprint excerpts from their scores. We also express thanks to composers Hiroyuki Itoh, Hiroyuki Yamamoto, Shirotomo Aizawa, Marty Regan, and Koji Nakano for supplying recordings and copies of their musical scores. For the chapter on computer music, we extend our gratitude to Takayuki Rai, Daichi Ando, Shintaro Imai, Naotoshi Osaka, and Hideko Kawamoto for sending us recordings of their music. Finally, we are grateful to *shakuhachi* virtuoso Retsuzan Tanabe, and composer Shirotomo Aizawa for writing about *Music of Japan Today 2007* for Japan's *Hogaku Journal*.

Thanks also to Cambridge Scholars Publishing for taking on this project, and especially Amanda Millar and Carol Koulikourdi for all of their work and advice.

Finally, we would like to dedicate this book to Kazuo and Minako Tanosaki, and Edwin and Janet Richards.

In the text that follows, we have attempted to be consistent in our use of the Hepburn system of transliteration of Japanese words. Also, following Western practice, we spell Japanese names first name first, last name last.

INTRODUCTION

This book is an outcome of work put forward by scholars, composers, and performers at the international symposium *Music of Japan Today 2007*, held in Baltimore, Maryland and Washington, DC from March 30-April 1. MOJT 2007 is part of a sequence of events we (Tanosaki and Richards) have established, over fifteen years, dedicated to the examination of cross-cultural elements within Japanese music. The first of these events (1992) was organized at Hamilton College in upstate New York – *Music of Japan Today: Tradition and Innovation*. This symposium was the first in the United States on contemporary Japanese music to couple scholarly presentations with a number of musical performances (including commissions and premieres), and integrated musicians and scholars from Japan, Hong Kong, and a variety of locations in the United States.[1]

Presenters (papers, workshops, panel discussion, performances) at MOJT '92 examined contemporary Japanese music (primarily notated music in the Western art-music tradition) that displayed "a cross-fertilization of aesthetics and musical characteristics from both East and West.....reflective of a variety of aspects of contemporary Japanese society, all of which are deeply rooted in an aesthetic, psychology, and culture that has evolved over many years."[2] The format of the symposium was designed to present views of insider and outsider (as defined by both ethnic/national and geographical/cultural identity), musician/scholar and non-musician/scholar, and music specialists who represented each step in the process from idea to sound: creator (composer), re-creator (performer), and listener/analyst. At the heart of the gathering were three distinguished Japanese composers, representing three different generations: Joji Yuasa (b.1929), Tokuhide Niimi (b.1948), and Masataka Matsuo (b.1959). These composers presented their musical ideas in several different formats: lectures, master-classes with performers, and a panel discussion, in addition to performances.

MOJT '92 led to five other symposia that we directed on topics of contemporary Japanese music (1994, '97, '99, '03, '07) – the first three at Hamilton College, with the most recent two at the University of Maryland, Baltimore County in Baltimore MD, and the Smithsonian National Asian Art Museum (Freer Gallery) in Washington DC.[3] Although the format remained fairly intact, these subsequent symposia were significantly shaped by the participants (many of them from the youngest generation of scholars). New topics arose, and older topics shifted in scope, refocusing the investigations. Since 1994, scholars from an expanding list of backgrounds and specialties have presented their observations at MOJT – anthropologists, sociologists, psychologists, theater historians, dancers, and music educators, as well as musicologists, ethnomusicologists, and theorists from Western Europe, South and Central America, Southeast Asia, Australia, and New Zealand have enriched the dialogue.

Additional perspectives have been advanced by Japanese composers/musicians not centered in Tokyo (Masao Honma, Mari Akagi), but in less cosmopolitan communities, where the position of traditional Japanese aesthetics and art in everyday life illuminates a different Japan. Also, an increased diversity of perceptions has been brought forth from composers ranging in age from their early thirties to late seventies. Equally important insights on Japan's music and its place within Asian music have likewise been provided by composers born and educated in the cultural milieus of Hong Kong (Richard Tsang), Macau (Bun-Ching Lam), and Vietnam (P.Q. Phan), as well as composers of Japan or other areas of Asia who immigrated or spent a significant amount of time living and creating music in the United States (Hiroyuki Itoh) or Europe (Isao Matsushita).

Also reflected in the background of MOJT participants during these fifteen years (as well as globally) is an increase in demographic inversion - the growing number of Japanese/Asian musicians studying Western music in the US and Europe, and American/Western musicians studying *hogaku* in Japan.[4] Some have returned to their home countries; others have immigrated. Japanese immigrants have assimilated in varying degrees to new cultures – yet, once outside Japan, a number of musicians have recognized a part of their (musical) thinking that is Japanese, and sought to preserve it and explore its artistic implications. The consequence is a rising number of what could be characterized as sophisticated bilingual cultural brokers. Convenient divisions of musical elements/ideas into East and West have become less distinct (if not impossible). The musical/aesthetic confluence within Japanese music today continues to evolve through a mounting number of conduits, including imitation, adaptation, assimilation, indigenization, transculturation (cross-fertilization), acculturation, syncretism, and synthesis.

The weight given performers' voices in MOJT is a direct outgrowth of our background as performers of contemporary music, especially of Japanese chamber music, since the mid-1980s.[5] To formulate a compelling and faithful interpretation for performance, one must "re-create" the composer's ideas as an insider, identify (as listener/analyst/scholar) the most essential characteristics of the musical work as an outsider, reconcile these views and effectively project the result. We have not only encouraged performers to participate in these symposia, with the hopes of stimulating performances of new repertoire and collaborations resulting in new compositions, but felt that their written/spoken ideas and discussion of this music was essential to a complete and meaningful picture of the topic. It is a significant process from notation on paper to the sound of a complete musical work, so in addition to traditional paper presentations on issues of performance practices (such as new sonic resources, including subtleties of timbre nuances and transformations appropriate to Japanese music), and notation (such as designing more appropriate representations of *portamenti*, silences, and ringing resonances), visiting performers have participated in master classes on particular works by a visiting composer (Nishimura – *Tritrope* for solo piano; Ichiyanagi *Paganini Personal* for solo marimba; Yuasa *Domains* for solo flute), and/or in a performance competition designed to help advance the music towards a place in the standard repertoire (Mayuzumi–*Bunraku*; Takemitsu–*Voice*). With regard to performances at MOJT 2007, close to 40 works of 20 Japanese composers were presented during the symposium, including ten works (four of them premieres) of the three guest composers. These performances included computer music by mid-career composers, chamber music for Western instruments, chamber music for Japanese instruments, and a work for a combined ensemble of Japanese and Western instruments.

This book, like the MOJT symposia, examines various topics concerning cross-cultural confluences in contemporary Japanese art-music through multiple approaches and views from composers, performers, and scholars. It is neither comprehensive in scope nor detail – a number of recent publications in English are available to provide a greater depth of historic, aesthetic, or cultural context.[6]

In Part I, three Japanese composers of international stature discuss their compositional techniques as well as aesthetic orientations, together with how these views have been constructed. Excerpts from interviews and the symposium's panel discussion, in addition to a brief analysis of Hiroyuki Itoh's *String Quartet* by theorist David Pacun, provide supportive material. The three composers represent a generation born after 1960 – mid-career composers who were pupils of leading composers from the postwar generations of Yuasa, Miyoshi, Ikebe, Noda, and Kondo.

Hiroyuki Itoh, a winner of international composition prizes in Europe and Japan (including the prestigious Akutagawa Award), has been commissioned and performed by major ensembles including the New Japan Philharmonic, the Nieuw Ensemble, and the Arditti Quartet. Hiroyuki Yamamoto, whose works have been performed at Forum '91 (Montreal), Gaudeamus Music Week '94 (Holland), and ISCM World Music Days (2000 in Luxembourg and 2001 in Yokohama), has received prizes for his work, including the Japan Music Competition, Toru Takemitsu Composition Award, and Akutagawa Award. Shirotomo Aizawa, winner of an Ataka Prize, and composition prize from the National Theater in Japan, has studied composition in Tokyo, Berlin, and Vienna, and conducting with Seiji Ozawa, among others.

The body of the book (Part II) contains nineteen essays by scholars and creative musicians, grouped under five broad sections, arranged in a general sort of chronological frame:

1. Politics and Music: Japan, World War II, and its Aftermath
2. Beyond Tradition: Recent Perspectives on Toru Takemitsu's Music and Legacy
3. Cross-Cultural Uses of Japanese and Western Instruments
4. Mid-Career Japanese Composers and their Work with Computer Music
5. Four Japanese Societies and their Current Music: Communities Within Japan, and "Offshore" Japan

The two essays in Section One focus on connections of the music and ideas of Japanese composers to Japan's politics before, during, and after the Second World War. David Pacun (*Style and Politics in Kosaku Yamada's Folksong Arrangements, 1917-1950*) provides an analysis of the relationship between composer Kosaku Yamada's deepening exploration of Japanese folksong (projecting an evocative sonic space that anticipates the explicit spatial characteristics of some post-war Japanese composition), and Japan's own budding militarism (considering whether it is possible to link changes in musical style to changes in society). Fuyuko Fukunaka (*A Japanese Zero-Hour?- Postwar Music and the "Re-making" of the Past*) examines individual composers' personal attempts to re-define themselves – their writings on the role(s) of (their) music during this time, possibly as evidence of their response to the ideological revolution "from above" – and, the twelve-tone technique of post-war composers as a catalyst for constructing a new identity.

Since his death in 1996, a number of important publications about the life and work of Takemitsu have been released. In Section Two, three papers present and analyze recent research – two of them concern contemporary readings of his music. Mitsuko Ono, a Japanese musicologist, discusses Takemitsu's use of *sawari* - a complex single sound containing many overtones, commonly heard in music for *biwa*, but which also exists in Takemitsu's music for Western instruments. She takes up the question of how Takemitsu's usage of *sawari* for Western instruments is different than that found in the traditional instrument repertoire. An essay by Hideaki Onishi examines three "Japanese garden" works of Takemitsu through a new set theory concept. According to Onishi, pitch structure in these compositions can be looked at as a seemingly random recurrence of a referential sonority and its derivatives, which is not dissimilar to the view of an object seen from various angles in a Japanese garden (a metaphor often used by Takemitsu with regard to a large number of his works). Finally, the role of the Western press in the emergence of Takemitsu as Japan's most recognized international composer is scrutinized by Peter Burt, a leading Takemitsu scholar and author of *The Music of Toru Takemitsu*.

The essays of Section Three investigate innovative, cross-cultural uses of Japanese and Western instruments, shaped by historical traditions, physical design, and acoustic characteristics and constraints. Musical examples from works of Yuasa, Hosokawa, K. Tanaka, Ishii, Mayuzumi, Nakano, Nishimura, Matsuo, and others are considered. Some of the writings also elaborate on collaborations between composers and performers. Groups of essays are organized according to instrumental families found in both Japanese and Western cultures – flutes, voice, and strings and piano.

Essays by both Stacey Fraser and Colin Holter focus on a single work that involves the voice (Koji Nakano's *Time Song II: Howling Through Time*; Joji Yuasa's *Observations on Weather Forecasts*). Both of these works move the voice outside of the bel canto tradition into extended technical and theatrical worlds. Holter reads Yuasa's work as a complex, dialogic exploration of television phenomena in a chamber music context, which is characterized not only by Yuasa's perspective on popular media, but by his lifelong relationship with *Noh*. Fraser discusses vocal gestures from Nakano's score that incorporate both Western and non-Western vocal techniques, and the composer's intention to portray the spiritual side of particular Japanese rituals associated with ceremonies.

Composer and *hogaku* performer Marty Regan (*Composing for the Shakuhachi*) offers some technical and practical resources for composers to explore the possibilities and constraints of the *shakuhachi*, with special attention paid towards new and innovative repertoire. With regard to the Western flute, Antares Boyle (*Flute Works of Toshio Hosokawa*) identifies and explores over-arching and recurring aesthetic concepts found in three solo flute works.

Grouped with writings here that involve string instruments is one which concentrates on a work for the piano (described as a "Western *koto*" during the Meiji era). Similar sonic ground is found among these instruments through their common usage in the music under investigation – percussive, plucked sounds, and nuances of timbre transformations (including resonances). Marty Regan introduces this group through his look at the *koto* (*Composing for the Twenty-One-String Koto*), including problems inherent in cross-cultural ensemble writing. Hugh Livingston describes the many techniques he has developed to realize sounds of traditional Asian instruments for the modern cello (*Adaptations of Performance Style from Early Modern Japan to the Contemporary Cello*), including narrator/*shamisen*/drums for use in Toshiro Mayuzumi's *Bunraku*. Different examples of *ma* are identified and discussed by Airi Yoshioka in violin works by Hosokawa, K. Tanaka, and Ishii (*"Ma" (sense of time) as Compositional Tool*). Finally, pianist Kazuko Tanosaki examines Joji Yuasa's concepts of temporality and cosmos reflected in his masterpiece for solo piano *Cosmos Haptic II: Transfiguration*.

The last essay of Section Three details performer/composer collaborations between several Japanese composers and E. Michael Richards (clarinet). He reveals how the resulting music represents consolidation of extended traditions: a merging of recent research into extended techniques for the Western clarinet, derived from acoustic principles of the instrument, with aesthetics, materials, and underlying musical syntax borrowed from traditional Japanese music and culture (*The Clarinet of the Twenty-First Century and Recent Music by Japanese Composers*).

Section Four describes the encounters of mid-career Japanese composers with computer music. A number of these composers, though born in Japan, have either trained or worked extensively in the United States or Europe (serious computer music studios for music and research were not established in Japan until the 1990s). These composers and their music include a tape work of Hideko Kawamoto, a violin and tape work of Karen Tanaka, interactive works by Atau Tanaka, and music for robots by Suguru Goto. A second group of computer composers (Daichi Ando, Shintaro Imai) trained at the Sonology Department at the Kunitachi College of Music (Tokyo), under the tutelage of Takayuki Rai and visiting

American professor Cort Lippe. Finally, Japanese composers who have trained and worked primarily in Japan are represented by Hiroyuki Yamamoto and Naotoshi Osaka.

Four sub-groups of Japanese society and their current music are examined in Section Five. David Hebert explores how music changes sonically and when crossing cultural boundaries during the adoption of the wind band genre in Japan (*Alchemy of Brass: Spirituality and Wind Music in Japan*). Yann Leblanc, a French anthropologist/ethnomusicologist, writes about links between sound and the body, sound and space in the work of sound artists within Tokyo's avant-garde music community - Toshiya Tsunoda, Toshimaru Nakamura, and Sachiko M (*Sonorous Bodies*). Identity paradoxes concerning Japanese composers living in England, trained in Western art-music, who are writing for Japanese *hogaku* instruments that are unfamiliar (performed by British musicians who have studied extensively in Japan), is discussed (*Identity Tactics of Japanese Composers in the Multicultural UK*) by Yumi Hara Cawkwell (a Japanese composer living in England). Finally, Noriko Manabe looks at cell phone *chaku-uta* (ringtones) and their role in the Japanese music market (*Ring My Bell: Cell Phones and the Japanese Music Market*). She argues how unique aspects of the Japanese cultural environment affect the development of this market, and identifies possible implications for other music markets.

Reading about the music discussed in *Music of Japan Today* is incomplete without an opportunity to hear it. This presents special problems since some of the music is not yet recorded, or recorded on small company labels. The reader is referred to the discography in this book on page 277, which includes websites with available scores and sound files. In addition, we have created a webpage, to be periodically updated, that contains sound-clips and further information about available recordings http://userpages.umbc.edu/~emrich/mfj2007.htm.

We hope that *Music of Japan Today* could be useful as supplemental reading for university undergraduate or graduate level courses on twentieth/twenty-first century music, Japanese, Asian, and World music and culture, and that it will, in some way, stimulate future research of the topics presented, as well as collaboration, artistic creation, and artistic re-creation in wide-ranging performances of music of Japan.

Notes

1. MOJT was structured differently from the well-known concert series in New York, *Music From Japan*, which did not present views from scholars.
2. topics did not only relate to notated music in the Western art-music tradition, but also popular music and *hogaku*. See http://home.sprintmail.com/~emrichards/musjapan.html for a list of presenters, abstracts, concert programs and notes, etc.
3. see Appendix A for listing of participants, paper topics, and works performed, or see http://userpages.umbc.edu/~emrich/MFJ2003.html for further information.
4. *hogaku* can be defined as traditional Japanese music, or music derived from "traditional" music, written for Japanese instruments. Richards and Tanosaki organized the symposium "Asian Music in America" in 1999 at Hamilton College, Clinton, New York.
5. see http://userpages.umbc.edu/~emrich/tanosakirichards.html
6. see Galliano 2003, a detailed historical study of Japanese art-music after the Meiji Restoration in the 19th century, and its development through the end of the 20th century. Galliano's book also addresses aesthetical and theoretical aspects of the music. Also see Everett and Lau 2004, a comparative study of Asian-influenced Western composers and Western-influenced Asian composers by music theorists, musicologists, composers, and ethnomusicologists.

References

Everett, Yayoi Uno and Frederick Lau. 2004. *Locating East Asia in Western Art Music*. Wesleyan U. Press.
Galliano, Luciana. 2003. *Yogaku: Japanese Music in the Twentieth Century*. The Scarecrow Press, Inc.

PART I

COMPOSER LECTURES AND DISCUSSIONS

Mid-career Japanese composers (born in the 1960s) are positioned historically as a bridge in the post-war transculturation and assimilation of Western art-music in Japan – too young to have participated in the avant-garde movements after the Second World War, yet old enough to have studied with some of the musical leaders of this first post-war generation.

Hiroyuki Itoh (b.1963), Hiroyuki Yamamoto (b.1967), and Shirotomo Aizawa (b.1962) are composers of international stature who represent three different backgrounds and aesthetic/musical orientations. Itoh, a student of Shin-Ichiro Ikebe in Japan, and Roger Reynolds, Joji Yuasa and Brian Ferneyhough in the United States, has developed a distinctive compositional voice, using primarily quarter-tones in "swaying, flickering" textures. His music is highly virtuosic, and some of his earlier work involves electronic resources as well as ideas expressed through complex and precise notation. Hiroyuki Yamamoto, a student of Jo Kondo, among others, composes virtuosic music that explores shifting cores of sound – it synthesizes elements from Japanese (heterophony) and European (textural) music, yet has a very personal voice that does not sound derivative. Shirotomo Aizawa, a student of Akira Miyoshi, Teruyuki Noda, and Makoto Shinohara, is also a conductor, and writes music for *hogaku* instruments, and for combined *hogaku* and Western instrument ensembles. His music relies on the subtleties of spectral merging in its quest for a synthesis of musical systems.

Hiroyuki Itoh (b. Sakata, Japan) studied music composition at the Tokyo College of Music, and earned a PhD in music from the University of California, San Diego in 1994. After residing in the United States for ten years, he returned to Japan, where he currently teaches at Nihon University and lives in Yokohama. Itoh has written works for solo instrument, chamber ensembles, and orchestra – much of it not only in a musical language of quarter-tones, but with dark textures and an elastic manipulation of time, among other characteristics. He has won prestigious international awards including the first prize at the Nuove Sincronie Competition (1995), a Stipendienpreis at the Darmstadt Ferienkurse

(1996), and the Akutagawa Composition Award for Orchestral Music (1998) in Japan. Itoh has been commissioned by the Suntory Music Foundation, the Akiyoshidai Festival, the Yokohama Culture Foundation, the Klangspuren Festival, and Music From Japan (New York), among others. His works have been performed at major festivals such as Darmstadt, Gaudeamus, ISCM World Music Days (2000 in Luxembourg, 2004 in Switzerland), Klangspuren, June in Buffalo, Akiyoshidai, and Takefu, and by orchestras and ensembles such as the New Japan Philharmonic, Tokyo City Philharmonic Orchestra, Kanagawa Philharmonic Orchestra, Izumi Sinfonietta Osaka, Art Respirant, Nieuw Ensemble, Klangforum Wien, and the Arditti Quartet.

Itoh's comments about his compositional process reveal that he tends to "use textural materials more often compared to many Western composers, who prefer motivic material."[1] He most often breaks his musical material apart into many pieces, rather than combining disparate parts into one. Two of Itoh's works performed at MOJT 2007 displayed some of his recent music. *Salamander 1b* for solo flute (2005) is a re-working of an earlier piece for solo piccolo (1995). The sonic image of the piece was inspired by the mythological reptile that is said to have lived in fire. "Despite this, a salamander is believed to be extremely cold. It is also believed to move very quickly. Once it is out of the fire, however, it dies immediately."[2] Itoh's writing in this piece employs quarter-tones extensively, and the musical materials are constantly changing speeds through complex rhythms that are meticulously notated. In *out of a blaze of light* (2007), a work for clarinet and piano that was premiered at MOJT 2007, Itoh composes a three part structure: an aggressive yet short introductory section where the clarinet's quarter-tone lines are picked up in the pedal resonances of the piano; a long middle section where multiple lines with complex rhythms between the two instruments are juxtaposed and overlapped (never phrasing together); and a final reflective slow/quiet section where the quarter-tone tremolo sequences of varying speeds and rhythms are again "reflected" in the piano resonances.

In his essay *Swaying Sensation and Fragile Beauty*, Itoh discusses the aesthetics from which his music grows – these principles have been dominant in all of his pieces during the last ten years. He points to examples within his compositional language found in *Mirror I* for twelve players (1997). Itoh also writes about the relationship of his aesthetics to the fact that he is a "Japanese" composer.

David Pacun presents an overview of Itoh's *String Quartet* (*Hiroyuki Itoh's String Quartet: Form, Style, and Content)*, written and premiered by the Arditti Quartet in 2002, which both draws upon and extends musical traditions through pitch/interval control, complex polyrhythmic textures, and quarter-tone harmonies. Pacun illustrates through musical examples from the *Quartet* many of the aesthetic/musical ideas mentioned by Itoh in his essay such as distorted time flow and complex superimposition of lines.

Hiroyuki Yamamoto (b. Yamagata Prefecture, Japan), was raised in Zushi City of Kanagawa Prefecture (southwest of Tokyo). He received both his bachelors (1990) and masters (1992) degrees in composition from the Tokyo National University of Fine Arts and Music. Yamamoto's honors and awards include third prize at the Japan Music Competition (1989), JSCM Composition Award (1996), Toru Takemitsu Composition Award (2002) and Akutagawa Award (2003). His works have been selected for Forum '91 (Montreal), Gaudeamus Music Week '94 (Holland), ISCM World Music Days (2000 in Luxembourg and 2001 in Yokohama) and performed by the Nieuw Ensemble (Amsterdam), Symphonieorchester des Bayerischen Rundfunks (Munich), Orchestre Philharmonique de Luxembourg, and the Tokyo Philharmonic Orchestra, among others. Yamamoto is a member of the composers' group TEMPUS NOVUM, which he helped to establish in 1990. He directed the Ensemble d'Ame (Tokyo) for four years from 1997. He currently teaches at Iwate University in Morioka City.

Three acoustic works of Yamamoto were performed at MOJT 2007. In the earliest of these works, *Saxophone The Relay* (1999) for solo alto saxophone, the composer shows an interest in ambiguous sounds by focusing on mechanical noises which are usually hidden behind the traditional sounds of the instrument. Yamamoto comments that

> "the saxophone's noise elements are louder than other wind instruments. But when we combine these noises and very beautiful soft sounds, this particular combined sound raises the saxophone to a special position."[3]

Matsumorphosis (2001) for solo violin is a one minute work written to celebrate composer Yori-aki Matsudaira's 70th birthday. Yamamoto uses the Morse code rhythm of Matsudaira's name to generate elements of the work such as articulations and sounds with different noise content. The source rhythm is hidden within these ambiguous elements. Finally, *The Wedge is Struck, the Fog Remains* (2006) for clarinet and piano, which was premiered at MOJT 2007, is constructed with shifting cores of sound between the two instruments. The clarinet part is written in quarter-tones, and Yamamoto uses complex polyrhythms and overlapping phrases in which the instruments never have rhythmic attacks together, as well as clarinet *portamenti* and muted pitches on the piano, sometimes among three voices (clarinet, piano left hand, piano right hand), to alter the "core of monody" that drives this through-composed piece forward.

Yamamoto discusses his compositional techniques before 2004 (accumulation of ambiguities) and after 2004 (monody with a core used to realize ambiguities) in his essay *My Compositional Technique and Thoughts on the Ambiguity of Sound.*

Shirotomo Aizawa, winner of the Ataka Prize, and composition prize from the National Theater in Japan, completed his undergraduate and graduate studies in music composition under full scholarship at the Tokyo National University of Fine Arts and Music. He studied composition with Teruyuki Noda, Akira Miyoshi, Yuzuru Shimaoka, Koichi Uzaki and Makoto Shinohara. Aizawa also studied conducting with F. Travis, Kotaro Sato, Yoko Matsuo, Chiyuki Murakata, and Seiji Ozawa in Tokyo. He undertook further studies in conducting and composition in Berlin and Vienna.

Two premieres by Aizawa were presented at MOJT 2007. In *Time of Time* for clarinet and percussion,

"harmonic overtones from metal percussion rise from, and emphasize, multiphonic sounds and microtones from the clarinet. This idea, which I used for the first time in this work, replaces the chronological concept that I formerly practiced with works combining Japanese traditional instruments and Western musical instruments."[4]

Influenced by Boulez, Grissey, Murail, Webern, Shinohara, and Takemitsu's *November Steps*, Aizawa's *Deposition for shakuhachi and Western instruments* (clarinet, violin, cello, piano, percussion) combines two musical systems with delicate colors that are carefully placed so that their overtone spectra merge. The title (meaning "evaporation") serves as a metaphor for this method of fusion.

In his essay (*Syncretism in Cross-Cultural Ensembles*), Aizawa looks at the problems and their possible solutions in writing for *hogaku* and Western instrument ensembles, including notation, and specific influences on his music.

Notes

1. from Composer Panel Discussion, Music of Japan Today 2007, March 31.
2. from program note by Hiroyuki Itoh on CD *Swaying time, Trembling time*, MSCD-0019, MusicScape, Tokyo, Japan, 2006.
3. from program note by Hiroyuki Yamamoto (March 31, 2007)
4. from program note by Shirotomo Aizawa (March 31, 2007)

CHAPTER ONE

SWAYING SENSATION AND FRAGILE BEAUTY[1]

HIROYUKI ITOH

Last year, my portrait CD was released by the Japanese label MusicScape. This CD includes six pieces (two solos, two chamber pieces, and two orchestral works) that I composed between 1995 and 2004. The CD is subtitled *Swaying time, Trembling time*, which describes one of the major characteristics of my music. This essay will attempt to introduce my music and the aesthetics that underlie my work.

The piece I am going to discuss first is *Mirror I* for twelve players (flute, oboe, clarinet, mandolin, guitar, harp, piano, percussion, violin, viola, violoncello, and double bass). I wrote this piece in 1997. The performers on the CD are the Nieuw Ensemble conducted by Ed Spanjaard (a live recording from a concert in Amsterdam in 1998). The total duration of the piece is about twelve minutes.

In *Mirror I*, I established my musical language in which a "swaying sensation" and "fragile beauty" play important roles. (These two notions have been dominant in all of my pieces for the past ten years. This does not mean that I have composed the same piece again and again, but that these ideas can be found to varying degrees in each of my works.)

Swaying, trembling, wavering, shimmering, or flickering images of trees, water, fire, lights, shadows, and so on, inspire me as I begin a new composition. These images trigger concrete sonic images and let my music breathe. They also compel me to gaze deeply into our existence and listen to our inner voices.

In actual pieces, such materials as repeated notes, trills, and tremolos, that change their speeds constantly, are quite frequently used to realize the images mentioned above. The successions of the repeated notes, trills, and tremolos constitute lines. These lines—having their own internal speeds— are superimposed one on another, intertwine, and create the sensation of a more complex and multi-layered time flow (Figure 1-1, p.10-11). For this reason, rather complex rhythms are meticulously notated in the score.

Sways and trembles are amplified by the extensive use of quarter-tones. (In all pieces on the portrait CD except for the last one, quarter-tones are used extensively.) Because of the fingering and embouchure difficulties as well as the spectral complexity, a certain fragility (which constitutes the notion of beauty in the music) inevitably remains—no matter how superb the performers are—when playing quarter-tones as heard on this disc. Along with the orchestration and the complexity of the intertwining swaying lines, the extensive use of quarter-tones contributes to the dark, shadowy, distorted, and delicately nuanced, kaleidoscopic texture in this work.

My *String Quartet* was written in 2002 and premiered by the Arditti String Quartet in the same year in Takefu, Japan. The piece has been played by the quartet three times thus far, and the recording on my CD is from their second performance, which took place in Switzerland during the ISCM World Music Days festival in 2004.

In regard to fragility, the *String Quartet* has probably reached the furthest extreme in my work so far. Beauty could only emerge with satisfaction when every subtle detail is worked out to perfection and to the extremes of human capabilities in performance. I am extremely pleased with the performance of this piece on the disc.

I have had some insightful positive reviews of the piece and I will cite one of them:

> "Hiroyuki Itoh has developed a sound language at the same time irritating and iridescent, and who with microtones has pulled the firm ground away, though brings the chords to an entirely unique luminosity. How the Arditti Quartet let the final sound in pianissimo shimmer, belonged to the most intense moments of the evening."[2]

By now, some of you might be wondering about my aesthetics as related to the fact that I am a "Japanese" composer. I do not use or borrow materials from traditional Japanese music in a direct manner. Most of my works are written for Western instruments using Western notation (except for two pieces in which I used traditional Japanese instruments such as the *sho* and *koto*).[3] Nonetheless, I am conscious that I am a Japanese composer.

From my experiences living in the U.S. for almost ten years, there are many universals that we share no matter what ethnic background we have. However, I also believe that, when it comes to a deeper understanding, language plays an important role. As you know, there are many things that do not translate well between two different languages. When we see a certain thing, we might react differently depending upon the language we speak. We could even say that language defines culture. When I compose, I think about things in Japanese. I consciously deal with the essential features found in my language and culture. One of the issues that I have been particularly dealing with is the abstract and fundamental framework of sensitivities, perceptions, systems of logic, and preferences.

Looking back at the activities of Japanese composers after World War II, some composers dealt with Japanese tradition more seriously than others. Yoritsune Matsudaira (1907-2001) is known for his excellent adaptations of *gagaku* music in such orchestral pieces as *Theme and Variations* for piano and orchestra (1951). Toshiro Mayuzumi (1929-1997) effectively transcribed both the sounds of *shamisen* and the chanting of *gidayu-bushi* for violoncello solo in *Bunraku* (1962). In his monumental piece *November Steps* (1967), in which solo *shakuhachi* and solo *biwa* are pitted against a full orchestra, Toru Takemitsu (1930-1996) treated Japanese instruments and Western instruments totally differently and juxtaposed them against each other (without trying to mix them too much). The *shakuhachi* and *biwa* sound like traditional Japanese music, whereas the orchestra sounds more or less like Western contemporary music in this piece. Joji Yuasa (b. 1929) has dealt with the literature of Zeami, Basho, and Buson, and successfully established his own musical language—being rather abstract, though Japanese, it has a strong connection with the music of *Noh*—in such orchestral pieces as *Scenes from Basho* (1980).

In the 1980's and onward, composers Toshio Hosokawa (b. 1955) and Akira Nishimura (b. 1953) have firmly and successfully established their musical languages that have connections with Japanese cultural traditions (in Nishimura's case, Asian cultural traditions) in more abstract and yet obviously noticeable manners. I should emphasize that one of the reasons why Hosokawa and Nishimura are more successful than others in terms of artistic cultural identification, is that they have digested the core of the traditions and have used them in abstract and uniquely individual ways.

Returning to my own music, I consciously deal in my work with a sense of elastic time, sustained tension, distortion, fragility, instability, uncertainty, subtlety, ambiguity, dark texture, structures made from juxtapositions, etc., all of which you can find in Japanese culture quite readily. I deal with these features probably in even more abstract ways than Hosokawa and Nishimura. Ultimately, however, it is not important for me if my music is perceived by the audience as Japanese or not. My higher goal is to create an undoubtedly "Itoh-esque" sonic world which is deep, multidimensional, noble, moving, rich, and beautiful.

Thank you very much for listening.

Notes

1. This article is based on a lecture given at the Music of Japan Today at the University of Maryland, Baltimore County on the 31st of March, 2007. Some parts of the article are developed from my writings in the liner notes of my portrait CD (*HIROYUKI ITOH Swaying time, Trembling time*, MSCD-0019, MusicScape, Tokyo, Japan, 2006).

2. Jürg Huber, *Neue Zürcher Zeitung* (13 November, 2004, Zürich, originally in German, translated by Hiroyuki Itoh with Steven Kazuo Takasugi)

3. *Aki no Kure* (*The Dusk of Autumn*) for 20-string *koto* (2002) and *Standing Still in a Winter Garden* for recorder and *sho* (2003).

Figure 1-1: Itoh *Mirror I* (m.10-15)

Figure 1-1 (continued)

CHAPTER TWO

HIROYUKI ITOH'S *STRING QUARTET*: FORM, STYLE, AND CONTENT[1]

DAVID PACUN

As Itoh notes in Chapter One, the *String Quartet* (2002) represents his most extreme exploration into juxtaposing "the stable and the structured" with "the unstable and fragile."[2] Here, complex polyrhythmic textures and quarter-tone harmonies that develop with surprising subtly create an array of "dark, shadowy, floating, and delicately nuanced kaleidoscopic texture[s]." Drawing upon tradition as much as extending it, this single movement work comprises a startling addition to the quartet repertoire.

Central to the *Quartet* is the idea of "distorted time flow." As Itoh writes, precisely notated "repeated notes, constantly changing their speed of repetition, become lines" and these lines, in turn, "superimpose [on] one another, intertwine, or interfere, creating frictions and conflicts."[3] Figure 2-1 provides a short excerpt of one such line, a figure central to the development of the quartet as a whole.[4] Despite the rhythmic complexity and quarter-tone alterations, the excerpt divides into two roughly parallel four-bar phrases. The parallelism between the phrases is especially evident at the conclusion wherein the phrase 2 G-E inverts and transposes the phrase 1 E+-G+, the quarter-tone difference, however, undercutting the sense of closure.[5]

Figure 2-1: Itoh, *String Quartet*, violin I (m. 54-60)

Each phrase subdivides into a pair of two-measure figures built upon the principle of rhythmic decay, as initially quick subdivisions devolve into longer values: quintuplets to sixteenths, sixteenths to triplets, triplets to eighths, dotted eighths or quarters. Supporting this written-out *ritardando*, the dynamics decrease. Mirroring the rhythmic decay, the melody gradually wedges outward in quasi-sequential fashion, the interval between the upper and lower pitches steadily increasing: G+-G (¼-tone), G-A (whole-step), A-F+ (small major third), E+-G+ (minor third).[6]

As noted by Itoh, pitch repetitions play a crucial role in the formation of these lines. While changes of pitch can correlate with changes in rhythm (division, subdivision), more often the two are offset to extraordinary effect. In measures 54-55 for instance, Itoh superimposes a pattern of three-repeated notes above the shift from quintuplets to sixteenths. (*Tenuto* articulations subtly weight the starting note in each group of three.[7]) These three-note groupings alter the rhythmic sense of the segment by emphasizing the recurring attack points, rather than the underlying meter. Hence, what the ear perceives are two groups of three evenly space notes (G+G+G+ and GGG, the last G extended slightly), followed by two more groups of three evenly spaced notes (AAA and F+F+F+), each of these one fifth slower. As syncopated values predominate toward the ends, each phrase does not cadence so much as decay to a point of rest. While the quartet is not overtly programmatic, these gestures are highly evocative and picturesque.

Figures similar to those seen above arise throughout the quartet, some chained into long and complex passages that develop, perhaps surprisingly, according to classical procedures. For instance, the violin I melody in measures 17-27 is constructed along the lines of a Haydnesque sentence. (Figure 2-2: phrasing and some articulation marks have been omitted.) Here a basic motive (m. 17-19) first repeats in varied form (m. 19-20), then fragments and drives, in a two-step process (m. 21-23 and m. 24-27), to the concluding apex on C#6. As with the excerpt discussed above, this final C# functions not so much as a structural cadence as the point where the phrase dissolves, its internal processes having run their course.

Figure 2-2: Itoh, *String Quartet*, violin I simplified (m. 17-27)

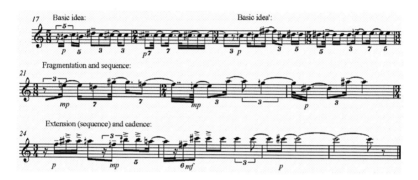

Texturally, the quartet explores the full gamut of instrumental combinations. Often, a single instrument will take the role of *primer inter pares* ("first among equals"), but complex passages involving four independent lines are not uncommon; two instances where the instruments move entirely in rhythmic unison will be discussed later. Despite this variety, the predominant texture divides the ensemble in half, with two fast moving lines in rhythmic unison supported by two slower lines also moving in rhythmic unison. As the slower lines often feature parallel motion (the intervals between the parts varying by quarter-tone), the local effect resembles the *cantus firmus* technique found in four-voice isorhythmic motets. Owing to internal repeats, the quartet sometimes projects a free, passacaglia-like form.

These aspects of form and texture are seen in the quartet's opening phrase. As shown in Figure 2-3 (the Roman numerals below each staff are my own and are explained below), a relatively faster and free flowing line in the upper strings is set against a slower moving "cantus" in the lower strings. Here again, the melody evolves as a loose, zig-zagging sequence of descending quarter- and semitones sighs (A+-A, B-A#+, C#-C), which gradually wedges outward, the intervals of transposition increasing with each leg (whole step, small minor third). Building to the first melodic apex, C#5 in m. 2.5, the rhythms first gain slightly in impetus, then subside into longer values at which point the gesture comes to a rest.[8] Beneath this complexly notated but, in some sense, simple idea, the two lower strings descend in rough parallel motion. As the lower string *cantus* releases its momentum (m. 3), the violins I and II restate their measure 2 cadential dyad (G+-C) an octave higher and with a quarter-tone alteration in the violin I (C+).

Figure 2-3: Itoh, *String Quartet*, m. 1-9

Interestingly, wedging also controls the accompanimental tessitura. Most importantly, the interval between the outer voices gradually expands from a large minor sixth (8.5 semitones) to a compound major second (14 semitones) by the end of measure 2. But, the intervals between each pair of instruments also expands: the interval between violins I and II grows from a major second (G+-A+), to a minor third (G#-B), then major third (A-C#), small perfect fourth (G+-C4.5 semitones), and finally a large perfect fourth (G-C+ or 5.5). The lower parts initially outline a rough parallel motion, but likewise project their widest interval, a large perfect fourth (G+-C# or 5.5 semitones), at the close.

As may be clear from the above discussion, despite the use of twenty-four tones space, the *Quartet* is still pitch centric—the cadential role of C#(+/-) in the opening phrases being, perhaps, even obvious. (See m. 2, 3, 19, 25-27 [vln. I], m. 3 and 8 [vla], m. 16 [vln. II].[9]) Moreover, the melodic notes typically rub against pitches in the accompaniment without settling into them (i.e. B against C+; A#+ against B+, C# against D+; C+ against C#). In this way, the violin line presents a search for resolution which never comes, or rather ends in a resting point equally, if not more dissonant than the start.

Albeit in highly contextualized and flexible ways, this pitch centricity appears to involve dyads as well. For instance, even though the upper and lower parts evolve according to different rhythmic lines, the pitch space projects a rough palindrome. Here, the measure 1 C#-G+ and C-G+ dyads (cello and violin II) return in reverse order in m. 2 (violin I and II =C-G+), and m. 3 (viola and cello=C#-G+).[10] The final chord builds upon this pitch complex, stacking the first two dyads formed by the violin II and cello (C#-G+ and C+-G) into a Bartok-like construction of two large perfect fourths, a quarter-tone apart. Supporting this reading, the cello's C#-C+-C is reworked as the violin I's cadence C#-C-C+.

The 'C'/'G' axis seen above also exerts influence in the second phrase. Beginning as a modified repeat of the opening (with the cello *tacet*), the phrase develops with the violin I ascending steadily, attaining C+5 (supported by a G in the violin II) at measure 8. The violin I cadence outlines the exact intervallic pattern (quarter-tone down followed by whole-step up) found in measure 1, the pitches transposed up by minor third. Below, the viola outlines a descent similar to that found in the first phrase (F+-C# vs F-C#), suggesting a passacaglia-like construction. In confirmation, the violin II and viola's cadential pitches, F# and C#+, echo the viola and cello's opening interval, only transposed up quarter-tone.

The above pitch-centricity is balanced, perhaps offset, by a remarkable exploration of the possible quarter-tone harmonies. Myles Skinner (one of the few scholars to explore quarter-tone space in detail) writes that the number of possible quarter-tone chords is unfathomably large, comprising 352,671 unique sets. Hence, while there are only 12 possible trichords in twelve-tone space (Forte's set classes 3-1 through 3-12), there are 48 in twenty-four tone (quarter-tone) space, and the totals only grow from there. Shifting to tetrachords, 256 possible sets arise in quarter-tone space, more than the entire total of possible chords in twelve-tone space.[11]

Given this wide range of possible harmonies, it is not surprising that Itoh explores only a small segment of the available quarter-tone set classes in any one phrase.[12] The chart below presents a set class analysis of m. 1-4 and m. 5-9. The Roman numerals correspond to those seen in example 3 (i.e. in m. 1 (i)=C#,F+l,G+,A; (ii)=C#,F+,G,A, etc.) and are unique to each phrase. The numbers 0-23 refer to twenty-four tones to the octave, and are not equivalent to set-classes in twelve-notes to the octave space. (Where sets reduce—all even numbers—the twelve-tone equivalent is shown in parenthesis.) Below each column, I have included interval vector totals for the entire phrase (a=10,b=11,c=12) again in twenty-four tone space (Ic^{24}). Other marks are explained below.

Set classes in mm. 1-4:

i	=	0,4,8,15
ii	=	0,3,7,15
iii	=	0,5,9,16
iv	=	0,3,9,16!
v	=	0,2,8,16!! (0,1,4,8)
vi	=	0,3,9,16!
vii	=	0,2,8,16!! (0,1,4,8)
viii	=	0,5,8,13
ix	=	0,2,8,11
x	=	0,5,9,14
xi	=	0,1,11,12 (sym.)

Set classes in mm. 5-9:

i	=	0,3,9
ii	=	0,2,8 (01,4)
iii	=	0,4,9
iv	=	0,5,12
v	=	0,6,15
		(sym.)
vi	=	0,6,13
vii	=	0,5,14
viii	=	0,3,13
ix	=	0,2,11
x	=	0,3,12
xi	=	0,1,9

Ic^{24} *1,2,3,4,5,6,7,8,9,a,b,c*
totals: 2,3,5,5,5,5,5,15,9,4,7,2

1,2,3,4,5,6,7,8,9,a,b,c
1,2,3,1,3,4,2,2,8,2,3,2

Even based upon this limited and preliminary analysis, several points seem clear. Above all, Itoh works primarily with distinctly quarter-tone chords: only three of the possible twenty-two chords can be reduced into twelve-tone sets.[13] Second, most of the chords are different.[14] This is particularly true in the second phrase, but even in the first, chord repetitions are limited to the brief sequence found between chords iv and vii (see ! and !!). Third, as might be expected in a slowly evolving texture, most of the chords are similar--that is, until the final cadence wherein seemingly distinct sets arise [(0,1,11,12) and (0,1,9)]. Finally, while all possible quartertone intervals are represented, a single interval tends to dominate each phrase—the major third (Ic^{24} '8') in mm. 1-4 and a large major third (Ic^{24} '9') in mm. 5-9. This is to be expected in a cantus firmus like setting with the lower voices moving in parallel motion, but the cantus intervals often recur with the melodic voice as well. For instance Ic^{24} '9' arises between the violin I and one of the other two parts—between the melody and one of the other voices—in the first chord in each of the first four pairs (i,iii,v,vii). A large major third appears between the violin II and viola, and thus supports the last three chords. Thus it may be possible to reduce or isolate Ic^{24} '9' in measures 5-9 as thus:

Vn I:	A+	A	A#+	B+		
Vn II:			F#+	G	F#——	
Vla:	F	E+			C#+——	
(chords)	i	iii	v	vi	ix – x – xi	

While such an analysis is preliminary and speculative, it does suggest a careful control of pitch and interval that broadly corresponds to the pitch centricity discussed above.

Although the quartet develops fluidly, with many interconnected passages and segments, it is possible to divide the work into seven sections. Each section elaborates a single main texture and concludes with a long held chord representing a point of rest, rather than a point of closure. The titles are my own but derive from the textural sense of the segments—the 'dances' elaborate equal pairs of instruments, the cadenzas offer more driving and energetic music with more soloistic writing; the interludes are by contrast slower and more introspective. Although the overall sense is more fluid than Figure 2-4 may suggest, the portions of the individual segments are similar, and moreover, combine to suggest a four-part design: two ternary form sections (dance-interlude-dance and cadenza-interlude-cadenza—the last cadenza contains the work's climax) framed by a short introduction and coda.

Figure 2-4: Formal Overview

Overall	‖	43	‖		74		‖
(Title)	Introduction	Dance 1		Interlude 1	Dance 2	
Section:	I	IIa		IIb	IIa'	
mm.	1-43 (43)	44-84 (40)		85-96 (11)	96-119 (23)	
Texture	vn solo (& vc solo) w/ vn 2 & vla	Pairs: Repeated note mel.		Chordal Melody (interactive)	Pairs: Rep. note melody	

‖		70		‖	53	‖
	Cadenza 1	Interlude 2	Cadenza 2	Dance 3	Coda
	IIIa	IIIb	IIIa	IIa'	IV (I'?)
	120-132 (12)	133-162 (29)	163-192 (29)	193-226 (34)	227-246 (19)
	vn 1 & vla Rhythmic canon w/ double stops	vc solo w/ vn & vla chords	Build to tutti rhythmic **Climax**	Pairs: Rep. note melody	mini-cadz, w/ sus. chords.

On the large-scale, two passages stand out as unique. In both the climax (cadenza 2) and coda, the four instruments settle into rhythmic unison. (Figures 2-5 and 2-6) At the climax, the four instruments reiterate a thickly clustered septachord (C# is stated in both the violin II and viola) at *fff* and *ffff*. As with the above examples, the rhythm gradually decays, while accents generally stress offbeats that cut against the underlying meter. The quartet's final passage is even more striking. Here, as the chords gradually augment in value (5-6-6-7-8-8 eighth notes, respectively) prior to the final held sonority, descending parallel perfect fifths between the viola and cello (C#-G#, B-F#) suggest an 'E' tonic; in fact the outer notes of the final chord are E and B. Yet each of the fifths is undercut by equally prevalent quarter-tone dyads. In the final chord, the A#+-F+ perfect fifth foils the E-B perfect fifth, creating a shimmering effect that disturbs the stability of the cadence. The resolution is thus tenuous, and even though the chord does not technically move, the quarter-tone harmonies create their sense of internal 'swaying' and 'trembling.'

As Itoh writes: "Swaying, trembling, wavering, shimmering, or flickering images of trees, water, fire, lights, shadows, mythological creatures, and so on, inspire me as I start a new piece. These images trigger concrete sonic images and let my music breathe. They also compel me to gaze deeply into our existence and listen to our inner voices."[15]

Figure 2-5: Itoh, *String Quartet* m.188-192

Figure 2-6: Itoh, *String Quartet*, m. 236-46

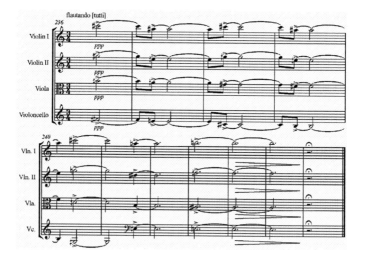

Notes

1. I would like to thank Lara Hoover, a graduate student in mathematics at Ithaca College (with a Music Minor from Ithaca College School of Music, 2007) for her help in dealing with the theoretical ramifications of working with twenty-four tones to the octave pitch space. A comprehensive overview of quarter-tone theory appears in Myles Skinner, *Quarter-Tones* (Dissertation: © 2005), available online at http://www.tierceron.com/diss/ diss.html, accessed 1/16/2008. See especially Chapter 1. (Owing to the nature of Itoh's score, some of my terminology and analytic notation differs from Skinner's.) Other important resources include articles in *Contemporary Music Review* 22 no. 1 and 2 (March/June 23), an issue dedicated to microtonal music. See especially Daniel James Wolf, "Alternative Tunings, Alternative Tonalities," (p. 3-15). Also helpful is Robert Hasegawa, "Tone Representation and Just Intervals in Contemporary Music," *Contemporary Music Review* 25 no. 3 (June 2006), p. 263-281.

2. Hiroyuki Itoh, *Swaying time, Trembling time*, (MusicScape: MSCD-0019, c. 2006.) "In terms of fragility, *String Quartet* has probably reached the furthest extreme in my entire oeuvre so far. The beauty of it could only emerge with satisfaction when every subtle detail is worked out to perfection and to the extremes of human capability when performing the work." (p. 6) Copies of the CD are available at: http://www.musicscape.net/index2.html.

3. Itoh, "Preface" to *String Quartet*, (2002). I would like to thank Hiroyuki Itoh for supplying me with a copy of the complete score.

4. Every effort has been made to reproduce Itoh's handwritten score as accurately as possible. However, owing to the score's complexity and software constraints, it has been necessary to simplify directions regarding string choice, use of vibrato, slurring, and articulation and dynamic marks. Where possible I have noted my simplifications in the example heading.

5. The '+' marks in my text indicate pitches raised by a quartertone: C+=a quartertone above C; C#+=a quartertone above C#, or three quartertones above C. Itoh does not use quartertone flats in his score.

6. Here, the adjectives 'small' and 'large' refer to the quartertone alterations: a semitone plus a quartertone is a 'large semitone'; a minor third minus a quartertone is a 'small minor third.' Technically, a large minor third is enharmonically equivalent to a small major third; this interval is sometimes referred to as a 'neutral third—halfway between major and minor. However, owing to the quartet's relative pitch centricity, I have preferred to retain some reference to the interval size and quality.

7. Itoh specifies a serial-like gradation of accents; however accents are not treated to serial manipulations.

8. Technically, the rhythmic notation requires performers to distinguish between a remarkably precise range of note values. For instance using the common denominator of 21 (3x7), the opening violin rhythms would be a string of 14,13, then 15 twenty-first notes. In general, Itoh does not appear to utilize a rhythmic series, but proportional rhythms do arise. The latter half of violin phrase in measures 7-9 retrogrades the rhythmic proportions of the first half at two and a half

times the speed: using a common denominator of 30 division/quarter, the note values would be: 15-15-20-25 then 10-8-6-6, or (3-3-4-5) x 3 becomes (5-4-3-3) x 9. As Itoh states in the score preface, his quartertones are not to be understood as inflections of an underlying diatonic or chromatic (twelve notes to the octave) framework. The quartertones do not resolve into a normative twelve-note-per octave frame, but are omnipresent throughout and few chords in any phrase will fit into a purely 12-tone per octave space. When pure chromaticism does reign, the pitches often pack into tightly formed clusters that hide the chromatic framework. As will be discussed, Itoh is careful in his treatment of perfect consonances (5ths and octaves).

10. This palindrome seems manifest in the rough voice-exchange outlined between the cello and violin I: while the opening C#4 shifts up to C5, the A+4 shifts down to the A#3.

11. Skinner, *Quarter-Tones*, p. 30. Skinner calculates these totals using Forte's method, which allows for equivalence between inversionally related sets. Owing to the pitch-centric aspects of Itoh's *Quartet*, it is not clear that inversional equivalence is present or maintained. However, full consideration of this topic goes well beyond the scope of the present overview.

12. In this regard, Itoh may have taken Elliot Carter's *Third Quartet* (in which individual sections focus on distinct intervals) as a model.

13. For instance, if one divides quartertone space into two chromatic scales a quartertone apart (chr.0=C-C#-D-D#...and chr.1=C+-C#+-D+-D#...), most chords mix notes from both scales. Although the opening (m.1-4) is not systematic, the upper and lower strings alternate between chr0 and chr1; just as one pair settles into chr1 or chr0, the other moves out, negating a sense of pure chromatic space:

Vn I:	chr1	chr0	chr0	chr1	chr0	chr0	chr1
Vn II:	chr1	chr0	chr0	chr1	chr0	chr1	chr0
Vla:	chr1	chr1	chr0	chr1	chr1	chr0	
Vc:	chr0	chr1	chr0	chr1	chr0	chr1	

14. The next four measure phrase (m.10-13) is more selective (repeating three chords twice and containing two two-note chords) and focuses on a different interval (Ic^{24} '11'), the segment as a whole - a total of twenty-three three note sets - introduces 18 of the possible 48 three-note sets, more than half of the distinct 37 quartertone (not twelve-tone) sets.

15. Itoh, *Swaying time*, p. 6.

Chapter Three

My Compositional Technique and Thoughts on the Ambiguity of Sound

Hiroyuki Yamamoto

While composers and other musicians are aware of the long history of Western art-music, one area that is not taken as a focus of concern is "the ambiguity of sounds." Since music is written in a score, sound is symbolized on paper, and these symbols are realized by a person reading this score. However, a kind of simplification occurs (a hearing phenomenon) when the sound is symbolized in the score. In other words, part of the elements of the sound is not written. This includes not only matters of expression, such as nuances, but also the physics of the sound, as well as its basis. For example, when a particular sound is produced and then disappears, we can recognize "the sound disappeared at this particular moment." However, I think this perception is slightly different for each person, even though the symbol written in the score is constant.

I think that an ambiguous element is trimmed by an encoding of the sound. But the simplification of sound by encoding is only an example of having missed the ambiguity of the sound. My compositional interest is to intentionally extend "an ambiguous element" in my music. I was interested in the ambiguity of sound within music from a physics or psychological standpoint. And since 1995, I thought interesting and compelling music might be composed by expanding and developing this idea.

Especially, in my music before 2004, I intentionally produced "sounds to be heard ambiguously," and collected them to methodically use as materials for my music. Methods I have used include: writing the border of the sounds between perceivable or not perceivable; writing very fast phrases including much information in order to blur the recognition of the written notes; and generating noise in an irregular way.

As a result, my work became music that is an accumulation of ambiguities. In *Noli me Tangere* for saxophone and nine musical instruments which I composed in 2000, I created ambiguous relations between a soloist and ensemble. Not only does ambiguity occur through noises from special techniques of the instruments, but *portamenti* create ambiguities of pitch (these defeat the great historical importance European music attaches to pitch, and allows the music to stand outside "rule by number"). Also, I have used several mutes with brass instruments to promote unstable musical colors. I created ambiguity in multiple layers through various methods in this fashion. (Figure 3-1 - score is written in C)

Figure 3-1

In addition to this work, the technique and way of thinking just described is carried through in my other music of this time. Accumulation of ambiguities can provide a stream of ideas. If I continue to pursue this method, my music will become more and more complicated.

Certainly, as a sound becomes complicated, the music becomes ambiguous, but there is limited interest in the music if the audible ambiguity can be realized only by making it chaotic. I have gradually come to think that ambiguity which is more carefully controlled is necessary. In other words, I have to consider "what is definite" to understand "what is ambiguous." This is a matter of course.

As a result, since 2004 I have introduced a concept called "monody" into my compositions. The so-called "monody style" was a response to the complicated polyphony of Renaissance music in the seventeenth century. This way of thinking was very useful for me in solving my musical problem. The fact that a monodic style promoted such a big switch in musical expression in Western music history, convinced me that it could also serve as a turning point for me towards writing more convincing music.

In addition, the construction method of my music before 2003 put various ambiguous subject matter together in length and breadth. This is similar to the classical idea of combining a melody with harmony. Therefore, I thought to compose only a horizontal line to express "time" – a minimum element of the music for the idea that I had. It is equal to a way of thinking called "monody," as well.

My "monody" is not the same as the monody style after the 17th century. First, there is a sound that is the core, like a melody to express a horizontal line, and it is made from some combination of pitches. In other words, I let special techniques retreat from the leading role in the composition (if I do not take this course, ambiguity will cease to exist).

The sound of the core can change/vary like a melody. Cores become ambiguous through several methods. For example, the timing and rhythm of the sound of the core is altered by the combination of instruments. In addition, the sound of a pitch that is close to the core conflicts, and the result can be a blurred core. Cores become ambiguous in these ways, and only their outline remains.

Therefore the listener hears it as a central sound in the deep part of the music. However, it will be difficult to grasp precisely what kind of rhythm it was originally, and what original pitch the sound was. I control ambiguity and distinctness as a parameter, in a similar way to pitch.

It may go against the concept of monody when I complicate a composition by exploring an aspect of rhythm of a core. I may add a totally different rhythm at any time through a sound made from the same core - not solely by sliding the rhythm of the core (for example, it is another character if it is accented, creating another flow). Then it can be heard to clash and compete within, even though these sounds are made from the same core. Interestingly, it may even sound like counterpoint. In other words, it is polyphony-like, despite being monophonic.

Such a phenomena appears in *The Wedge is Struck, The Fog Remains* played during Music of Japan Today 2007. In Figure 3-2, the sound of the core changes from A flat, to G-A, to E-F, etc. G-A means that the sound of the core is blurred between A and G. The pitch of the two musical instruments (top stave = clarinet; bottom two staves = piano) is almost completely determined based on cores. However, the rhythm is considerably free.

Figure 3-2

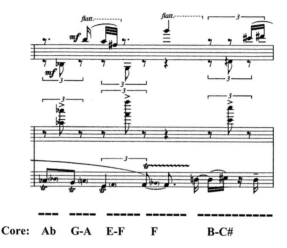

The upper part of the clarinet and the lower part of the piano (left hand) flow free of each other, creating counterpoint. However, the lower part of the clarinet and the upper part of the piano (right hand) ticks away at the completely same rhythm within a triplet. It is heard as three independent parts (counterpoint), even though they form monody based on a common core. Elements such as the reverberation of the hall or the articulation of the player increase in importance when an audience listens, and the music is heard in a more complex way than is apparent from just looking at the musical score (without sound).

In my current music, the idea of monody with a core that I use to realize ambiguities, suggests various possibilities. I do not know how I will develop this method in the future, but I trust that it is part of my musical voice that is contributing to my continued development as a composer.

CHAPTER FOUR

SYNCRETISM IN CROSS-CULTURAL ENSEMBLES

SHIROTOMO AIZAWA

Q: What are the differences in writing for *hogaku* instruments compared to Western instruments?

A: In contemporary music, there are many cases using special extended techniques for any instrument. Therefore, there is no difference between Western instruments and *hogaku* Japanese classic instruments, with regard to collaborative research and development of new instrumental possibilities.

Q: Why did you begin to write for *hogaku* instruments when your training was in Western music?

A: My mother was studying *koto*, so *hogaku* was near to me since my youth. Because of this reason, I took classes in *hogaku* and ethnomusicology as well as composition lessons during my time at the university. Eventually, I started to receive commissions for *hogaku* instruments.

Q: How has your music changed during your career composing for *hogaku* instruments?

A: There is no special change. *Hogakki* are instruments close to me, but when you compose, you must study deeply about every instrument. This point is the same whether it is Western instruments, other ethnic instruments, or electronic effects, etc. Also, I became strongly aware about Japan by using *hogaku* instruments - this point makes me aware of what is Western, while at the same time, opens the way to assimilation.

Q: What kind of difficulties do instrumental constraints of *hogaku* instruments present when combined with Western instruments? How is your approach to composing for *hogaku* and Western instruments different from Takemitsu (and other composers)? Give some specific musical examples from your scores (including *Deposition*).

A: When Western instruments and *hogaku* instruments are used in the same piece, it is always a difficult problem to decide how to combine the regular sense of rhythm of Western music, and the free (less regular) sense of rhythm of Japanese music.

In *November Steps*, by Toru Takemitsu, the Western orchestra and *hogaku* instruments begin at rehearsal number 2 by moving at the same time (top two lines are *shakuhachi* and *biwa*). After that, the *hogaku* instrument group (*biwa*, *shakuhachi*) move by their own sense of time/rhythm, while the orchestra moves to the precise sense of rhythm of the conductor. Therefore, from the top of Figure 4-1, two different instrument groups move in a different way, from the point of view of rhythm, and restart together at rehearsal number 3 on the next page.

Figure 4-1

©Edition Peters No.6629

To solve these different rhythmic tendencies, and to be able to situate more complicated relationships between Western instruments and *hogaku* instruments, I use two different kinds of arrows (with their angles) to show the relations of starting points, and broken lines to show the same stating points. An example of my use of both types of arrows (Figure 4-2) can be found in *Su-Ohu II* (1998, revised) for 2 *shakuhachi*, *koto* and 17-string *koto* (1 player), voice, and narrator.

Figure 4-2

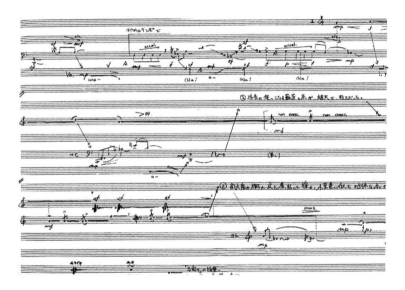

©Aizawa 「蘇芳II」 *Su-Ohu*、国立劇場創作賞

In *Deposition for Shakuhachi and Western instruments* (clarinet, violin, cello, piano, percussion), commissioned by UMBC, durations in the *shakuhachi* part are notated by horizontal lines, but changing points are precisely notated (proportionally) within the Western score. However, in order to satisfy both a sense of freedom and the preciseness (regularity) of two different groups of instruments, a conductor is needed.

Figure 4-3

©Aizawa *Deposition*, 2007

One more important theme that interests me is the microtonality of the *shakuhachi*, and the control of multiphonics which occur in the upper partials of the *shakuhachi*. I am interested in these points in all of my other works, and can say that I have reached a common interest with the "Spectral School" (musical movement originating in France in the 1970s which features the use of sound, including timbre, pitch, and rhythm of individual sounds, as a model for composition) through the analysis of the overtone spectrum of *hogaku* instruments.

Figure 4-4

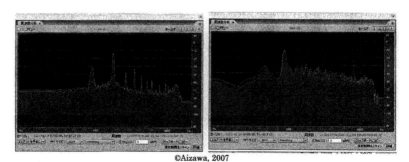

©Aizawa, 2007

In the spectrum analyses (on the previous page) of the same pitch, common differences between the Western flute (left) and *shakuhachi* (right) are clear. In the Western flute, partials (peaks) appear at the same distances. In the *shakuhachi*, the overtone cycle shows many tiny overtones, like the teeth of a saw. *Hogaku* players, with good training, can control these overtones in many different ways through sensitive air manipulation and small differences of finger positions.

Figure 4-5: Examples of notation of *shakuhachi* overtones

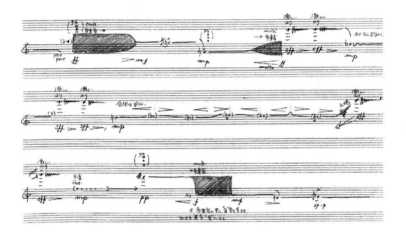

The score above is the beginning part of *Kouro-zen* (1991) for *shakuhachi* solo. The first note (Ab) is a note which doesn't exist on the D-*shakuhachi*, and a performer has to create the sound by *meri* (changing his/her embouchure from a different note) and/or by opening one-quarter of a tone-hole of the *shakuhachi*. As a result, this note becomes a microtone.

In the middle of this work, there is a designation for "multiphonics." But I didn't write precise upper pitches because *hogaku* instruments have big differences between each instrument, and it is impossible to recreate the same multiphonics on all different *shakuhachi* instruments. Therefore, I only designate "alternate fingerings" from which it is easy to create multiphonics, and the actual sounds are graphically notated. Also, in the case of a superior performer, it is possible for her/him to modulate partials continuously within multiphonics.

Q: How do you manage balance (volume) of *hogaku* and Western instruments in your ensemble music?

A: The dynamic range of *hogakki* is very wide compared with Western instruments. Also, their character is to have special spectra of overtones. Therefore, I must be careful during soft writing for *hogakki* to not cover them with Western instrument sounds or overtone spectra. In the loud area of *hogakki*, I must be careful to not erase Western instruments' sounds.

One area that I have to be more sensitive to than the balance of dynamics is in composing the pitches/scales which determine the tuning of the *hogaku* instruments. Dynamics must be chosen very carefully to avoid a strange feeling of incongruity when combined with the Western scales/tuning. If I am not careful, the *hogakki* will be heard as always out of tune with the Western instruments.

Q: What kind of effect does being Japanese have on music you compose?

A: When I compose, I use Western instruments and write Western Music. By using *hogaku* instruments, I sense strongly that I am a Japanese (Asian) person - not only geographically, but also culturally, and philosophically. I recognize these differences from the West, and attempt to put "myself" into my work.

It is said that globalization will make the world closer in distance and foster better communication. However, it should not result in everything becoming the same. It is necessary that each society becomes independent by having its own specialties, but the world as a whole needs to have harmony.

In composing, it is necessary to recognize strongly the character of *hogaku* (or Japan, Asian), and mix them with Western instruments and Western style. I think that when we deal with *hogaku*, contemporary composers have the necessity and responsibility to compose with a truly global point of view, unlike the time between the Meiji era and Showa era…..a time of camouflaged relationships between *hogaku* and composers. Such reconfirmation of myself, comes from the experience of using *hogaku* instruments, brought to life daily by the opposite stream of composition for Western instruments.

Q: What are influences from Western composers/pieces on your work *Deposition*? On your other pieces?

A: With regard to *Deposition*, many pieces of Boulez...many pieces of Gerard Grissey. I was also influenced by Makoto Shinohara. In other pieces....Webern....his approach towards composition, rather than any particular piece of Webern.

Naturally, there is no simple effect such as this composer's piece or such specific points of compositional technique. If I express my answer like a table of contents, Boulez influenced me by his control towards small parts of sounds. Also, the improvisational feeling of spontaneity, which I take in my *Deposition*. I don't use Boulez's total serialism method itself, but apply some of his techniques. First, when I determine the chord settings (group of sounds), I choose notes through serial methods. At the same time, I choose pitches from traditional *aitake* (chords) produced by the Japanese *sho* (there are 11 type of *aitake*).

Figure 4-6: *Sho aitake*

After these two procedures, I choose pitches in common, and construct a basic harmonic setting. In this harmonic setting, after the pitches construct a harmony by converging, they diverge in the manner of *teutsuri* used by a performer of the *sho* (in performance practice, due to the structure of the instrument, when one moves from one chord to another, a few notes precede the other pitches).[1] In Figure 4-7, the top stave is an example of a sequence of *aitake*; the bottom stave demonstrates how the first five *aitake* above might be realized through *teutsuri*.

Figure 4-7: sequence of *aitake* realized through *teutsuri*

Room for improvisatory sounds in live performance is also notated in the score in a planned fashion. Traditional notation is used in the score, up to the point where the intention can not be recognized by a performer.

I use my view of acoustics when I voice particular chords among instruments. For example, a concern could be how to float or sink the *shakuhachi* among the overtones of other Western instruments. In this case, I carefully voice the chords among the instruments. To make this effect work in my music, I may use *sul ponticello*, *tremolo*, and pedaling effects for Western instruments. Also, a *shakuhachi* player who has been trained to listen carefully (such as Retsuzan Tanabe, the soloist in *Deposition*) can produce overtones and eliminate unnecessary sounds, comparatively easily.

The effect of an ensemble's overtones is influenced greatly through the use of sensitive pitch and dynamics. During the performances at UMBC and the Smithsonian in Washington DC, I conducted myself, so I could control these freely during rehearsals. To test the acoustical effect, I record basic sounds, and check overtones visually with a spectral analysis application on my computer. This type of creation of acoustics which eyes the effect of overtones among instruments shares common ideas with the "spectral school" composers, Grissey and Murail.

One remaining problem concerns notation. Notation for an ensemble of Western and *hogaku* instruments has been already established by composers such as Makoto Shinohara. But, like the notation of overtones, this system remains a problem. In the case of *hogaku* instruments, unlike Western instruments, the differences among instruments are large, and it is not guaranteed that two players of the same instrument will create the same overtones by using the same fingering. Therefore, the ways to direct fingerings, and the way to direct the production of multiphonics are not consistently precise (or appropriate). This problem will be a future task for composers who are interested in the field of acoustics (including the problems of microtones and multiphonics).

Notes

1. Aizawa defines "converging" as "a state where numbers of a progression or oscillation become closer to the limit value." "Diverging" is the opposite motion.

PART II

ESSAYS ON CONTEMPORARY JAPANESE MUSIC

SECTION ONE

POLITICS AND MUSIC:
JAPAN, WORLD WAR II, AND ITS AFTERMATH

The two essays in this section address the effect on music and musicians of Japanese nationalism and militarism surrounding the Second World War (Imperial Japan and Postwar Japan). These investigations underline the political/social complexity of Japan's profound transition at the conclusion of the war in 1945, which contributed to moving a number of Japanese composers away from music of the past, and cleared the way for avant-garde ideas in the early 1950s.

One of the most successful and powerful figures of Western art-music in Japan during this time was Kosaku Yamada (1886-1965), who was not only a prolific composer, but a prominent conductor, organizer, and leader.[1] Born in Tokyo, he spent part of his early childhood in Yokosuka – a naval city southwest of Tokyo, where Yamada enjoyed watching and listening to military bands that frequently marched in the city. Yamada was also exposed to Protestant church hymns (by his mother), and the harmonies of the harmonium (owned by his parents). After a fire caused his family to lose everything, followed shortly by his father's death, and his own extended illness, Yamada moved to Okayama (in western Japan) at the age of 14, where his sister lived. His sister had married an Englishman (Edward Gauntlet) who was not only a high school English teacher, but an amateur musician who encouraged (emotionally and monetarily) Yamada's continually growing interest in Western music. Yamada attended the Tokyo Music School as a singer (composition was not taught until the 1930s), studying with German musicians who helped him enter music school in Berlin in 1910. Among his teachers in Berlin was Max Bruch. During his time in Berlin, Yamada created an orchestral symphony, symphonic poems, and a full-scale opera (the first Japanese to write Western music on this scale). After returning to Japan (there were no performance opportunities for him in Germany), he organized a temporary orchestra to perform his works. A trip to the United States followed in 1918-9, where he conducted two concerts of his music in Carnegie Hall, and met Rachmaninov and Prokofiev. His fame growing, Yamada's activities during the 1920s into the 30s included conducting the Berlin Philharmonic and Lenningrad Philharmonic, and forming an orchestra in Japan (which ultimately became the NHK Philharmonic) which he conducted in performances of standard Western repertoire (Mozart, Beethoven), music of young Japanese composers, his own works, and operas of Wagner. He also wrote numerous songs during this time (including collaboration with poet Hakshu Kitahara in creating songs like *Karatachi no hana, Kono michi,* and *Akatombo*).

Yamada gradually steered his composition focus to opera, thinking that music dramas rather than symphonies would be more accessible to Japanese familiar with *kabuki* and *Noh.* Yamada's

"....dream grew bigger towards the end of World War II. He thought of writing a grand opera *The Princess Shian-Fei* (based on Chinese history) and performing it in Beijing under Japanese occupation, in collaboration with the Chinese people. His intention was to demonstrate the quality of Asian musicians to the world, but Japan lost the war and the opera was left unfinished. (This was completed by his pupil Ikuma Dan and was first performed in 1981.)"[2]

The musical environment in the 1930s in Japan, within which Yamada worked, grew increasingly restrictive with the increase of extreme right-wing and military movements. The government encouraged a nationalist style of music that (Galliano 2002, 116) "took the glamorous, bombastic aspects of the European orchestra spiced up with a touch of Japanese folk music." Censorship was extended in all areas, including the arts. Popular songs were replaced by propaganda "songs of courage," and new compositions were commissioned (from Ibert, Strauss, and others, including Yamada) for a celebration of the 2600th anniversary of the empire (1940). Yamada's work from this project, *Kamikaze,* extolled the beauty of war (Galliano, 120).

David Pacun's essay (*Style and Politics in Kosaku Yamada's Folksong Arrangements, 1917-1950*) traces Kosaku Yamada's growing sensitivity to the modal and rhythmic shadings of Japanese folksong through examination of four groups of his arrangements. He also draws connections with Yamada's activities and compositions at the time that "establish suggestive paths that link the 'cultural' arrangements of the 1920s to the 'political' arrangements of the 1940s."

The Allied military occupation after the war (1945-1952) enacted sweeping changes in Japan – a new constitution based on the American model (which also included a clause forever renouncing war), and reforms in the administration of the state and justice, and in industrial relations and education were instituted. Artists were faced with the sudden freedom (and necessity) to articulate their own ideas for the assimilation of Western culture in their work.

Fuyuko Fukunaka examines the social and cultural climate surrounding Japan's musicians immediately after the war (*A Japanese Zero-Hour? - Postwar Music and the "Re-making" of the Past*), including efforts of leading music figures to "re-define" themselves in order to "prove worthy of a new Japan." She also looks closely at the public exchange in *The Tokyo Newspaper* between music critic Ginji Yamane and Kosaku Yamada, in which Yamane labeled Yamada "a war criminal," and at the twelve-tone technique of post-war composers as a catalyst for constructing a new identity.

Notes

1. in fact, Yamada played an important role in Western music taking root in Japan.
2. Morihide Katayama, Yamada, Kosaku Biography, http://www.naxos.com

References

Galliano, Luciana. 2003. *Yogaku: Japanese Music in the Twentieth Century*. The Scarecrow Press, Inc.
Katayama, Morihide. 2007. Yamada, Kosaku Biography. http://www.naxos.com
Pacun, David. 2006. "Thus we cultivate our own world, and thus we share it with others": Kosaku Yamada's visit to the United States in 1918-1919. *American Music* 24:1, 67-94.

CHAPTER FIVE

STYLE AND POLITICS IN KOSAKU YAMADA'S FOLKSONG ARRANGEMENTS, 1917-1950

DAVID PACUN

Between 1917 and 1950, composer Kosaku Yamada (1886-1965) arranged twenty-seven Japanese folksongs for voice and piano, including several with obbligato parts. Although these works comprise a small part of Yamada's enormous output (some 1500 works), they vary considerably in style and form, with the arrangements of the late 1920s displaying especially refined treatments. As folksong arrangements were popular in concerts, radio broadcasts, and film scores, the changes in style may owe to many factors, including Yamada's own maturing compositional voice. Yet owing to their position between East and West, between 'authentic' source and 'universal' technique, folksong arrangements had the potential to carry strong ideological implications.[1] In Japan of the late 1920s-1930s for instance, radical nationalist movements often espoused folk culture, including folk music, for its direct embodiment of the so-called 'Japanese Spirit' (*nihonteki narumono, nihonronjin*) (Harootunian 1990a, 1990b). And far from being silent in political affairs (as is implied in *New Grove*), Yamada was an early and active supporter of Japan's military regime.[2] In brief then, this paper investigates the interaction between Yamada's deepening exploration of Japanese folksong and his own growing militarism, and through this narrow lens hopes to shed light on the complex interaction between cultural nationalism (*minzoku-shugi*) and political nationalism (*kokumin-shugi*) in interwar Japan.[3]

As shown in Figure 5-8, Yamada's arrangements divide into approximately four groups; yet, neither the divisions nor the chronology are uniform.[4] For instance, three of the four Pacific War arrangements (see group 4) originated in larger works, some from the late 1920s, and Yamada produced no vocal and piano arrangements between 1932 and 1943, the years during which radical nationalism exerted its greatest impact on Japanese society. Thus, it is unclear whether the lacuna in arrangements represents a break in style and ideology, or whether some hidden path bridges the divide. Before addressing this question, it is vital to examine the four groups of arrangements in greater detail.

I) The Fischer Arrangements (1917-1918)

As I have written elsewhere, Yamada's arrangements for Carl Fischer were aimed at amateur American audiences who, in keeping with the vogue for *Japonisme*, desired 'authentic' Japanese music—but only if presented in 'civilized' Western form.[5] Yamada subtitled each arrangement "transcribed and modernized by…," thus giving lie to their dual esthetic intents. Internationally, World War I raged on in Europe, and Yamada often posed in military uniform as a cultural ambassador from allied Japan.[6] Not surprisingly, critics viewed his arrangements as representative of authentic Japanese music, and positioned them as a bridge between two culturally distinct, if allied, nations.

'Counting Song' exposes Yamada's early treatment (Figure 5-1). A simple children's song in strophic form, the syllabic melody is straightforward in design and rhythm. Yamada's accompaniment is correspondingly simple, beginning with a light octave doubling in the left hand and gently syncopated chords in the right, then shifting to light, *koto*-esque rolls. Harmonically, ii∅6/5-I progressions evoke the required 'Japanese' atmosphere, but Yamada avoids clashes between melody and harmony by treating the "final" G of the melody as scale degree 2 in f minor, rather than the tonic in a Phrygian-based mode.[7] Save for "Fisherman's Song," whose modernesque ostinato anticipates Yamada's mature arrangement style, all six arrangements have much in common with those made by Yamada's contemporaries in the West.

Figure 5-1: Yamada *Counting Song* m. 5-10

II) The Miura Arrangements (1922-1924)

The four arrangements for soprano Tamaki Miura, who had just returned to Japan following a tour of the United States and Europe, gain in intensity and richness.[8] Dense, heterophonic effects dominate "Himematsu," but "Kuruka" goes further, its irregular, syncopated melody hovering gently above a dense, if four-square, *ostinato* (Figure 5-2). Textural shifts now demarcate and enliven the strophic treatment. Composed for modern connoisseurs and professional singers, these arrangements seem less afraid of themselves and more outward looking. In fact, Miura performed them throughout her career.

Figure 5-2: Yamada *Kuruka Kuruka* m. 3-8

III) The 'Fujiwara' Arrangements (1927-1931):

Written over a broader span, the third group reveals a deeper probing of Japanese folksong. Yamada set complex *oiwake bushi*, transcribed two previously unrecorded melodies—thus taking on the role of ethnographer—and composed increasingly unique accompaniments. In "Oshoro Takashima" for instance, the right hand tremolo and resonant *ostinato* clearly aim to match the frothy intensity of the highly ornamented melody. (Figure 5-3)

Figure 5-3: Yamada *Oshoro Takashima* m. 5-9

In "Chugoku Komoriuta," by contrast, a mercurial blend of common-practice ('Western') and modal ('Japanese') harmonies is placed within a subtly crafted theme and variations. Each new strophe is enriched with poignant dissonances and understated alterations in phrase structure. Here the setting creates a dark subtext to the original melody, turning lullaby into art song, *minyo* into *kakyoku*. In "Hakone Hachiriwa," perhaps Yamada's best arrangement, two gestures—an ascending anacrusis figure and a iv-I (ii∅6/5-i) cadence—recur in freely evolving forms. Owing to the understated harmonic flow (there is no structural dominant) and abrupt registral shifts, the setting projects not so much a sense of time but a sense of space, evoking, at once symbolically and literally, the immensity of nature and a journey across the expansive Hakone landscape itself.[9] (Figure 5-4)

Figure 5-4: Yamada *Hakone Hachiriwa* m. 1-11

IV) The Pacific War Arrangements of 1943 (1929-1943)

The four arrangements first published during the Pacific War appeal to grander scales, and utilize more transparent musical gestures. In 1943, Yamada supplied the already flush "Oshoro Takashima" with a heterophonic flute counterpoint and added an elaborate introduction and coda, the latter sadly overblown. (Figure 5-5) In "Funauta," arranged for Yamada's 1940 opera "Kurofune," the melody floats in above a long Wagnerian chromatic scale—a gesture found nowhere else in Yamada's folksong arrangements. Here, the accompaniment functions as independent musical scenery.

Figure 5-5: Yamada *Oshoro Takashima* revised version, coda (tacet vocal part not shown)

Likewise, in the newly revised "Oryoko Bushi," the simple offbeat chordal accompaniment recalls that found in the 1918 "Counting Song." (Figure 5-6) Critically, the source melody was a Japanese boat song sung on the Amnok-kang (river) between Korea and Manchuria, the site of intense Japanese industrialization and several famous battles during the Japan-Russian war. Yamada's decision to include this arrangement in his 1943 compilation can only be read, I think, as a symbol of Japan's cultural conquest of East Asia.

Figure 5-6: Yamada *Oryoko Bushi* m. 1-8

If the first three groups of arrangements trace a steady growth in richness and density with the most original works coming in the late 1920s, the extent to which the Pacific War arrangements—some dating nevertheless from the 1920s—further or retreat from this trajectory is difficult to gauge. On the one hand they extend the mid-period style through new counterpoints, dramatic gestures, and operatic contexts. On the other they simplify the surface and structure through generic rhythms and extraneous material such as the banal, overwrought coda in "Oshoro Takashima."

Still, the four arrangement groups do correlate, albeit roughly, with their respective historical settings, edging us toward a political hermeneutics of musical style. The simplified nature of the American set fits within the paradigm of 'tempered exoticism' prevalent in Western culture at the time; the progressive arrangements of popular tunes undertaken for Miura embody something of 'Taisho chic;' the intense and sensitive arrangements dating from the later 1920s reflect then nascent movements that had begun to look more deeply into Japan's ancient and folk traditions; the less subtle aspects of the final group maybe best attributed to a country at war. And in turn, these correlations suggest a further division between the two inner groups, composed mainly for performers, and the two outer groups, whose *raison d'etre* stems more from public/political contexts—Western exoticism in the Fischer set, cultural superiority in the Pacific War compilation. Without denying multiple meanings, it is possible, then, to characterize the inner arrangements as examples of cultural nationalism (*minzoku-shugi*), the outer arrangements as examples of political nationalism (*kokumin-shugi*).

This analysis is no doubt reductive, and rests on a perhaps too facile equivalence between "society" and "music."[10] Yet, Yamada's own activities and compositions establish suggestive links between the 'cultural' arrangements of the 1920s to the 'political' arrangements of the 1940s. For instance in the years surrounding the arrangements of 1927-1931, Yamada delved into Japan's cultural past with increasing purpose and scale. He directed music for new *kabuki* plays, saw the premiere of his own *kabuki*-based opera "Ochitaru tennyo" (composed originally in 1913), and began work on his most famous opera, "Kurofune," fashioned after the colorful legend of Okichi, a tea-house girl hired to "nurse" Townsend Harris during his negotiations for the first Treaty of Commerce between the US and Japan (1854-1856); Yamada's arrangement of "Funauta" for this opera appeared in his 1943 compilation.[11]

In 1931, Yamada mined the *shinnai* and *kabuki Akegarasu* for his opera/ballet, *Ayame*. Here, the score included two folksongs ("Hakone

Hachiriwa" and "O-edo Nihonbashi"), and utilized a *kabuki* ensemble in the final double love-suicide. Composed in Paris for the progressive directors Michel Benois and Fyodar Komissarzhevsky, Yamada nevertheless stated that he was inspired by the timbre and intonation of the *shamisen*, and at one point argued that owing to 'the restrictions in tone imposed by the twelve notes of the piano…Western music [was] unable to express the deep subtleties of Japanese music.' Yamada further quipped: "All pianos should be scrapped and never introduced again…but I am afraid the piano manufacturers would not agree to this."[12]

A reactionary stance is even more explicit in remarks Yamada published just prior to *Kurofune*'s 1940 premiere. Specifically, Yamada vented his "long-standing dissatisfaction and even anger" over Orientalist works such as 'Madame Butterfly' and 'Iris, stating that' "at last I came to believe it my duty to write myself an opera on a Japanese theme in which the errors in these works would be corrected."[13] In fact, "Kurofune" was part of a conscious effort to shroud Okichi in a samurai-like aura, as a symbol of sacrifice for the nation; even her remarkable concluding plea for peace between Japan and America blends aspects of cultural and political nationalism.[14] Within such a context, the presence of folksong(s) must have carried strong ideological implications.[15]

It is particularly relevant, then, that shortly after *Ayame*, Yamada composed his first explicit piece of militaristic music, one drawn upon contemporary events. During the 'Shanghai Incident' of 1932, three Japanese soldiers, all from farming villages, sacrificed themselves in suicide attack.[16] Throughout the 1930s, heroic acts by common folk garnered enormous media attention, and Yamada responded to this one with a short *gunka* ('military song'), "Human Bullets—Three Brave Warriors," published by *The Asahi Shinbum* in 1932.[17] The poem (by one Tsutomu Nakano) is typical of heroic ballads—both Japanese and Western—but Yamada's melody draws heavily upon Taki Rentaro's emblematic "Kojo no tsuki," a song that, while technically *kakyoku* (lied), was often seen as *minyo* (folksong).[18] (Figures 5-7a and 5-7b) *Gunka* had long comprised a part of the public's steady diet of Western music, but the impact of Yamada's "Human Bullets," as recorded by *enka* star Koga Masao, appears to have been substantial (Young 1998, 77-8).[19]

Figure 5-7a: Yamada *Human Bullets* (melody only), m. 1-4

Figure 5-7b: Rentaro *Kojo no Tsuki* (melody only), m. 1-4

Following "Human bullets," Yamada turned increasingly toward modern media, composing scores for numerous propagandistic films including Mizoguchi's "Dawn to Manchuria" (now lost) and Arnold Fanck's "The Daughter of the Samurai."[20] Here, Yamada employed a full range of musical styles: impressionistic music for landscapes, popular tunes to accompany the heroine, march music for factory scenes, and of course folk music. In the denouement, cherry blossoms overlap the heartbroken heroine as she ascends a volcano intent on suicide; and in the background she envisions children singing "Sakura." After her fiancé intervenes to save her, the couple moves to Manchuko (Manchuria), where they help settle Japan's most famous colony under the watchful eye of a heavily armed Japanese soldier.

Melodrama aside, the list of Yamada's nationalistic activities is substantial: he played leading roles in music federations allied to the government, traveled himself to Manchuria as part of Japan's pen-brigade (1937) and, during the Pacific War, functioned as a 'musical ambassador' to Japan's East Asian colonies (thus duplicating his 1918 role, if from the 'opposite' side).[21] Returning from the Philippines in 1943, Yamada voiced plans to compose an opera based upon the Philippine folk legend 'Sampaguita,' altering the tale (see below) to suit Japan's 'Greater East Asian' ideology. The announcement in *The Japan Times* directly enjoined the ideals of music, especially those rooted in national identity, to Japan's imperialist ideology:

> "Romantic traits are ideally interwoven with patriotic ideas and national characteristics in the story in 'Sampaguita.' The love between chieftain Lakan Galing and princess Liwayway 'reaches its climax when Lakan Galing is called away to fight for the honor of his country which is invaded by white men [sic: in most versions, rival tribes].' Lakan dies in battle, and Liwayway follows him to the grave, on which a white flower blooms, the

Sampaguita....The selection of this story...is highly significant, manifesting as it does the will of the composer to contribute toward the creation of a new culture for Greater East Asia....If such an opera composed by Japan's foremost musician with a traditional Filipino legend as its subject could materialize through the collaboration of the musicians and artists of both countries, the close cultural ties already linking Japan and the Philippines will undoubtedly be further forged."[22]

It is not known whether Yamada intended to utilize 'authentic' Philippine folk music in realizing the score, but it would hardly be surprising if he did it, and certainly not difficult not to read such a score as direct evidence of the transformation of cultural nationalism into the political variety.[23]

If it is too simplistic to read a direct evolution from cultural works using folksong, to national works using folksong, to mass-media works (movies, *gunka*) using or based upon folksong, to (a planned) imperialist opera based upon an 'exotic' folk legend from a colonized island, there are still several ways in which Yamada's folksong arrangements of the late 1920s lay the ground work for his propagandistic *gunka*, film scores, and projected opera. One concerns how the later arrangements evoke what Darrell Davis (1996, 237) has termed the 'monumental style:' the "appropriation of Japan's traditions to cast a sacramental light on the past and inspire people in the present."[24] "Oshoro Takashima" certainly evokes an atmosphere worthy of the 'Japanese spirit;' "Hakone Hachiriwa" a quasi-religious one."

More subtly, H.D. Harootunian (2000, 213) describes the transformation of cultural nationalism into political nationalism as an inversion (italicized insert is mine):

"[But] what appeared as a huge rescue operation to recall difference...was inverted to become a discourse devoted to upholding a unique cultural identity rooted in the racial specificity of myth and the presumption of ethnic homogeneity. When the experiences unearthed by the desire to resituate involuntary memory were subjected to appropriation and put into the service of public memory [*for instance via folksong arrangement?*], they risked slipping into the very process of reification they were supposed to counteract. Worse, they became the building blocks of an ideology of cultural exceptionalism and fascism."[25]

Perhaps this type of inversion, or the means through which it took place, is present in Yamada's own compositional record. Although many different song genres existed in interwar Japan, the lines between them were permeable. *Shôka* blurred into *gunka* (Yamada published a set of educational songs in 1931 just prior to "Human Bullets") and, as shown earlier, 'Human Bullets' itself drew upon the melodic tropes of "Kojo no Tsuki," a work taken as *minyo* despite its modern origin.[26] Yamada's most famous lieder ("Karatachi no Hana") occupy a similarly vague space between popular song (*kayokyoku*) and lieder (*kakyoku*). In brief, Yamada may have viewed *shôka, gunka, kakyoku* and *minyo* as equivalent forms of 'national' music, with folksong arrangement (*henkyoku*) situated ideally in between.[27] In any case, the point is not abstract. Not only did modern media provide sites wherein these forms of music could interact, but interwar recitals often concluded with Japanese folksong arrangements, thus presenting a vivid re-enactment of the communal body (*kyodotai*) itself, one that united composer, audience and performer in a common, authenticized, and imaginary Japanese past.[28]

There is at least one other sense in which Yamada's folksong arrangements foreshadow Japan's deepening nationalism. As noted above, in the late 1920s and early 1930s, Yamada began to use folksong in large-scale compositions. This treatment prefigures that found in the numerous propagandistic oratorios, cantatas and symphonic poems written under the fascist regime in the later 1930s and 1940s. In these works, a folksong or theme validated the work's Japanese content, while the Romantic style assured its emotional intensity. Albeit on a smaller scale, Yamada's folksong arrangements of the 1940s, with their obvious, grandiose effects, fit precisely into this esthetic mold and complete the frame.[29]

To conclude, the limited account posited above offers hypothetical paths, not unavoidable teleologies. But the analysis does help us to understand how one composer envisioned the complex politics and esthetics of the period as a unity—or better, reveal to us how he created a sense of unity through music. While it may be puzzling that Yamada's own stylistic pluralism didn't establish a stronger bulkhead against the idealized esthetics of Japan's fascist regime—folksong arrangement is hardly pure, at least not in the traditional sense—perhaps the idea of an easy exit on the road to militant nationalism is too simple. Although Yamada is sometimes portrayed as unaffected by his time (Harich-Schneider 1973, 545), he was, in fact, steeped in it, and a composer who yoked his music to the ship of state without bothering to consider what brackish reach of shoal lay await in the turbulent sea. While one can debate the extent to which time and compositional subtlety insulate Yamada's best arrangements from moral challenge—1928 is not 1943, but then in some ways it is—let us hope that we can enjoy the fruits of the past without repeating it errors.

Figure 5-8

Figure 5-8: Yamada's Folksong Arrangements for Voice and Piano (and obbligato insts.). Source: *Yamada Collected Works*, edited by Nobuko Goto, v. 9, 1924 'arrangements' for a Ministry of Education shōka, *Revitalization of Words of Old Songs*, omitted; vol. included Yamada's arrangement of Rentaro, "Kojo no Tsuki," c. 1917. (Volume illustrated by Yumeji Takehisa.)

Title	Date comp. (m/d)	Date 1st Published	Genre/Origin	Notes
For Carl Fischer Publishers. ("transcribed and modernized by")				
Cradle Song	1918 (3/4)	1919	Komoriuta/ Lullaby	
Sakura Sakura*	1918 (3/4)	–	Popular song	Omitted from publication
Flower Song	1918 (3/14)	1919	Shamisen	
Fisherman's Song	1918 (3/15)	1919	Boat song (Oiwake bushi)	Notes on each piece by Fred. H. Martens. Texts in English and Japanese.
Counting Song	1918 (3/23)	1919	Children's Song	
Imayo	1918 (3/23)*	1919	Buddist chant	
Song of the Pleasure Seekers	1918 (3/23)	1919	Pleasure quarters song	
For Tamaki Miura				
Himematsu	1922 (6/20 or 7/20)	1922	Children's song	(In Messager's *Mad. Chrysanthème*.)
Kuruka Kuruka	1922 (6/21?)	1922	Shamisen nagauta	By Kineya Rokuzaemon 9th, d. 1819.
Sakura Sakura*	1922	1922	Popular song	Rev. from 1918 version. (In *M.C.*)
Kinmya Monya	1922 (6/21?)	1922	Children's song	Lyrics contain nonsense syllables
For Fujiwara Yoshie				
Oshōro Takashima*	1927 (7/3)	1927	Hokkaido Fisherman's song	(Wax Recording avail. c. 1901-13.)
Hakone Hachiriwa*	1927 (8/9)	1927	Oiwake bushi	
Chūgoku Komoriuta	1928 (4/4)	1928	Lullaby from Chūgoku region	Transcribed from singer Ueno Taeyuki
Temariuta	1928	1928	Children's song ('hand ball')	Transcribed from singer Toyama Kunihiko
Sado Okesa	1928 (5/28)	1928	Sado Island folksong/Niigata(?)	First arr. with violin & drum
Funa uta*	1929	1943	Fisherman's Song	For *Kurofune*, Act III. Premiered 1940
Nagamochi uta	1931	1943	Famous Wedding song	
Published in *18 Japanese Folksongs* (1943)				
Oshōro Takashima*	1942/43	1943	Hokkaido Fisherman's Song	New flute cpt., intro. & coda; for Mariko Y.
Inna Bushi	1943	1943	From Nagano Prefecture.	
Ōryōkō Bushi*	1943 (1928)	1943	Japanese boating song from Korea	Simplified from draft for orch.& v., 1928.
Funa uta*	1943 (1929)	1943	Fisherman's song	Same as 1929 draft for *Kurofune*.
Hakone Hachiwa*	1950	1950	Oiwake Bushi	With new violin & bell parts.

*= two different versions composed.

Notes

1. Richard Taruskin, "Nationalism," in *Grove Music Online* accessed 02/08/2007. However, Taruskin does not treat Japanese nationalism. See also Robert F. Waters, "Emulation and Influence: *Japonisme* and Western Music in *fin de siècle* Paris," *The Music Review* 55 no. 3: 214-226.

2. Support for Japan's military regime was wide spread among intellectuals. See Keene 1984; Mayo, Rimer, and Kerkham 2001; and on music, Herd 2004 and Galliano 2003.

3. On *minzoku-shugi* and *kokumin-shugi* see Yayoi Uno Everett's review of Luciana Galliano, *Yogaku: Japanese Music in the Twentieth Century*, in *Asian Music*, Winter/Spring 2006: 139-140; Kevin M. Doak, "Building National Identity through Ethnicity: Ethnology in Wartime Japan and After," *Journal of Japanese Studies* 27, no. 1: 1-39;____, "Ethnic Nationalism and Romanticism in Early Twentieth-Century Japan," *Journal of Japanese Studies* 22, no. 1: 77-103; Yano 1998. General accounts include H.D. Harootunian 1974; and Shillony 1981.

4. Yamada's approach to arranging may have been influenced by his teacher Max Bruch. Christopher Fifield, *Max Bruch: His Life and Works*, (The Boydell Press, 1988), 48.

5. "'Thus we cultivate our own World, thus we share it with others: Kósçak Yamada's Visit to the United States, 1918-19," *American Music* 24, no. 1: 67-94 Yamada undertook the arrangements to help fund his visit but they generated little if any royalties.

6. Yamada stated (somewhat awkwardly): "The more intimate alliance and the identity of aspirations of the great nations, at the present leagued together for the achievement of world freedom, among them the United States and Japan, promises a closer and more intimate mutual interest in their arts." "Koscak Yamada Talks of Japanese Music and Musical Conditions (An Interview by Frederick H. Martens)," *The Musical Observer*, Dec. 1918: 14-15; See also Jiuji Kasai's intermission speech as related in "Japanese Conducts Own Native Works," *The New York Times*, Oct 1918? (NYPL Clippings file).

7. David W. Hughes, "Japanese 'New Folk Songs,' Old and New," *Asian Music* 22, no. 1: 1-49.

8. Miura was internationally renowned for her portrayal of 'Butterfly.' See Mari Yoshihara, "The Flight of the Japanese Butterfly: Orientalism, Nationalism, and Performances of Japanese Womanhood," *American Quarterly* Volume 56, no. 4: 975-1001.

9. In my original paper, I suggested that Yamada's use of space here anticipated the postwar esthetic of *ma*, but questioned this usage as it seemed to play into the trap, laid by Western essentialism, that Japanese music must sound or be audibly Japanese. As Yumi Calkwell's paper demonstrated, essentialist expectations continue to haunt Japanese composers, and Yamada was exposed to these sorts of expectations early in his career (see fn. 6). I do believe that 'space' provides a compelling metaphor for Yamada's setting of 'Hakone,' but cannot wonder if a trace of 'ma' remains in my discussion.

10. Saburo Moroi's *Symphony no. 3* constitutes a relevant example. Dating from 1944, the symphony's Romantic language may be easily read through a wartime lens. Yet as Morihide Katayama suggests (Naxos 8.557162 liner notes), the symphony may reflect the nation's growing consciousness of death, suggesting (perhaps) a more universal theme.

11. Harris's role is listed as the American consul. While his portrayal is positive, his actual behavior (under the veil of asking for a nurse, he requested a mistress/prostitute) and his role in the negotiations could have been presented in ways that would further inflame Japanese nationalism (Statler 1969).

12. "Koscak Yamada's Views on Music Told: Declares Western Music is Restricted by Notes on the Piano," *The Japan Times* (hereafter *TJT*), March 24, 1931: 1.

13. Koscak Yamada, "The Opera 'Dawn' or 'Black Ships,'" *Contemporary Japan* 9, no. 11: 1432. Yamada's complaint extends back to 1918 (H.E. Krehbiel, "Music: A Revelation of Japanese Music at Carnegie Hall," *New York Tribune*, Oct. 17, 1918). Although "Kurofune" is sometimes characterized as 'Madame Butterfly from a Japanese perspective,' its plot and characterizations differ substantially. Okichi resists not only the town governor, who wants Okichi to seduce Harris, but also her samurai lover Yoshida, who asks her to assassinate him.

14. Okichi's final lines (*The cannon roar, the cannon roar/They are not the cannon of war/They foretell the coming of morrow's peace!*) appear to have added in 1939 or 1940. Compare Koscak Yamada, "The Opera 'Dawn' or 'Black Ships,'" 1437-1438, with Koscak Yamada [sic Noel Percy], *Yoake (Dawn) or The Black Ships*, manuscript copy of original [?] English libretto (date unknown, perhaps late 1920s or early 1930s).

15. Despite obvious nationalistic strains in Yamada's symphonic poem 'Kamikaze' (premiered in 1940), the work did not produce the intended effect. (I.J. Fischer, "Symphony Concert is Great Success," *TJT*, November 27, 1940: 8.)

16. Peter High (2003, 37) relates that "[t]he late film researcher Yamamoto Kikuo develops the interesting thesis that the Human Bomb Patriots myth played an active role in the ideological conditioning of the Japanese people. All three men had come from impoverished homes. In the popular imagination they were identified as the epitome of the traditionalist theory that true human virtue comes from the combination of *Hin-Kô-Chû.* (poverty, filial piety, and loyalty)."

17. *The Asahi Shimbun* had established a competition for poems about the attack. The first stanza reads: "Over the bodies of war comrades/For the sake of their fatherland, for the sake/Of his Majesty, their lives dedicated./Advanced, ah the loyal hearts, three heroes with their bombs." ("'Three Heroes With Their Bombs' Is Theme of Prize-Winning Song; Composer Gets 500 [yen]," *TJT*, March 17, 1932: 1.)

18. Yamada published an arrangement of it in his 1924 Ministry of Education *shôka*, "Revitalizations of the Words of Old Songs."

19. On early *gunka* see Ikuma Dan, "The Influence of Japanese Traditional Music on the Development of Western Music in Japan," trans. Dorothy G Britton, *Transactions of the Asiatic Society of Japan* 8: 211; and Tôyô Nakamura "Early

pop song writers and their backgrounds," trans. John Dolan, *Popular Music* 10, no. 3: 271.

20. Mizoguchi remembered his film as "a nightmare born from a political idea rather than an artistic one." (As cited in High, *Imperial Screen*, 34.)

21. See for instance "Iguchi Outlines Vital Role of Japan in Musical World: Japanese Music is Spreading to the Southern Regions, and It Is Nippon's Duty to Lead the Peoples There to Find and Create Their Own National Music," *TJT*, July 14, 1943: 5.

22. "Sampaguita, Philippine Classic, Is Basis of New Opera, Written by Koscak Yamada," *TJT*, December 23, 1943: 3. Interestingly, the legend itself maybe the product of native writers' own search for a national identity while under Spanish rule.

23. ....And as a more than faint echo of the exoticism and essentialism practiced in the West.

24. On 'spiritism' in Japanese films, see High, *Imperial Screen*, 198-99, 382+.

25. Elsewhere (p. 300-2) Harootunian highlights persistent 'contradictions' and 'oscillations' between tradition and modernity.

26. On the relationship between *shôka* and *gunka*, see Ury Eppstein, "School Songs Before and After the War. From 'Children Tank Soldiers' to 'Everyone a Good Child,'" *Monumenta Nipponica* 42 no. 4: 431-447; on popular song, see Yano, "Defining a Nation."

27. However, David Hughes reads the demise of new folksong (*shin-minyô*) in the 1930s *against* Japan's burgeoning nationalism. ("Japanese 'New Folk Songs,'" 5.)

28. See also remarks by Percy Noel (librettist for 'Kurofune') in *When Japan Fights*, (The Hokuseido Press, 1937), 235.

29. As a product of Meiji Japan and Meiji education, Yamada may have viewed his music in terms of the ideal of national progress, whatever that progress might be. His early symphonic poems possess suggestive titles: 'Victory and Peace,' 'Ode to Meiji,' 'Prelude to Kimigayo.' In any case, he made no attempt to counter Japan's turn toward imperialism.

References

Davis, Darrell W. 1996. *Picturing Japaneseness: Monumental Style, National Identity, Japanese Film*. New York: Columbia University Press.

Galliano, Luciana. 2003. *Yogaku: Japanese Music in the Twentieth Century*. Scarecrow Press.

Harich-Schneider, Eta. 1973. *A History of Japanese Music*. London: Oxford University Press.

Harootunian, H.D. 2000. *Overcome By Modernity: History, Culture, and Community in Interwar Japan*. Princeton: Princeton University Press.

—. 1990a. Figuring the Folk: History, Poetics, and Representation. *Mirror of Modernity: Invented Traditions of Modern Japan.* ed. Stephen Vlastos. Berkeley: University of California Press. 144-62.

—. 1990b. Disciplinizing Native Knowledge and Producing Place: Yanagita Kunio, Origuchi Shinobu, Takata Yasuma. *Culture and Identity: Japanese Intellectuals During the Interwar Years.* ed. J. Thomas Rimer. Princeton: Princeton University Press.

—. 1974. Between Politics and Culture: Authority and the Ambiguities of Intellectual Choice in Imperial Japan. *Japan in Crisis: Essays on Taishô Democracy.* ed. Bernard S. Silberman and H.D. Harootunian. Princeton: Princeton University Press.

Herd, Judith Ann. 2004. The Cultural Politics of Japan's Modern Music: Nostalgia, Nationalism, and Identify in the Interwar Years. *Locating East Asia in Western Art Music.* ed. Yayoi Uno Everett and Frederick Lau. Middletown: Wesleyan University Press. 40-56.

High, Peter. 2003. *The Imperial Screen: Japanese Film Culture in the Fifteen Years' War, 1931-1945.* University of Wisconsin Press.

Keene, Donald. 1984. *Dawn to the West: Japanese Literature in the Modern Era.* New York: Henry Holt and Company.

Mayo, Marlene J. and J. Thomas Rimer, H. Eleanor Kerkham eds. 2001. *War, Occupation, and Creativity: Japan and East Asia 1920-1960.* Honolulu: Univ. of Hawaii Press.

Shillony, Ben-Ami. 1981. *Politics and Culture in Wartime Japan.* Oxford: Clarendon Press.

Statler, Oliver. 1969. *Shimoda Story.* Random House.

Yano, Christine R. 1998. Defining the Modern Nation in Popular Song. *Japan's Competing Modernities: Issues in Culture and Democracy, 1900-1930.* ed. Sharon A. Minichiello. Honolulu: University of Hawaii Press. 247-266.

CHAPTER SIX

A JAPANESE ZERO-HOUR? - POSTWAR MUSIC AND THE "RE-MAKING" OF THE PAST

FUYUKO FUKUNAKA

In the September 1946 issue of *Ongaku Geijutsu* [*The Musical Art*] appeared an essay by the prominent music historian, Sadao Tsuchida. It is entitled "Creation from Nothing" and opens with an empathic phrase, "the joy at being able to feel the great might with which to create something visible out of nothing" (Tsuchida 1946, 2). The urge for a renewed start stressed in the essay echoes the notion of total artistic freedom embraced by Boulez and other European figures around the same time— retrospectively captured in his oft-cited phrase suggestive of the zero-hour myth, "finding nothing in front of us" (Boulez 1971, 7). Yet Tsuchida also reminds that such "joy" could be had only by embracing "a cold reality where tradition, history, [and] existing values [. . .] are [. . .] abandoned in a lifeless wasteland [. . .]" (Tsuchida 1946, 2). Indeed, he distances himself from the unreserved optimism abundant in print in Japan's music scenes following the end of the war, one example of which, dating from October 1945, reads thus: "We [musicians] must play a part in enlightening our people [. . .] towards reconstructing the nation with a sense of hope and determination. This is the direction where our music should be headed" (Horiuchi 1945, 2). Devoid of condescending sentiments marking similar essays that collectively identify "us musicians" as a signpost for a new Japan, Tsuchida's rhetoric lacks a sense of euphoria, instead maintaining incisive tones throughout. In Tokyo, its musical life had begun anew in September 1945 when the Japan Symphony Orchestra (now the NHK Symphony Orchestra) resumed its concert series at the Hibiya Public Hall, symbolically located only a few blocks away from the GHQ/SCAP occupation authorities. Yet Tsuchida perhaps meant his essay to be a bitter warning that the rewriting of Japanese music in its truest sense had not yet begun.

The present paper looks at the social and cultural climates of Japan's music scenes immediately following its defeat, as well as the nature of self-reinvention sought after by some of the leading music figures in an attempt to prove themselves worthy of a new Japan. The study of contemporary documents, from composers' writings to GHQ/SCAP papers, reveals that the collectively-embraced "new beginning" in reality was slow to come. There were several contributing factors: for one, Japan's music sector did not undergo GHQ/SCAP purging policies as extensive as those exercised in other domains. One should also note the absence of a Darmstadt equivalent, where the *younger* figures would have mandated a total aversion to past ideologies, both technical and aesthetic. Darmstadt is indeed an interesting parallel: with the Schoenbergian dodecaphonic writing introduced in Japan on the one hand, and the post-Webern serial system eagerly pursued in Europe on the other, serialism seems to have stood for contrasting notions: in Japan, for a purely *technical* means that would speak for a framework for "new music"; in Europe, for an *aesthetic* premise that would entirely revise the notion of "music-writing." This difference, albeit symbolic, mirrors the emotional construct of "post" in the word "postwar" that Japanese musicians eagerly sought to affix to their music, as will be examined below.

On 2 September 1945, the same day the instruments of Japan's surrender were signed, the State Secretary James Byrnes spoke in Washington of "the need for the psychological demilitarization of the Japanese [. . .], which is more important than physical disarmament."[1] Foreshadowing the United States Initial Post-Surrender Policy for Japan issued in late September,[2] Byrnes thus urged revision in areas where things were less visible. Only a month later, the magazine *Ongaku Chishiki* [*The Musical Knowledge*] announced the *voluntary* dissolution of the Japanese Music Culture Association.[3] This corporate body had been restructured out of a multi-sectional organization called the Alliance for the Promotion of the New System in Music in November 1941, which itself had been founded in November 1940 after the dissolution of the Contemporary Composers' Federation of Japan and of other organizations, the former being the Japanese branch of ISCM. As a pretext for the creation of the Japanese Music Culture Association, the Alliance was a product of the totalitarian "one-field, one-organization" scheme, founded as part of the government's attempt to consolidate the so-called New System, a political framework for promoting imperialist military campaigns. An organization promoting musical activities through publishing music and organizing auditions and concerts, the Japanese Music Culture Association in turn functioned in close collaboration with government officials and remained under their tight control, especially that of the notorious Information Bureau. From its inception, the Association held an indispensable function in instrumentalizing music for constructing imperialist propaganda. For example, the *Ongaku Bunka Shimbun* [*Music Culture News*], the newsletter published by the Association, led discussion of whether to physically destroy musical scores of US and British composers, and the need for drastic measures was argued for in the 1 July 1943 edition, since "we must hate not only our enemy, but also what they create" (Yamazumi 1976, 153). In 1943 the Association took on an additional role as an agent for the Metropolitan Police Commissioner, holding the exclusive authority over the issuance of mandatory concert permits (Takahashi 2002, 108-9). Given its history as such, the dissolution of the Association in October 1945, to many, stood for a symbolic end of wartime musical life.

If the Association's dissolution marked, to music circles, a hastened break with the past, another incident of similar nature took place in December the same year in a manner more visible to the public. *The Tokyo Shimbun* [*The Tokyo Newspaper*] printed an essay written by the prominent music critic Ginji Yamane, entitled "The Unqualified Intermediary." In it Yamane called the composer Kosaku Yamada (1886-1965) "a war criminal" and questioned the validity of his senior membership in the Japan Music Federation, the postwar successor of the Association (Yamane 1945, 2). Yamane's accusations against Yamada ranged widely: that Yamada persecuted Jewish musicians living in Japan during the war years, manipulated the Association to consolidate his standing, and later ingratiated himself with GHQ/SCAP in an attempt to play down his war-time activities. This was the first piece of the three-piece essay by Yamane and, interestingly enough, Yamada's response appeared in the same paper on the day the first essay by Yamane was printed. In his response "Who Really Is a War Criminal?" Yamada argues that he could not be singled out, as virtually every Japanese musician had supported Japan's militarist policies. Yamada then tactically shifted the focus of the argument, saying that "we now must devote ourselves to resuscitating our nation through noble activities," instead of resorting to unproductive finger-pointing (Yamada 1945, 2).

Present-day readings of this incident vary. For example, Iwao Takahashi in his recent book chronicling his activities as a concert agent before, during, and after the war paints a picture of Yamada as an innocent by-stander whose fame was exploited by the militarist government for propagandistic purposes (Takahashi 2002, 145-51). Several music historians, on the other hand, consider Yamada voluntarily involving himself in militarist campaigns during the war (Sasaki 1976, 169; Komiya 2001, 132-6). In all fairness, facts fail to speak of Yamada as a reluctant collaborator: in 1940, even prior to the foundation of the Association, Yamada appointed himself president of the Performers' Association founded under the auspices of the Metropolitan Police Department. By taking up the role of issuing *mandatory* permits to performers, including orchestral musicians, this organization enabled itself to place Tokyo's performance scenes under their strict control. In the following year, Yamada established the Music Service Force consisting of performers registered with the Performers' Association and organized concerts for the purpose of "provid[ing] people living under harsh conditions with comfort and relief," visiting army bases and arsenals.[4] Indeed, several contemporaries of Yamada have documented him as proudly donning a military uniform and a saber, and taking a visible role in militarist activities under the slogan of "Our music is our weapon."[5] Josef Rosenstock is one such person. A German of Jewish origin, and conductor of the Japan Symphony Orchestra between 1936 and 1946 who remained in Japan throughout the war years, Rosenstock contributed an essay to a non-music weekly journal in January 1946, where he singled out Yamada as someone who had led Japan's war-time music sector in accordance with the "Nazi" ideologies (Rosenstock 1946, 12).

The inconvenient truth, however, is that many other musicians of prominent standing adopted the imperialist propaganda during the war as well, at least as documented through contemporary writings. Yamane himself is the author of an essay "Our Project as People's Movement" published in the January 1943 issue of *Ongaku Bunka* [*The Music Culture*]. There he calls on composers to "write brave, robust new songs with which to boost the morale of our soldiers nobly devoted to destroying the Allied Powers" (Yamane 1943, 37). Although later expelled on the grounds of his alleged past as a communist sympathizer, Yamane was also a founding member of the Association and a signatory of its Statement of Intent, a document that is replete with unambiguously imperialist rhetoric (Akiyama 2003, 327-8). As for composers, Shukichi Mitsukuri (1895-1971), Yasuji Kiyose (1900-1981), and Saburo Moroi (1903-1977), all of prominent standing, fulfilled a central role in administering the Association's composers wing. Elsewhere, the music critic Akimitsu Yoshimoto took as prominent a role in persecuting Jewish musicians in Japan, arguing that "Japan's music scenes have been desecrated by Jewish conspiracies," and called for Rosenstock's resignation (Yoshimoto 1942, 39), long before the Association issued a recommendation to refrain from hiring non-Japanese performers of non-German or Italian origin (Takahashi 2002, 116).

The Yamada incident ended up only in the naming of names, instead of prompting the entire music sector to self-examine its roles in propagandizing culture during the war years--but why? With the benefit of hindsight, it perhaps mirrored the wishful thinking among musicians, Yamane among them, that some external force would somehow help cleanse postwar Japanese music of its painful past. Yamane's accusations appeared in the month when, in anticipation of the Tokyo Trial, the International Prosecution Section was erected within GHQ/SCAP. In addition, with the announcement in early October of the creation of the Government Section within GHQ whose responsibilities were to include "the removal of ultranationalists," extensive purging procedures in the public sector had been set on track by December.[6] In other words, Yamane put out his essay when there was considerable momentum towards, to cite John Dower's expression, "revolution from above" (Dower 1999, *passim.*).

If Yamane's accusations were motivated only by his personal enmity towards Yamada as suggested by some (Takahashi 2002, 151; Akiyama 2003, 365-78), then his wish was ultimately fulfilled when the recently-erected Tokyo Metropolitan Philharmonic Orchestra, partially funded by the city of Tokyo and with Yamada as its first president, was abruptly closed by GHQ in July 1946. A conference report of CIE (Civil Information and Education Section) from around the same time, in fact, reveals that the case of Yamada was being discussed within CIE, with a good deal of information on his wartime activities already collected (Figure 6-1). Other than Yamada's case, however, no drastic "revolution from above" really took place.[7] One may even claim that, apart from the extensive curriculum reform in music, the GHQ/SCAP policies that most affected Japan's music sector were those on the purging of the education sector, with CIE having begun in late October the extensive removal of "suspected" teachers from schools, both public and private.[8] The exact number of music teachers removed from their positions has not been located anywhere in related documents; however, an attempt to discharge eleven professors by the Tokyo Academy of Music (now the Tokyo National University of Fine Arts and Music) in July 1946 was a widely-publicized incident.[9] Applicants for new academic positions were also subjected to screening. Some even voluntarily asked for closer investigation by CIE officials.[10] What remained of the imperialist rhetoric that had so deeply pervaded pre-war music magazines, on the other hand, did not intrigue GHQ/SCAP obviously: Table 6-1 is a list of articles in classical music magazines that went through post-publication censorship. Compared to the extensive censorship imposed on other domains by CCD, the Civil Censorship Detachment,[11] this list is inexplicably short, bypassing writings by those who had mounted ultra-nationalistic expressions in pre-war magazines and newspapers.[12]

Table 6-1

> 1. Yoshihiko ARISAKA, "The Newly-Born Record Industry," *Ongaku no tomo* 4 (January 1946).
> 2. Shizuko KASAGI, "Singing as My Life," *Ongaku no Tomo* 4 (July 1946).
> 3. Shiro FUKAI, "On Respect for Technique," *Ongaku Geijutsu* 4 (December 1946).
> 4. Hidemaro KONOE, "Beethoven's Symphonies," *Ongaku* 3(January 1948).
> 5. Takeo MURATA, "What Critics Should Do," *Ongaku* 3 (January 1948).
> 6. Keizo HORIGUCHI, "Bach's *Brandenburg Concerto*," *Ongaku no Tomo* 7 (January 1949).

(Source: "The Prange Collection Database" (on-line data-base), published by Waseda University, The Institute for 20th-Century Media Studies, at http://www.prangedb.jp)

    In hindsight, this is one version of "postwar" Japanese music, a version where the agents responsible for creating the future anew were also the agents that had constituted the past. As a result, the "post" in a truer sense failed to take hold. This "failure" was perhaps a leading factor behind the emergence of composers' groups that rapidly sprouted between 1945 and 1950. In place of a conclusion, I shall briefly touch upon one of these groups, *Shinsei-kai* (the Group of New Voice), and its members, Yoshiro Irino (1921-1980) and Minao Shibata (1916-1996), who drew upon twelve-tone composition for their post-war departure.[13]
    The roots of twelve-tone music in Japan may be traced chiefly to two currents. One was a cluster of interests that surfaced in the 1930s: this can best be seen in the short-lived journal *Ongaku Kenkyu* [*Music Research*] that mounted a special issue in 1937 devoted to Schoenberg, although discussions of twelve-tone music there remained general. Those interested included Isao Nobutoki (1887-1965), who reportedly lent a number of Schoenberg scores to Saburo Moroi, the composer whose pupils formed

the *Shinsei-kai* in 1946.[14] The other current appeared after the war, when Kunio Toda (1915-2003), later a member of the *Shinsei-kai*, returned to Japan in 1948 after incarceration in French Saigon, with a copy of Leibowitz's *Schoenberg et son école* (Shibata 1995, 227). Literature published in the first half of the 1950s on twelve-tone composition is an interesting testimony to its contemporary contextualization. The March 1955 issue of *Geijutu Shincho* [*New Currents in the Arts*], for example, discusses the system through the metaphor "language," i.e. solely as a means for expression, not as expression itself (Fukai et al. 1955, 202-6). As if echoing this, Irino, who had written an introductory book on twelve-tone music, offered an evolutional context of the system (Irino 1953, 12). After positing that what is important is the composer's *idea* expressed, not techniques, Irino states that "twelve-tone music is based on the system Schoenberg invented, that is to say, is born *directly* out of German music tradition." He then draws a parallel between compositional technique and language, arguing that "the question is, where to find the means most suited for expressing one's own creative *ideas* [italics added]" (Irino 1955, 45). These sentences thus underscore the notion that the serial technique came along as a result of some evolutional logic, of which one's *creative* thinking should be independent. In other words, Irino and Shibata seem to have embraced the serial technique as secondary to what Irino called "idea," implying that this "idea,"—whatever that was to mean—was of somewhat elevated status, and something to remain intact from external stylistic or technical contextualization.

What contention does this formula imply when it comes to "music" and "war"?: that many had been "forced" to frame their music in militarist style; many, likewise, had to compose to propagandistic text against their will; yet their musical "idea" itself had been intact, and it now found the means of expression in line with the international vocabulary. Such naiveté as to separate the "content" from inconvenient external framework may in part explain why it took Japan's music sector almost thirty years to vet in detail what contributions music had made in creating the all-nation support system towards ultranationalist campaigns during the war.[15] The idea that music could exist independently from all social and political happenings still seems to resist refutation in Japan. Given this, closer examination of Japan's wartime musical life may provide us with something more than a source of finger-pointing: something that makes us ask ourselves, again, why we "do" music.

Figure 6-1. GHQ/SCAP Conference Report, dated 19 July 1946 (The Japan National Diet Library, the Politics and Law Division, microfiche#: CIE(A) 00398, page 8-C)

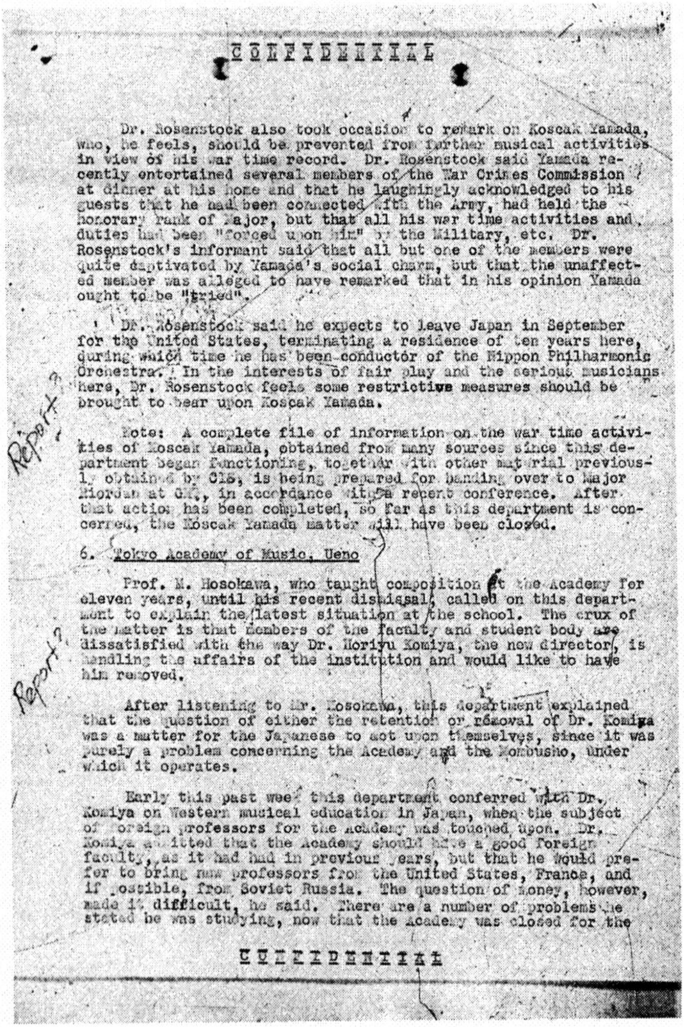

CONFIDENTIAL

Dr. Rosenstock also took occasion to remark on Koscak Yamada, who, he feels, should be prevented from further musical activities in view of his war time record. Dr. Rosenstock said Yamada recently entertained several members of the War Crimes Commission at dinner at his home and that he laughingly acknowledged to his guests that he had been connected with the Army, had held the honorary rank of Major, but that all his war time activities and duties had been "forced upon him" by the Military, etc. Dr. Rosenstock's informant said that all but one of the members were quite captivated by Yamada's social charm, but that the unaffected member was alleged to have remarked that in his opinion Yamada ought to be "tried".

Dr. Rosenstock said he expects to leave Japan in September for the United States, terminating a residence of ten years here, during which time he has been conductor of the Nippon Philharmonic Orchestra. In the interests of fair play and the serious musicians here, Dr. Rosenstock feels some restrictive measures should be brought to bear upon Koscak Yamada.

Note: A complete file of information on the war time activities of Koscak Yamada, obtained from many sources since this department began functioning, together with other material previously obtained by CIS, is being prepared for handing over to Major Riordan at GHQ, in accordance with a recent conference. After that action has been completed, so far as this department is concerned, the Koscak Yamada matter will have been closed.

6. Tokyo Academy of Music, Ueno

Prof. M. Hosokawa, who taught composition at the Academy for eleven years, until his recent dismissal, called on this department to explain the latest situation at the school. The crux of the matter is that members of the faculty and student body are dissatisfied with the way Dr. Horiyu Komiya, the new director, is handling the affairs of the institution and would like to have him removed.

After listening to Mr. Hosokawa, this department explained that the question of either the retention or removal of Dr. Komiya was a matter for the Japanese to act upon themselves, since it was purely a problem concerning the Academy and the Mombusho, under which it operates.

Early this past week this department conferred with Dr. Komiya on Western musical education in Japan, when the subject of foreign professors for the Academy was touched upon. Dr. Komiya admitted that the Academy should have a good foreign faculty, as it had had in previous years, but that he would prefer to bring new professors from the United States, France, and if possible, from Soviet Russia. The question of money, however, made it difficult, he said. There are a number of problems he stated he was studying, now that the Academy was closed for the

CONFIDENTIAL

Notes

1. Jichi-Daigaku, ed. *Sengo Jichishi* [*The History of Postwar Self-Government*], vol. 6 (Tokyo: Jichi-Daigaku, 1964), 8.

2. Refer to SWNCC (State- War- Navy- Coordinating Committee) Document #150/4, cited in: ibid, 13.

3. Tetsuo Maruyama, "Ongaku-kai tenbo [The Outlook of Music Scenes]," *Ongaku Chishiki* [*The Musical Knowledge*] 3 (November 1945), 2.

4. N. a., "Ongaku kenshintai kessei saru [The Music Service Force has been erected]," *Gekkan Gakufu* [*Music Monthly*] 30 (October 1941), 106.

5. This popular phrase may be spotted in many music periodicals published during the war years, e.g., Hideo Hiraide, "Ongaku wa gunju-hin nari [Our Music is Our Weapon]," *Ongaku Kurabu* [*Music Club*] 7 (August 1940), 6.

6. Jichi-Daigaku, 60-1.

7. One may compare it against the extensive purging that ICD, the US Information Control Division, exercised in occupied Germany, through compiling comprehensive black, grey, and white lists of suspected former Nazi-sympathizers in the field of music. See David Monod, *Settling Scores* (Chapel Hill: The University of North Carolina Press, 2005), 40-49.

8. This began in accordance with the GHQ document known as "Memorandum on investigation, exclusion, and permission of teachers and officials in the education sector (SCAPIN 212)," issued on 30 October 1945 and quoted in: Takashi Momose, *Jiten: Showa Sengo-ki no Nihon: Senryo to Kaikaku* [*Handbook: Japan in the Postwar Era: Occupation and Reform*] (Tokyo: Yoshikawa Kobunkan, 1995), 110-11. The official directive on purging in all sectors was issued on 4 January 1946 as SCAPIN 550: Jichi-Daigaku, 55-60.

9. Documented in a CIE weekly report dated 26 July 1946, doc. # CIE(A)-06399 (The Japan National Diet Library, Politics and Law Division).

10. The composer Shukichi Mitsukuri was one such case. A CIE conference report dated 19 July 1946 documents that Rosenstock, whose pupil Mitsukuri was, visited the CIE and indicated the composer's wish to have his war-time records thoroughly reviewed. Conference Report, dated 19 July 1946 (The Japan National Diet Library, Politics and Law Division, doc.#: CIE (A) 00398).

11. This was a division within CIS, the Civil Intelligence Section. The censorship was at times conducted jointly with the CIE.

12. This includes the prominent critics Araebisu Nomura and Akimitsu Yoshimoto, and the composer Osamu Shimizu. See, for example, Yoshimoto, "Hyakunen senso-da! Nihon wa korede yoika! [It is a Hundred-Year War! What Should Japan Do?]," *Ongaku no Tomo* [*The Friends of Music*] 2 (December 1942), 39.

13. Irino and Shibata are generally credited with first having "used" the twelve-tone technique in Japan. Irino's first composition using the technique, the String Sextet, dates from 1950, while Shibata's, *Morning Song* dates from 1952.

14. It is interesting that, while privately studying Schoenberg's music, Nobutoki composed the highly tonal, homophonic symphonic cantata entitled *Kaido Tohsei*

[*Passage in the Sea, to conquer the East*], performed at a concert in 1940 celebrating the 2600th anniversary of imperial Japan. See: Kenzo Nakajima, *Ongaku to Watakushi* [*Music and I*] (Tokyo: Kodansha, 1974), 173.

15. Akiyama's aforementioned publication, which is a collection of essays originally published in the magazine *Ongaku Geijutsu* [*Musical Art*] between January 1974 and December 1978, was the first attempt at looking back to the roles played by composers and music critics in the propagandizing of music during the war years.

References

Akiyama, Kuniharu. 2003. *Showa no sakkyoku-ka tachi* [Composers in the Showa Era]. Tokyo: Misuzu Publishing. 327-28.

Boulez, Pierre. 1945. Où en est-on? *Revue musicale* 276-7 (1971): 7-9.

Dower, John. 1999. *Embracing Defeat*. New York: W. W. Norton.

Fukai, Shiro, Yoshiro Irino, Kenzo Nakajima, and Hidekazu Yoshida. "Nijusseiki no meisaku [Masterpieces of the 20th Century]." *Geijutsu Shinchou* [*New Currents in the Arts*]. No vol. # (March 1955): 186-208

Hiraide, Hideo. 1940. Ongaku wa gunju-hin nari [Our Music is Our Weapon]. *Ongaku Kurabu* [*Music Club*] 7 (August 1940): 6.

Horiuchi, Keizo. 1945. Ongaku wa donaruka [What with Our music?]. *Ongaku Chishiki* [*The Musical Knowledge*] 3 (October 1945): 2.

Irino, Yoshiro. 1953. *Juni-On no Ongaku* [*Twelve-Tone Music*]. Tokyo: Hayakawa Publishing.

—. 1955. Naze juni-on ongaku o jissen suruka [Why I Compose Twelve-Tone Music]. *Geijutu Shincho* [*New Currents in the Arts*] (February 1955): 44-6.

Jichi-Daigaku, ed. 1964. *Sengo Jichishi* [*The History of Postwar Self-Government*]. Vol. 6. Tokyo: Jichi-Daigaku.

Komiya, Tamie. 2001. *Kin-gendai nihon no ongakushi* [*The Music History of Modern Japan*]. Tokyo: Ongaku no sekai-sha.

Maruyama, Tetsuo. 1945. Ongaku-kai tenbo [The Outlook of Music Scenes]. *Ongaku Chishiki* [*The Musical Knowledge*] 3 (November 1945): 2.

Rosenstock, Josef. 1946. Shin-nihon no ongaku [The Music of New Japan]. *Shukan Shin-Nihon* [*New Japan Weekly*] (1 Jan 1946): 10-13.

Sasaki, Hikaru. 2001. Ongaku-ka to senso-sekinin [Musicians and their War-time Responsibility]. In *Kindai Nihon to Ongaku* [*Contemporary Japan and its Music*]. Nihon Ongaku Buyo Kaigi, ed. Tokyo: Ayumi Publishing.

Shibata, Minao. 1995. *Waga Ongaku, Waga Jinsei* [My Music, My Life]. Tokyo: Iwanami.

Takahashi, Iwao. 2002. *Showa Gekido no Ongaku Monogatari* [*The Dynamic History of Music in the Showa Era*] Tokyo: Asahi Publishing.

Tsuchida, Sadao. 1946. Mu kara no sozo [Creation from Nothing]. *Ongaku Geijutsu* [The Musical Art]. (September1946): 2-5.

Yamada, Kosaku. 1945. Hatashite darega senso-hanzaisha ka [Who Really is a War Criminal?]. *The Tokyo Shimbun* (23 December 1945): 2.

Yamane. Ginji. 1943. Kokumin undo to shite no kikaku [Our Project as People's Movement]. *Ongaku Bunka* [*The Music Culture*] 1 (December 1943): 37.

—. 1945. Shikaku-naki chukai-sha [The Unqualified Intermediary]. *The Tokyo Shimbun* [*Tokyo Newspaper*] (23 December 1945): 2.

Yamazumi, Masami. 1976. Taiheiyo-senso kaishi toji no ongaku to ongaku kyoiku [Music and Music Education at the Beginning of the Pacific War]. In *Kindai Nihon to Ongaku* [*Contemporary Japan and Music*], Nihon Ongaku Buyo Kaigi, ed. Tokyo: Ayumi Publishing.

Yoshimoto, Akimitsu. 1942. Hyakunen senso-da! Nihon wa korede yoika! [It is a Hundred-Year War! What Should Japan Do?]. *Ongaku no Tomo* [The Friends of Music] 2 (December 1942): 39.

SECTION TWO

BEYOND TRADITION:
RECENT PERSPECTIVES ON TAKEMITSU'S
MUSIC AND LEGACY

The music and ideas of Toru Takemitsu (1930-1996) continue to attract worldwide attention among musicians and scholars, more than ten years after his death. One reason, in addition to the quality of his music, is the poetic and metaphorical nature of his words concerning his music, which leaves much for others to interpret. Another is the almost cult-like status that he attained, especially outside of Japan, which still holds today.

Early in his musical career, Takemitsu stayed away from overt references to, or influence from, Japanese traditional music or aesthetics (Galliano 2003). However, along with his colleagues in the *Jikken Kobo*, Yuasa and Fukushima, he became conscious of how Japanese culture in general was so deeply connected to his thinking. In his attempt to develop a new music (Galliano, 160), Takemitsu used his "Japanese approach to art to find new and different musical categories, procedures, and structures." He embraced a sophisticated and sensitive use of sound, at first stimulated by French impressionist music, but also drawn from aesthetic principles of Japanese culture and art. One of these principles is a focus on the beauty within characteristics of individual sounds from nature. Takemitsu writes (1995, 56-7):

> "I think that as a people who developed the concept of 'attaining Buddha-hood in a single sound' (*Ichion Jobutsu*), the Japanese found more meaning in listening to the innate quality of sound rather than using sound as a means of expression."

Because of the belief that humans should exist as a part of nature rather than conquer nature, Japanese aesthetics also celebrates natural sound that includes noise components. Attitudes towards timbre in Western art-music have traditionally favored a pure, innate, static quality. In traditional Japanese music, the acceptance of noise is in stark contrast to this concept.

Japanese view timbre as a temporal, changing phenomenon – a shifting of sound ….a dynamic state.

A term used to describe a complex, single sound containing many overtones (and noise components) is *sawari* – a phenomenon commonly heard in sounds of the *biwa* and *shamisen*. (*sawari* refers to the prioritization of sound in Japanese traditional music in contrast to the emphasis on harmony and the elimination of noise in Western music) Mitsuko Ono, a Japanese musicologist who has translated a number of writings by and about Takemitsu, discusses Takemitsu's use of *sawari* in his music (*Toru Takemitsu and the Japanese Sound of Sawari*). In her exploration, she explains how Takemitsu's usage is different than that found in the Japanese traditional instrument repertoire, and shows examples of original sounds in Takemitsu's works for Western instruments that resemble *sawari* but are no longer *sawari* itself.

Another element of Japanese culture that reflects a close connection to nature is the Japanese style of garden design – *kaiyushiki*. In addition to trees and shrubs, the Japanese garden makes artistic use of rocks, sand, artificial hills, ponds, and flowing water – no detail dominates over any other. In contrast to the geometrically arranged trees and rocks of a Western-style garden, the Japanese garden traditionally creates a scenic composition that mimics nature (even scenes from outside the garden "frame" can often be viewed as part of its composition - the garden becomes part of "outside" nature). It is to be experienced by walking/wandering through it (in a non-linear rather than linear sense of time), not from the outside, blending the notion of space with that of time.

Takemitsu often used the Japanese garden as a metaphor when talking about his musical aesthetics. Hideaki Onishi has found, through set-theory analysis, that three of Takemitsu's orchestral works (*Fantasma/Cantos*, *Spirit Garden*, *Dream/Window*) in which he refers to a Japanese garden (in either the title or program notes) can be viewed as "a seemingly random recurrence of a referential sonority and its derivatives, which is not dissimilar to the view of an object seen from various angles in a Japanese garden." To reach this conclusion, Onishi has developed a superset/subset network that is more locally conceived than, though similar to, Allen Forte's concept of set complex K and subcomplex Kh.

Finally, Peter Burt examines the role of the Western press in the genesis of Takemitsu's status as pre-eminent Japanese composer of the post-war period (*Music in the Bathtub: Reading Takemitsu's Music Through Western Criticism*). In particular, Burt finds that some negative readings serve to emphasize the positive qualities they distort and misrepresent.

References

Burt, Peter. 2001. *The Music of Toru Takemitsu*. Cambridge University Press.

Galliano, Luciana. 2003. *Yogaku: Japanese Music in the Twentieth Century*. The Scarecrow Press, Inc.

Koozin, Timothy. 2002. Traversing distances: pitch organization, gesture and imagery in the late works of Tōru Takemitsu. *Contemporary Music Review* 21:4. 17–34.

Ministry of Foreign Affairs. 2007. *Japanese Gardens*. Kodansha International Ltd.
http://www.soundintermedia.co.uk/treeline-online/gardens.html

Nuss, Steven, 2002. Hearing 'Japanese', hearing Takemitsu. *Contemporary Music Review* 21:4. 35–71.

Ohtake, Noriko. 1993. *Creative sources for the Music of Toru Takemitsu*. Scolar Press.

Parkes, Graham. 1995. Ways of Japanese Thinking. *Japanese Aesthetics and Culture: A Reader*. Ed. Nancy G. Hume. Albany St University of New York Press.

Takemitsu, Toru. 1995. *Confronting Silence*. Berkeley, CA: Fallen Leaf Press.

Takemitsu, Toru with Cronin, Tania & Tann, Hilary. 1989. Afterword. *Perspectives of New Music* 27:2. 205–214.

Takemitsu, Toru (trans. Adachi, Sumi with Reynolds, Roger). 1992. Mirrors. *Perspectives of New Music* 30:1. 36–80.

—. (trans. Hugh de Ferranti). 1994. One Sound. *Contemporary Music Review* 8:2. 3–4.

—. 1989. Contemporary Music in Japan. *Perspectives of New Music*, vol. 27:2. 198–204.

CHAPTER SEVEN

TORU TAKEMITSU AND THE JAPANESE
SOUND OF *SAWARI*

MITSUKO ONO

Takemitsu and the Japanese sound of *sawari*

Many composers in Japan create their music with reference to Japanese traditional music - for example, *Noh* or folk song. Japanese composer Toru Takemitsu (1930-96) also had an interest in traditional music. One of his unique points as a composer was that he had approached the sound of traditional music. It is true that Takemitsu composed for Japanese instruments - but he composed only seven pieces for traditional Japanese instruments out of nearly 200 concert works.[1] It was works for the musical instruments of the West that Takemitsu devoted his energies to creating. He composed much music for films, TV dramas, and stage drama, but here I will refer only to the concert works. In this summary, I will consider the traditional Japanese sound in which Takemitsu was interested, what the difference is between traditional music and Takemitsu's music, and discuss how Takemitsu thought about *sawari*.

What is *sawari*?

What is the sound with which Takemitsu was concerned? It was a tone that Japanese call *sawari*. *Sawari* is a sound rich in reverberations. It is a delicate, complex sound. The *shamisen* is one of the traditional Japanese instruments, a three-stringed plucked lute. When one hears it close to a player (listen to the sound of a *shamisen* player tuning up), its delicate and complex sound is very surprising. Many sounds are contained in one sound. It is one sound but the reverberation contains many sounds simultaneously. I had heard *shamisen* music on the radio and at the theater. However, when I heard it close to the player, I noticed this sound.

Moreover, the overtones of a *shamisen* sound are complex because three strings resonate at the same time, and it is perceived as a sound near noise or unpitched sound.

This complex sound is called *sawari* in Japan. The word *sawari* comes from the verb "*sawaru*" in Japanese. If translated into English, it means "touch." *Sawari* relates to overtones. So, *sawari* is a useful sound for tuning. If the player does not tune the instrument well, he or she does not produce this *sawari* sound. It is said between players, "if a person can get a beautiful *sawari*, he or she might be a master." We can see the same sound device in *biwa*, which is another type of Japanese lute. Both *biwa* and *shamisen* originated in China. However, *sawari* is not associated with the *biwa* and *shamisen* in China. The Japanese musicologist Eishi Kikkawa, observed *sawari* and wrote that the instrument accomplished its "Japanisation" when *sawari* was added.

Sawari is used as a Japanese musical term in the following three, roughly separate meanings:

1) The special sound phenomenon produced by the *biwa* and *shamisen*.
2) The important part of a work or play. If we see only the famous scenes in a *kabuki* play, we say "seeing only the *sawari*."
3) An alloy of tin, silver and copper.
3-1) A bowl made of this alloy. It is used as a pitcher, or a flower bowl. Because the sound produced by striking it is clear, it is used as a prayer bell in Buddhism.
3-2) The reed of the *sho*, a musical instrument of traditional court music, is made of this alloy.

All meanings of *sawari* relate to aesthetics. In 1943, Eishi Kikkawa wrote interesting observations about the aesthetic considerations of *sawari*. Kikkawa began his thesis by stating, "*sawari* seems like a trifling matter. It is true. But I have enthusiasm for it." He continued, "*sawari* is one example of the Japanese aesthetic notion '*sabi*' applied to aural art."[2]

Sabi: the Japanese aesthetic

"*Sabi*" is a term that is used in the Japanese poetic form *haiku*, and in the other arts. The idea is that one finds beauty in change or deterioration by the passage of time. At the same time, it is the idea of leaving self-will and personal feelings behind and uniting with nature. Patina, green rust, could be said to have a similar beauty if one tries to think of an English example.

Why did Kikkawa begin his *sawari* thesis with the very modest words "*sawari* seems like a trifling matter. It is true. But...?" It is because *sawari* is common practice for the player and is axiomatic, a matter of course. *Biwa* music and *shamisen* music is originally vocal music. The song or narrator is the main focus. Musical instruments are accompaniment. Besides, *sawari* exists as a sound that supports music with its shadow.

In such traditional music, there were no purely instrumental works. But in the 1960's, composition for Japanese instruments changed. Composers who wrote music in Western style began to write music for traditional Japanese instruments. For example, Makoto Moroi composed *Chikurai goshou* for *shakuhachi* (1964), and Toru Takemitsu wrote *Eclipse* (1966) for *shakuhachi* and *biwa*.

Many composers in Japan wrote music for traditional Japanese instruments in the 1960's. This is related to the music of John Cage. In the 1960's, they found that the traditional music of Japan had ideas in common with Cage's ideas of music through chance operations.

Tradition and Takemitsu

How did Takemitsu reflect on tradition? I see *November Steps* for *biwa*, *shakuhachi* and orchestra as Takemitsu's most important work. He received a commission from the New York Philharmonic for this piece. One year before composing *November Steps*, Takemitsu composed a piece called *Eclipse* for *biwa* and *shakuhachi*. The combination of two instruments such as *biwa* and *shakuhachi* is Takemitsu's original idea - not a traditional one.

In *November Steps*, Takemitsu had the Japanese instruments appear alternately with the orchestra. Both *biwa* and *shakuhachi* are written in graphic notation, and there are detailed instructions about the performance.[3] However, neither the rhythm nor the tempo is indicated. The decision when to play one sound and the following sound was entrusted to the player.

Looking at the *biwa* part, the song or narrator that is the main voice with traditional *biwa* music is removed. As a result, the sound of *biwa* with *sawari* stands out, even with one sound. A feature of his instructions to the *biwa* player are, for example, directions to make a percussion-like sound: "hit the body of the instrument with the plectrum, or finger, fist or palm"; or "rub upward all strings while hitting the body of the instrument lightly with the plectrum". Another instruction is to make a microtone-like sound through *portamento*.

Looking at the *shakuhachi* part, one finds many notations which relate to noise: "play with voice," "jump upward or downward an extreme distance," "tap the whole of the instrument strongly with the fingers," "*muraiki*" (the traditional *shakuhachi* instruction to blow with a lot of breath), and so on.

The combination of *biwa* and *shakuhachi* does not exist in traditional music. It is an ensemble by which Takemitsu expressed a complex sound like *sawari* from both a stringed instrument and wind instrument. Takemitsu makes the sound of *sawari* stand out more than the sounds used in traditional music.

The use of two Japanese instruments reveals Takemitsu's aim. He wanted to show us the sound that traditional Japanese instruments have, and the instruments of the orchestra don't have. Yet it does not mean that he was satisfied with traditional Japanese music. Takemitsu criticized present-day Japanese traditional music. His point of view was radical - he affirmed "Traditional music is corrupt."[4] In those days (1967), and even today, the *biwa* is unpopular, and the number of those carrying on the tradition has decreased. On the other hand, the *shamisen*, which has a complex sound like the *biwa*, is an indispensable musical instrument as accompaniment for *kabuki* plays. If it is used in chamber music, the sound and the *sawari* are common practice for the player as a matter of course. The *shakuhachi* is popular now, but the tendency with which the *shakuhachi* is played in a Western style like a flute is growing.

Beyond Tradition

At the world premiere in the United States, *November Steps* caused a sensation. It was performed continuously the following year in the Netherlands and France, and established Takemitsu's reputation in Europe. Though it received high acclaim, Takemitsu devoted his life to composing music not for *sawari* instruments, but for Western instruments that have no *sawari*. Observing the pieces after *November Steps*, of the 70s, 80s and 90s, we can find a lot of places where reverberations play an important role. There is one term that is used more and more frequently. That is *dying away*. We find this term not only at the end of the piece, but also in many other parts of his music. In such places, Takemitsu uses the musical term *diminuendo*.

Takemitsu Compositions for Western Instruments
that have no S*awari*

Rain Spell for chamber ensemble (1982): "dying away", "very spatially"/ *riverrun* for piano and orchestra (1984): "dying away", "let ring" / *Les yeux clos II* for piano (1988): "al niente" / *Itinerant* for flute (1989): "al niente" / *Visions* for orchestra (1990): "al niente"/ *Air* for flute (1995): "al niente."

Figure 7-1: *Rain Spell* (for fl [alto.fl], cl, hp, pf, vib, 1982) G; "dying away"

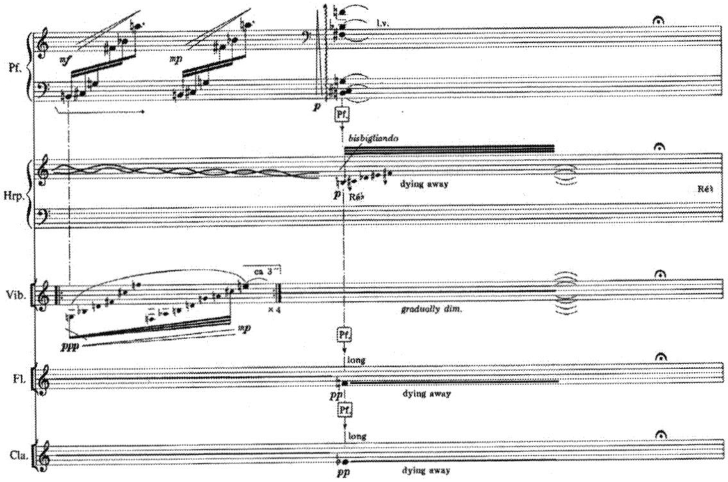

©1983, Schott Music Co. Ltd., Tokyo.
Reprinted by permission of Schott Music Co. Ltd., Tokyo

In such places, the act of listening to the sound is awakened in the performer and the listener. We listen to the sound of reverberation and listen to it until it gradually unites with the sound of the natural environment surrounding us. Some musicians say, "I don't know when I should cut the tone."[5] Such reverberations of the sound are important factors influencing the tempo of the piece. It is essential for the performer to listen to the sound well because the sound changes according to the humidity and the size of the performance place. I can say, even when he does not use Japanese instruments with *sawari*, *sawari* lives in Takemitsu's music as an important aesthetic; listening to the reverberations and listening to the change of the sound as time flows.

As previously introduced, *sawari* is used as a Japanese musical term with three meanings. However, Takemitsu seems to trace the word *sawari* to its origin. Takemitsu describes *sawari* in one of his essays as follows.

"The meaning of *sawari* originally comes from 'to touch others'. And one of the first meanings of *sawari* is to take the remarkable and excellent method that others have. (…) I think the meaning that the word *sawari* has is a more intense and dynamic attitude than we imagine today. I think *sawari* is not a fixed aesthetic idea, but a need in doing something, that is to say, a need in ordinary life."[6]

In realizing that Takemitsu was a composer who was heir to the musical ideas of Debussy and Messiaen, who loved jazz, and who was influenced by the ideas of John Cage, this way of thinking may apply to the whole creation of Takemitsu. He put a high value on the chance that people can "*sawaru*" or "touch" others. Perhaps I should say not "*sawaru*" nor "touch" others but use another English phrase. He was thinking of communication with each other. He communicated with many film directors, painters, poets. He participated in many music festivals and also directed some music festivals where we could communicate with the participants. And what is more, he announced his opinion to the reader as a general editor of several magazines in Japan.

In Takemitsu's works, I can find an aesthetic connected with the tradition of Japan. However, the aesthetic is one led by radically considering sound, and not one led from the concept of a national identity (Japan). There is an original Takemitsu world there.

Notes

1. *Eclipse* for *biwa* and *shakuhachi* (1966), *November Steps* for biwa, *shakuhachi* and orchestra (1967), *Distance* for oboe and *sho* (1972), *In an Autumn Garden* for *gagaku* (1973/79), *Autumn* for *biwa*, *shakuhachi* and orchestra (1973), *Voyage* for 3 *biwas* (1973), *Ceremonial* for *sho* and orchestra (1992).
2. The completion of *sangen* [*shamisen*] in Japan. *Nihon shogaku shinkoukai kenkyu houkoku*, Vol.21.
3. As Ferranti pointed out, Takemitsu wrote the parts of the traditional instruments in five-line staff notation (Ferranti, Hugh de. Takemitsu's *biwa. A Way a Lone*. Akademia Music Ltd., Tokyo, 2002.). However, Takemitsu adopted graphic notation in publication. I think it is Takemitsu's wish to play and listen to the sound which cannot be shown in Western conventional writing style.
4. *Mirror of trees, mirror of grass*, Tokyo: Shincho sha, 1975, p.154
5. For example, Nobuko Imai said so in *Takemitsu Toru wo kataru 15 no shogen* (15 people talking about Takemitsu); Shogakukan, 2007.
6. *Mirror of trees, mirror of grass*, p.104

Chapter Eight

Excursions into Takemitsu's Japanese Garden: An Application of the Superset/Subset Network to the Analysis of Three Orchestral Compositions

Hideaki Onishi

Introduction

Toru Takemitsu was as productive a writer as a composer, and one of the topics in his numerous writings was the universal nature of music. Music for him was something that stood beyond all kinds of differences (2000, 3:80), and he repeatedly expressed his wish to be a cosmopolitan with "the body of a whale to swim freely in the sea that had no East or West."[1] Yet at the same time Takemitsu seemed unable to completely free himself from his true origin as Japanese, insisting that his music was Japanese and different from that of the West (Takemitsu 2000, 4:266). This somewhat ambivalent attitude of Takemitsu towards his origin, rather common among Japanese of his and later generations, should not affect our appreciation and evaluation of what he has left us, although it has admittedly given a certain framework in which it is performed, listened to, and discussed. For example, many would associate Takemitsu's name with *November Steps* for *biwa*, *shakuhachi*, and orchestra (1967), although he called for this particular instrumentation in only one other work.[2] Moreover, the number of his compositions that employ any Japanese instrument is far smaller than that of his works that do not.[3] The situation has been similar in academia, and a number of studies have paid attention primarily to the so-called Japanese-ness of his music from various angles.[4]

This study is an attempt to show that the two seemingly opposing views are actually reconcilable when documentation of Takemitsu's writings and analysis of his music are successfully combined, taking into account the relationship between the concept of the Japanese garden and the formal structure of his works. Blindly following the composer's writings can be misleading, but they can provide us with valuable clues if scrutinized carefully and compared with musical facts.[5]

The Japanese Garden and Formal Structure of Takemitsu's Music

It has been pointed out that Takemitsu's music has no recognizable form, or no form at all, for that matter. Peter Burt, for instance, relates this "absence of imposed 'form'…at a higher structural level" with the "avoidance of imposed syntax at the microstructural level" or what is often called the "oneness of sound" in traditional Japanese music (Burt 2001, 252).[6] Takemitsu himself admitted this alleged lack of musical form, although this does not mean that he tried to avoid any formal scheme in his music. Rather, he sought a way to compose without having to resort to the teleological and unidirectional narrative underlying traditional forms of Western music (Tachibana 1992, 267-8): "I have not liked to follow formal conventions such as sonata, and have had a desire to write a piece without a clear formal outline since my earliest stage as a composer. I have preferred music without a clear-cut edge, I do not know why, but that's what I have felt. I have always wanted to write 'something between some things,' not 'some thing' itself."[7]

Takemitsu did not give us a full account of "something between some things," but instead, as was often the case with his metaphorical writings, compared his music with such non-musical objects as the dream, *emaki* (Japanese picture scroll), and, above all, the Japanese garden.[8] As a matter of fact, it gradually became his obsession to "compose a musical garden," and many orchestral and other works after the mid-1980s are results of such an endeavor. According to the composer, the formal structure of these works is "modeled on a Japanese garden."[9] This modeling process is never a simple one, since it involves the translation of the spatial aspect of garden into the temporal aspect of music. Takemitsu tried to solve this problem by designing his garden as a correlative of time that one spends in the garden. More specifically, this kind of temporality is realized through melodic or harmonic events that represent various objects in the garden -- as the composer describes: "If you walk through a garden, the elements are always the same: paths, rocks, trees, grass. But as you walk through, each element looks different depending on your perspective.... Instrumental color, notes, rhythms are like the elements of a garden."[10] The main musical events usually appear at the beginning of the piece and return again and again with different instrumentation, register, dynamics, and nuance, but never undergo variation in the traditional sense. Table 1 lists only those works where Takemitsu specifically mentions garden in the title and/or program notes, although a lot more can potentially be included here:[11]

Table 8-1: "Garden Series" Compositions by Toru Takemitsu

Arc for piano and orchestra (1963-66/76)
The Dorian Horizon for seventeen strings (1966)
In an Autumn Garden for *gagaku* orchestra (1973/79)
Garden Rain (1974)
A Flock Descends into the Pentagonal Garden for orchestra (1977)
Dream/Window for orchestra (1985)
A Minneapolis Garden (environmental music, 1986)
A String Around Autumn for viola and orchestra (1989)
Fantasma/Cantos for clarinet and orchestra (1991)
Quotation of Dream—Say sea, take me! for two pianos and orchestra (1991)
Between Tides for violin, cello, and piano (1993)
Spirit Garden for orchestra (1994)
Fantasma/Cantos II for trombone and orchestra (1994)
Path—In Memoriam Witold Lutoslawski for trumpet (1994)
A Bird came down the Walk for viola and piano (1994)
Spectral Canticle for violin, guitar, and orchestra (1995)

I have chosen three orchestral compositions from Table 8-1 for this study as they were composed over a significant time span (three to six years in between) and written for slightly different instrumental formations: *Dream/Window* (with flute, clarinet, and string quartet as solo instrumental group), *Fantasma/Cantos*, and *Spirit Garden*.

Analysis: Superset/Subset Network and Its Applications

There have been a couple of studies of different methodologies to examine the formal structure of Takemitsu's music in relation to the Japanese garden, although it has not been made entirely clear yet how musical events are laid out temporally in this specific context (Koh 1998;

Takahashi 2001). A clue seems to be found in Takemitsu's own words
(Tachibana 1993, 242):

> "When I compose, I think with something like a mass of sound. Many
> people seem to start from a melodic or rhythmic idea, but in my case a
> sonority comes up to my mind. Sometimes it has a concrete and definitive
> form and sometimes it emerges as an obscure imagery."[12]

PC-set analysis seems suitable to the objectives here, as it makes it
possible to grasp each "mass of sound" in an abstract form and to compare
it with others in a precise and objective manner. As a matter of fact,
several studies through this methodology have already made an important
contribution to Takemitsu scholarship during the past two decades.[13]
Although I have made some changes, the way I have adopted pc-set theory
here is similar to methods of Timothy Koozin and Hidetoshi Fukuchi, in
particular, who have produced a thorough analysis of the piano works by
Takemitsu.

(1) Previous analyses have not always shown clear criteria for the
choice of pitch classes to be included in a pc set at a certain moment of
music, which in turn has given the impression that the choice was made
more or less arbitrarily. This also seems to contradict the way we listen to
music, since it would be difficult to extract certain notes from the entire
texture and leave out the others, unless the two groups are clearly
distinguished from each other by instrumentation, register, or some other
means. As Nicholas Cook said (1989, 117), "one of the most crucial
questions we can ask about any theory of music . . . is how it relates to the
perceptual experience of the listener." In spite of the insights that these
analyses were able to offer, the question remained whether pc sets that
were formed this way were really in operation. I maintain that, in order to
avoid any pre-analytical bias that would result from such exclusions, all
notes (with fixed pitch) should be considered in the analysis.

(2) In relation to the above point, previous studies have had a tendency
to limit the maximum cardinality of a pc set to five or six (except for some
common cases such as 8-28), although, again, this may contradict our
listening habit if there are other notes to be heard together with the set.
Such a limitation may overlook important pc sets of larger cardinality that
are truly in operation and prefer its nonessential subsets and/or other
arbitrary sets. By contrast, I have taken all the notes with fixed pitch into
account and examined various possibilities for different segmentations and
groupings to find pc sets of cardinality three to twelve.

(3) Regardless of methodology, many previous studies have focused on
certain sections of a composition rather than its entirety. Narrowing down

the analytical scope is helpful, especially when focusing on the small-scale organization, as has been proved. Since my primary objective is to examine the formal structure of Takemitsu's music in relation to the concept of the Japanese garden, though, I have taken entire compositions into considerations.

It is crucial to establish strict rules of segmentation in order to secure the objectivity of an analysis.[14] I have segmented the three chosen works largely in terms of vertical sonorities to examine the temporal aspect of Takemitsu's garden music. Separating the vertical from horizontal events turned out to be not as complicated as it first seemed, since there is something rather traditional in his otherwise meticulous and subtly colorful orchestration, in the sense that the music often consists of a simple combination of melody and accompanying harmony. Figure 8-1 is a typical example of the texture that predominates Takemitsu's music. The cardinality of a chord varies greatly, usually from three to ten (and sometimes even up to twelve to form the chromatic aggregate), as does the duration, normally from a sixteenth note up to several measures.

Figure 8-1

m. 104-5
Takemitsu FANTASMA/CANTOS
© 1991 Schott Music Co. Ltd, Tokyo
Used by permission of European American Music Distributors LLC,
sole U.S. and Canadian agent for Schott Music.

Most of the pc sets obtained as a result of such segmentation are
related through the superset-subset relationship to well-known sets such as
the whole-tone, diatonic, and octatonic sets, but, more importantly, also to
a set that is unique to each of the three works: 8-24 (0124568T) octad
[8,9,10,0,1,2,4,6] in *Dream/Window*; 6-Z39 (023458) hexad [2,4,5,6,7,10]
in *Fantasma/Cantos*; and 5-Z38 (01258) pentad [6,9,0,1,2] in *Spirit
Garden*. I have grouped all possible supersets and subsets (both those

which appeared in the work and those which did not) for each of these referential sets as a virtual network, which I shall call the *superset/subset network*. The superset/subset networks constructed from the 8-24 octad, 6-Z39 hexad, 5-Z38 pentad, whole-tone set (6-35), diatonic set (7-35), and octatonic set (8-28) are shown in Appendix 1.

Table 8-2: Takemitsu, *Spirit Garden*, m.1-18, small-scale structure[15]

Measure	Chord	Set Class	0	1	2	3	4	5	6	7	8	9	10	11	W	SG	D	O
1	1-4	4-19	0	1				5				9						
	1	4-19		1	2				6				10					
	2	4-24				3				7		9		11	W			
	3	4-19	0				4	5			8							
	4	4-24		1				5		7		9			W			
	5	5-28		1		3				7		9	10					O
	6	5-26		1		3		5	6			9						
2	7	5-28	0		2				6		8	9						O
3	1	4-19		1	2				6				10					
	2	4-24				3				7		9		11	W			
	3	4-19	0				4	5			8							
4		4-19		1	2				6				10					
5	1	4-19	0	1				5				9						
	2	4-24			2				6		8		10		W			
	3	4-19				3	4			7				11				
6	1	4-19	0	1				5				9						
5	1	4-20		1	2				6			9				SG	D	
	2	4-26	0			3		5			8						D	O
	3	4-Z29					4	5		7				11			D	O
6	1	4-19			2	3			6				10					
	2	7-22	0	1	2			5	6		8	9			T_0			
8-9		5-21		1	2			5	6			9						
9-10		5-33	0		2		4		6		8				W			
11-12		5-21		1	2			5	6			9						
12-13		5-33	0		2		4		6		8				W			
14	1	6-20		1	2			5	6			9	10					
	2	6-Z28	0		2	3		5	6			9	10					
15	1	6-20		1	2			5	6			9	10					
	2	6-Z28	0		2	3		5	6			9	10					
	3	7-22	0	1	2			5	6		8	9			T_0			
16-18		8-24	0	1	2		4	5	6		8		10			SG		
16		5-21		1	2			5	6			9						
17-18		5-33	0		2		4		6		8				W			

Viewed through the superset/subset network, each of Takemitsu's three orchestral works can be regarded as an alternation of pc sets belonging to different networks. The opening of *Spirit Garden* (see m.1-19) and its small-scale (chord-to-chord) analysis in Table 8-2. This chord-to-chord analysis provides the basis on which to view the middle- and large-scale structure. The small-scale structure is subsumed under the

larger motion of music through various means: (1) *Combination* - adds all
the pc sets present into one set, especially when the duration of each set is
short and the same group of sets appears repeatedly in the same order to
accompany the same musical idea. The first three chords in measure 1 (4-
19 [10,1,2,6], 4-24 [7,9,11,3], and 4-19 [4,5,8,0]) have been combined into
the chromatic aggregate (12-1 [0,1,2,3,4,5,6,7,8,9,10,11]) this way; (2)
Inclusion - makes it possible for a superset to subsume all of its subsets
and become the middle-scale structure. For example, 7-22 septad
[0,1,2,5,6,8,9] includes 5-21 pentad [1,2,5,6,9] and therefore provides its
middle-scale structure (not shown in examples); and (3) *Representation* -
when a section contains several pc sets that are related to one set through
both superset and subset relationships, it can represent the section and
become the middle-scale structure (even though it is not the set of
maximum cardinality). This is seen, for example, at the beginning of
Dream/Window   (m.1-3)   where   the   Dream/Window   Octad
[8,9,10,0,1,2,4,6] in m.2 grows out of a 4-16 tetrad [9,10,2,4] in m.1 and
further into a 10-4 decad [8,9,10,11,0,1,2,4,5,6] in m.3 but its sonorous
identity is not lost:

The result of such a reduction process of Table 8-2 is shown in Table
8-3 (next page). At this level, the real harmonic motions begin to take
shape with corresponding melodic events, the Spirit Garden Pentad (the
"Main Theme" that is to appear in mm. 19ff) and the chromatic aggregate
(with the "12-Tone Chorale" in m.3).

The continuation of this reduction process enables us to see the entire
composition from an even larger perspective. The large-scale structure of
Dream/Window, *Fantasma/Cantos*, and *Spirit Garden* are shown in Table
8-5.[16] The harmonic and melodic events are now fully in tandem with each
other, while many of the surface events that we actually hear have been
absorbed into this large motion. In contrast to the uniqueness of the
referential sets (8-24, 6-Z39, and 5-Z38), the large-scale structures of the
three works are not as unusual as they may have seemed at first. They are
all based on the same structural principle, though do not follow exactly the
identical formal scheme. A limited number of melodic and harmonic
events return during the course of the piece, seemingly not following a
predetermined course. This apparent randomness that contributes to the
non-linearity and non-directionality of the music is actually carefully
planned. These features are not so dissimilar to what we experience when
we stroll around in a Japanese garden, although they are entirely
sustainable without such an extra-musical association. The referential set
of each work is varied through changes in timbre, instrumentation,
dynamics, transposition, and, last but not least, operations such as addition

and subtraction of pitch classes, as if objects in the Japanese garden such as rocks and trees change their shapes and colors according to the distance and angle from which they are seen. *Dream/Window, Fantasma/Cantos,* and *Spirit Garden* thus realize the spatial layout of the Japanese garden in their horizontal (temporal) aspect.

Table 8-3: Takemitsu, *Spirit Garden*, m.1-18, middle-scale structure

Measure	Chord	Set Class	Normal Form	W	SG	D	O	12	Reduction to large-scale structure
1	1-4	4-19	[9,0,1,5]						
	1-3	12-1	[0,1,2,3,4,5,6,7,8,9,10,11]					12	12-1
	4	4-24	[5,7,9,1]						
	5	5-28	[7,9,10,1,3]				O		6-34 [1,3,5,7,9,10]
	6	5-26	[1,3,5,6,9]						
2	7	5-28	[6,8,9,0,2]				O		
6	3-5	12-1	[0,1,2,3,4,5,6,7,8,9,10,11]					12	12-1
	1	7-22	[0,1,2,5,6,8,9]		T_0				8-19 [0,1,2,4,5,6,8,9]
	2								
8-13		8-19	[0,1,2,4,5,6,8,9]		T_0				
14	1	6-20	[1,2,5,6,9,10]						9-11
15	2	6-Z28	[9,10,0,,2,3,6]						[8,9,10,0,1,2,3,5,6]
15	3	7-22	[0,1,2,5,6,8,9]		T_0				
16-18		8-24	[0,1,2,4,5,6,8,10]	W	SG				9-12
		8-19	[0,1,2,4,5,6,8,9]		T_0				[0,1,2,4,5,6,8,9,10]

Concluding Thoughts

Takemitsu devoted the last dozen years of his life to designing Japanese gardens in music, of which the three orchestral compositions that I have analyzed here are but an example. Transplanting something spatial to something temporal is in no way a straightforward task, but Takemitsu realized the labyrinthine design of the Japanese garden through seemingly random recurrences of sonorous events. We feel lost there, even though the music is carefully planned and organized. According to John Rahn, Takemitsu's music is "a non-structured experience of something structured. It is a structure with no structure."[17] As Takemitsu continued to search for the ideal form of a musical garden, he explored the same formal principle in other works, such as *I Hear Water Dreaming, A String around Autumn, Quotation of Dream—Say Sea, Take me!,* and *Fantasma/Cantos II.*

The foregoing analysis does not give a definite answer to the question as to how these "garden" works should be listened to (as absolute or program music), nor does it intend to do so. Of particular interest in this regard is, again, Takemitsu's own comment: "When planning most pieces, I make sketches of a garden."[18] If these sketches become available to researchers, it would be an intriguing project to try to identify which garden piece by Takemitsu corresponds to which (real or virtual) garden, and in what manner.

Table 8-4: Tables of Superset/Subset Networks

1. Superset/Subset Network of 8-24 (*Dream/Window*)[19]

Decad [3]: 10-2 (2); 10-4 (3); 10-6 (1)
Nonad [3]: 9-6 (1); 9-8 (2); 9-12 (1)
Itself [1]: 8-24 (1)
Heptad [4]: 7-13 (2); 7-26 (2); 7-30 (2); 7-33 (2)
Hexad (13): 6-4 (1); 6-Z10 (2); 6-15 (2); 6-16 (2); 6-21 (4); 6-22 (4); 6-Z26 (1); 6-31 (2); 6-34 (4); 6-35 (1); 6-Z43 (2); 6-Z46 (2); 6-Z49 (1)
Pentad [20]: 5-3 (2); 5-6 (2); 5-8 (2); 5-9 (4); 5-11 (4); 5-13 (4); 5-15 (2); 5-16 (2); 5-18 (2); 5-20 (2); 5-21 (2); 5-24 (4); 5-26 (4); 5-27 (2); 5-28 (4); 5-30 (4); 5-32 (2); 5-33 (6); 5-34 (2); 5-38 (2)
Tetrad [22]: 4-2 (4); 4-3 (1); 4-4 (2); 4-5 (4); 4-7 (2); 4-8 (1); 4-11 (4); 4-12 (4); 4-14 (2); 4-Z15 (4); 4-16 (4); 4-17 (2); 4-18 (2); 4-19 (4); 4-20 (2); 4-21 (6); 4-22 (4); 4-24 (6); 4-25 (3); 4-26 (1); 4-27 (4); 4-Z29 (4)
Triad [11]: 3-1 (2); 3-2 (4); 3-3 (6); 3-4 (6); 3-5 (4); 3-6 (6); 3-7 (4); 3-8 (12); 3-10 (2); 3-11 (6); 3-12 (2)
Dyad [6]: 2-1 (4); 2-2 (6); 2-3 (4); 2-4 (7); 2-5 (4); 2-6 (3)

2. Superset/Subset Network of 6-Z39 (*Fantasma/Cantos*)

Decad [6]: 10-1 (3); 10-2 (3); 10-3 (3); 10-4 (3); 10-5 (2); 10-6 (1)
Nonad [11]: 9-1 (1); 9-2 (2); 9-3 (4); 9-4 (2); 9-5 (1); 9-6 (2); 9-7 (1); 9-8 (2); 9-9 (1); 9-10 (1); 9-11 (2)
Octad [13]: 8-2 (2), 8-3 (1); 8-4 (1); 8-7 (1), 8-11 (1); 8-12 (2); 8-14 (1); 8-16 (1); 8-17 (1); 8-18 (1); 8-21 (1); 8-22 (1); 8-Z29 (1)
Hepad [6]: 7-3 (1); 7-8 (1); 7-11 (1); 7-16 (1), 7-Z18 (1), 7-24 (1)
Itself [1]: 6-Z39 (1)
Pentad [6]: 5-2 (1), 5-4 (1); 5-13 (1); 5-25 (1); 5-26 (1); 5-Z37 (1)
Tetrad [13]: 4-1 (1); 4-2 (1); 4-4 (2); 4-5 (1); 4-10 (1); 4-11 (1); 4-12 (1); 4-13 (1); 4-19 (2); 4-24 (1); 4-26 (1); 4-27 (1); 4-Z29 (1)

Triad [11]: 3-1 (2); 3-2 (3); 3-3 (2); 3-4 (2); 3-5 (1); 3-6 (1); 3-7 (3); 3-8 (2); 3-10 (1); 3-11 (2); 3-12 (1)
Dyad [6]: 2-1 (3); 2-2 (3); 2-3 (3); 2-4 (3); 2-5 (2); 2-6 (1)

3: Superset/Subset Network of 5-Z38 (*Spirit Garden*)

Decad [6]: 10-1 (1); 10-2 (1); 10-3 (1); 10-4 (1); 10-5 (1); 10-6 (1)
Nonad [12]: 9-1 (1); 9-2 (1); 9-3 (1); 9-4 (1); 9-5 (1); 9-6 (1); 9-7 (1); 9-8 (1); 9-9 (1); 9-10 (1); 9-11 (1); 9-12 (1)
Octad [24]: 8-2 (1); 8-3 (1); 8-4 (1); 8-5 (1); 8-6 (1); 8-7 (1); 8-8 (1); 8-9 (1); 8-10 (1); 8-11 (1); 8-12 (1); 8-13 (1); 8-14 (1); 8-Z15 (1); 8-16 (1); 8-17 (1); 8-18 (1); 8-19 (1); 8-20 (1); 8-22 (1); 8-23 (1); 8-24 (1); 8-27 (1); 8-Z29 (1)
Hepad [18]: 7-3 (1); 7-7 (1); 7-10 (1); 7-13 (1); 7-14 (1); 7-16 (1); 7-17 (1); 7-Z18 (1); 7-19 (1); 7-20 (1); 7-21 (1); 7-22 (1); 7-23 (1); 7-26 (1); 7-29 (1); 7-30 (1); 7-Z36 (1); 7-Z38 (1)
Hexad [7]: 6-15 (1); 6-18 (1); 6-Z40 (1); 6-Z42 (1); 6-Z43 (1); 6-Z44 (1); 6-Z46 (1)
Itself [1]: 5-Z38 (1)
Tetrad [5]: 4-4 (1); 4-5 (1); 4-18 (1); 4-20 (1); 4-27 (1)
Triad [8]: 3-1 (1); 3-3 (1); 3-4 (2); 3-5 (1); 3-7 (1); 3-8 (1); 3-10 (1); 3-11 (2)
Dyad [6]: 2-1 (2); 2-2 (1); 2-3 (2); 2-4 (2); 2-5 (2); 2-6 (1)

4: Superset/Subset Network of the Whole-Tone Collection (6-35)

Decad [3]: 10-2 (6); 10-4 (6); 10-6 (3)
Nonad [3]: 9-6 (6); 9-8 (12); 9-12 (2)
Octad [3]: 8-21 (6); 8-24 (6); 8-25 (3)
Heptad [1]: 7-33 (6)
Itself [1]: 6-35 (1)
Pentad [1]: 5-33 (6)
Tetrad [3]: 4-21 (6); 4-24 (6); 4-25 (3)
Triad [3]: 3-6 (6); 3-8 (12); 3-12 (2)
Dyad [3]: 2-2 (6); 2-4 (6); 2-6 (3)

5: Superset/Subset Network of the Diatonic Collection (7-35)

Decad [4]: 10-2 (3); 10-3 (2); 10-4 (1); 10-5 (4)
Nonad [4]: 9-6 (1); 9-7 (3); 9-9 (4); 9-11 (2)
Octad [3]: 8-22 (2); 8-23 (2); 8-26 (1)

Itself [1]: 7-35 (1)

Hexad [4]: 6-Z25 (2); 6-Z26 (1); 6-32 (2); 6-33 (2)

Pentad [9]: 5-12 (1); 5-20 (2); 5-23 (4); 5-24 (2); 5-25 (2); 5-27 (4); 5-29 (2); 5-34 (1); 5-35 (3)

Tetrad [13]: 4-8 (1); 4-10 (2); 4-11 (4); 4-13 (2); 4-14 (4); 4-16 (2); 4-20 (2); 4-21 (1); 4-22 (6); 4-23 (4); 4-26 (3); 4-27 (2). 4-Z29 (2)

Triad [9]: 3-2 (4), 3-4 (4), 3-5 (2); 3-6 (3); 3-7 (8); 3-8 (2); 3-9 (5); 3-10 (1); 3-11 (6)

Dyad [6]: 2-1 (2), 2-2 (5); 2-3 (4); 2-4 (3); 2-5 (6); 2-6 (1)

6: Superset/Subset Network of the Octatonic Collection (8-28)

Decad [2]: 10-3 (4); 10-6 (2)

Nonad [1]: 9-10 (4)

Itself [1]: 8-28 (1)

Heptad [1]: 7-31 (8)

Hexad [6]: 6-13 (4); 6-Z23 (4); 6-27 (8); 6-30 (4); 6-Z49 (4); 6-Z50 (4)

Pentad [7]: 5-10 (8); 5-16 (8); 5-19 (8); 5-25 (8); 5-28 (8); 5-31 (8); 5-32 (8)

Tetrad [13]: 4-3 (4); 4-9 (2); 4-10 (4); 4-12 (8); 4-13 (8); 4-Z15 (8); 4-17 (4); 4-18 (8); 4-25 (2); 4-26 (4); 4-27 (8); 4-28 (2); 4-Z29 (8)

Triad [7]: 3-2 (8); 3-3 (8); 3-5 (8); 3-7 (8); 3-8 (8); 3-10 (8); 3-11 (8)

Dyad [6]: 2-1 (4); 2-2 (4); 2-3 (8); 2-4 (4); 2-5 (4); 2-6 (4)

Table 8-5: Large-Scale Structure of Three Orchestral Works by Takemitsu

1: Large-Scale Structure of *Dream/Window*

	mm.	set class	normal form	W	D	DW	O	12	musical event	Place(s)
A	1-10	4-16	[9,10,2,4]		D	DW			Harmonic	1
		8-24	[8,9,10,0,1,2,4,6]		T_0				Pitch 2	2
		10-4	[8,9,10,11,0,1,2,4,5,6]		D	DW			(HP 2)	3
	11-23	12-1	[0,1,2,3,4,5,6,7,8,9,10,11]					12	Harmonic Pitch 1 (HP 1)	11-13
		8-24	[8,9,10,11,0,1,2,4,5,6]		T_0				HP 2	14-15 / 15-18
		4-Z29	[1,2,4,8]		D	DW	O		6-34 Ascent / HP 2	20-21/22 / 21
B	24-30	10-6	[2,3,4,5,6,8,9,10,11,0]			DW	O		6-34 Ascent at T_{10}	26
		6-34	[9,10,0,2,4,6]			DW			HP 2	29-30
C	31-38	12-1	[0,1,2,3,4,5,6,7,8,9,10,11]					12	7-4 Ascent / HP 1	30-35 / 31-35
D	39-44	10-4	[11,0,1,2,3,4,5,7,8,9]			DW			7-4 Ascent at T_1 / 6-34 Ascent	38-42 / 39-41
E	45-54	10-6	[11,0,1,2,3,5,6,7,8,9]			DW	O			
F	55-61	12-1	[0,1,2,3,4,5,6,7,8,9,10,11]					12	HP 1	55-57
		8-22	[8,9,10,11,1,2,4,6]						HP 2 at T_2	55
		7-24	[9,10,11,0,3,5,7]						HP 2 at T_1	
G	62-70								Espressivo Melody	62-67
		8-28	[2,3,5,6,8,9,11,0]				O		HP 2 at T_1 / HP 2 at T_4	67/70 / 70
H	71-74	8-24	[6,7,8,10,11,0,2,4]		T_{10}					
I	75-84	4-19	[6,7,10,2]			DW				
J	85-91	8-24	T_9, T_{10}, T_{11}, T_1			DW			HP 2 at T_1	88/89-90
K	92-104	8-24	[7,8,9,11,0,1,3,5		T_{11}					
		7-31	[3,5,6,8,9,11,0]				O			
L	105-109	8-24	[8,9,10,0,1,2,4,6]		T_0				HP 2	105/107
		8-24	[6,7,8,10,11,0,2,4]		T_{10}				HP 2 at T_{10}	108

	Measures	Set class	Pitch set			Trans			Description	Pages
M	110-128								6-15 Ascent	115-116
									7-4 Ascent at T_1	117-122
									6-15 Ascent at T_4	123-128
N	129-139	8-24	[8,9,10,0,1,2,4,6]			T_0			HP 2	134
										135
									HP 1	136-138
		12-1	[0,1,2,3,4,5,6,7,8,9,10,11]					12	6-15 Ascent	137
									HP 1	137-138
O	140-146	6-33	[7,9,10,0,2,4]						HP 2 (vertical)	141-142
		10-4							HP 2	145
P	147-156								7-4 Ascent at T_4	146-148
									6-15 Ascent at T_3	148
									Espressivo Melody	149-154
Q	157-166	4-24	[6,8,10,2]			T_0			6-15 Ascent at T_4	157
										158
		10-1	[7,8,9,10,11,0,1,2,3,4]						HP 2 at T_8	159
										159
		6-34	[9,10,0,2,4,6]						HP 2	165
		8-24	[8,9,10,0,1,2,4,6]							
R	167-175	7-33	[4,5,6,8,10,0,2]	W		DW				
S	176-185	4-16	[9,10,2,4]		D	DW			HP 2	176
		8-24	[8,9,10,0,1,2,4,6]			T_0				177
		10-4	[8,9,10,11,0,1,2,4,5,6]			T_0				178
T	186-188	8-28	[1,2,4,5,7,8,10,11]				O			
U	189-198	8-24	[8,9,10,0,1,2,4,6]			T_0			HP 2 (vertical)	191-196
		7-35	[4,5,7,9,10,0,2]		D				HP 2 (varied)	196

2: Large-Scale Structures of *Fantasma/Cantos*

measure #	set class	PC/SC Region20	normal form	W	F/C	D	O	musical event
1-3	9-8	PC	[2,3,4,6,7,8,9,10,0]	W'	F/C			
4-9/1	6-Z39	SC			F/C			Main Theme
11-12/1	7-Z38	PC	[8,9,11,0,2,3,4]					
12/2-5	9-10	SC			F/C		O	
14-18/1	6-Z39				F/C			
18/5-20	9-10		[11,0,1,2,3,5,6,8,9]				O	
21	6-Z39	PC	[1,3,4,5,6,9]	T_{11}				
22-23	8-27		[5,6,8,9,11,0,1,3]					
24-25	8-22		[7,8,9,10,0,1,3,5]			D		
26-28	6-33	SC				D		Main Theme
29-36	9-11	PC	[3,4,5,7,8,9,10,0,1]		F/C	D		
37-38	6-Z39	SC			F/C			Secondary Theme 1
39-40	4-Z29	PC	[1,5,7,8]	w'	F/C	D	O	Secondary Theme 2
41-45	8-19		[0,1,2,4,5,6,8,9]					
46-47/1	6-Z39	SC			F/C			
47/2-49					F/C			Secondary Theme 1
50-51	9-11	PC	[2,3,4,6,7,8,9,11,0]		F/C	D		
52-53	6-Z39	SC			F/C			MT
55-56					F/C			
57-60	4-Z29	PC	[0,4,6,7]	w'	F/C	D	O	
61-64	8-27							
65-66	5-Z37	SC			F/C			
67-68	6-Z39				F/C			Secondary Theme 1
70-74/1	7-26	PC	[4,6,8,9,10,0,1]					
74/2-4	6-15	SC						
75-76	8-7		[4,5,6,7,8,9,0,1]		F/C			
77-84	4-Z29	PC	[0,4,6,7]	w'	F/C	D	O	
85-88	6-15		[10,11,0,2,3,6]					
90/1-2	7-21	SC						
90/3-92/1	7-34	PC	[5,6,8,9,11,1,3]					Main Theme
92/2-93	7-11	SC			F/C			
94-95	8-17				F/C			
97-100	4-22	PC	[2,4,6,9]	w'		D		
101-103	5-25	SC			F/C	D	O	
104-105	6-Z39				F/C			Main Theme
106	9-8	PC	[1,2,3,4,5,7,8,9,11]	W'	F/C			
107-117	4-Z29		[1,5,7,8]	w'	F/C	D	O	
118-122	6-34		[6,8,10,0,2,3]	w'				
123-125	6-Z39	SC			F/C			Main Theme

126-132	9-8	PC	[2,3,4,6,7,8,9,10,0]	W'	F/C			
133-141	6-35		[0,2,4,6,8,10]	W				
142-148	6-Z39	SC			F/C			Main Theme
149-151	8-27	PC	[9,10,11,1,2,4,5,7]					
152-157	6-Z39	SC			F/C			
172-173					F/C			Secondary Theme 1
186-189	4-22	PC	[2,4,6,9]	w'		D		
190-192	5-25	SC			F/C	D	O	
193-194	6-Z39				F/C			Main Theme
195	9-8	PC	[1,2,3,4,5,7,8,9,11]	W'	F/C			
196-206	4-Z29		[1,5,7,8]	w'	F/C	D	O	
207-211	6-34	PC	[6,8,10,0,2,3]	w'				
212-214	9-8		[2,3,4,6,7,8,9,10,0]	W'	F/C			
215-220/1	6-Z39	SC			F/C			Main Theme
222-223/1	7-Z38	PC	[8,9,11,0,2,3,4]					
223/2-5	9-10	SC			F/C		O	
225-227	6-Z39	PC	[3,5,6,7,8,11]		T_1			

3: Large-Scale Structure of *Spirit Garden*

	measure number	set class	normal form	w	SG	D	O	12	musical event
	1-3	12-1	[0,1,2,3,4,5,6,7,8,9,10,11]					12	Opening Theme
	4-6	6-34	[1,3,5,7,9,10]	w'					
	3-6/1	12-1	[0,1,2,3,4,5,6,7,8,9,10,11]					12	12-Tone Chorale at T_0 and T_{11}
	6/2-13	8-19	[0,1,2,4,5,6,8,9]		T_0				Signal
	14-15	9-11	[8,9,10,0,1,2,3,5,6]		T_0	D			Signal
	16-18	9-12	[0,1,2,4,5,6,8,9,10]	W'	T_0				Signal and sustained chord
	19-26	5-Z38	[6,9,0,1,2]		T_0				Main Theme and Main Theme'
A	27-28	12-1	[0,1,2,3,4,5,6,7,8,9,10,11]					12	12-Tone Chorale at T_0
	29-30	9-8	[0,1,2,3,4,6,8,9,10]	W'	T_0				Secondary Theme
	32-34/3	12-1	[0,1,2,3,4,5,6,7,8,9,10,11]					12	12-Tone Chorale at T_{11}
B	34/4-39	8-21	[7,8,9,10,11,1,3,5]	W'					
	40-42	12-1	[0,1,2,3,4,5,6,7,8,9,10,11]					12	12-Tone Chorale at T_4 and T_7
	43-45	9-8	[5,6,7,9,10,11,0,1,3]	W'					Secondary Theme at T_9
C	46-49	9-8	[10,11,0,2,3,4,5,6,8]	W'					Opening Theme (with E in the bass)
D	54-58/1	7-16	[9,10,0,1,2,3,6]		T_0				Main Theme
	62-65	9-8	[11,0,1,2,3,5,6,7,9]	W'					Secondary Theme
	66-67	9-10	[6,7,8,9,10,0,1,3,4]				3		
E	67-69	12-1	[0,1,2,3,4,5,6,7,8,9,10,11]					12	12-Tone Chorale at T_4
	71-72	11-1	[4,5,6,7,8,9,10,11,0,1,2]					12	12-Tone Chorale (without 3)
	73-74	8-22	(N/A)			D			8-22 set-class region
	75-81	9-12	[0,1,2,4,5,6,8,9,10]	W'	T_0				Melodic Ascent 2
	84-86	7-33	[2,3,4,6,8,10,0]	W'					Main Theme, first half
G	87-89	11-1	[6,7,8,9,10,11,0,1,2,3,4]					12	12-Tone Chorale (without 5)
	90-92	12-1	[0,1,2,3,4,5,6,7,8,9,10,11]					12	12-Tone Chorale at T_{10} (tutti)
	95-98	8-28	[0,1,3,4,6,7,9,10]				3		
H	99-100	12-1	[0,1,2,3,4,5,6,7,8,9,10,11]					12	12-Tone Chorale at T_4, varied

									(tutti)
J	101-104	9-8	[0,1,2,4,5,6,7,8,10]	W'					(with Melodic Ascent)
K	105-109	8-19	[0,1,2,4,5,6,8,9]		T_0				Signal
L	113/3-117	9-10	2,3,4,5,6,8,9,11,0				2		Octatonic Chorale
M	118-119	6-35	[0,2,4,6,8,10]	W'					
	120-122	9-8	8,9,10,0,1,2,3,4,6	W'	T_0				Main Theme
	123-124	5-Z38	[6,9,0,1,2]		T_0				
	125-128								Main Theme'
	129-130	12-1	[0,1,2,3,4,5,6,7,8,9,10,11]					12	12-Tone Chorale at T_0
N	131-133	6-35	[0,2,4,6,8,10]	W					
	134-137	5-Z38	[6,9,0,1,2]		T_0				Main Theme
	138	7-33	[8,9,10,0,2,4,6]	W'					Main Theme"
	139-141	9-10	[0,1,2,3,4,6,7,9,10]		T_0		3		(non-harmonized)
	141-142	8-19	[0,1,2,4,5,6,8,9]		T_0				Signal
	143-147	9-10	[0,1,2,3,4,6,7,9,10]		T_0		3		Main Theme'
	148	12-1	[0,1,2,3,4,5,6,7,8,9,10,11]					12	12-Tone Chorale at T_0
O	154-155								
	156-159	7-26	[9,10,0,1,2,4,6]		T_0				Octatonic Chorale at T_{11} (incomplete)
P	162-164/2	7-31	[9,10,0,1,3,4,6]				3		
Q	167-171	8-24	[8,9,10,0,1,2,4,6]	W'	SG				
	173-175/3	12-1	[0,1,2,3,4,5,6,7,8,9,10,11]					12	12-Tone Chorale at T_{11}
	175/4-180	8-21	[7,8,9,10,11,1,3,5]	W'					
	181-183	12-1	[0,1,2,3,4,5,6,7,8,9,10,11]					12	12-Tone Chorale at T_4 and T_7
R	184-186	9-8	[5,6,7,9,10,11,0,1,3]	W'	T_9				Secondary Theme at T_9
	188-190	6-Z28	[5,6,8,10,11,2]						
S	195-198	5-Z38	[6,9,0,1,2]		T_0				Main Theme'
	201-202	8-21	[7,8,9,10,11,1,3,5]		SG				
T	203	8-19	[1,2,4,5,6,8,9,10]		SG				Octatonic Chorale at T_8 (fragment)
	206/3-210	9-10	[2,3,4,5,6,8,9,11,0]				2		Octatonic Chorale
	211-214	8-19	[0,1,2,4,5,6,8,9]		T_0				Signal

Notes

1. All translations from this collection are by the present author, unless otherwise noted.

2. The other work is *Autumn* (1973).

3. Among more than 120 works (except for the film scores), only seven include traditional Japanese instruments: *November Steps*, *Autumn*, *In an Autumn Garden* (*gagaku* ensemble), *Ceremonial—An Autumn Ode* (sho and orchestra), *Eclipse* (*biwa* and *shakuhachi*), *Distance* (oboe and *sho*), and *Voyage* (three *biwas*).

4. See, for example, Wilson 1982, Jin 1987, Wu 1987, Koozin 1988 and 1993, Koh 1998, Takahashi 2001, Burt 2001, and Nuss 2002.

5. See, for example, "Forum Session of the Sydney University Takemitsu Symposium," in: De Ferranti and Narazaki, eds. *A Way a Lone*: 234-48; and "Toru Takemitsu and Composition in Japan" Panel Discussion 4, the Musicological Society of Japan 57th Annual Meeting, 28 October 2006, Kyushu University (http://www.design.kyushu-u.ac.jp/~sn/msjq2006/takemitsu.html; in Japanese).

6. The oneness of sound is, according to Roger Reynolds (1992, 30), a quality that "traditionally resides far less in a chronological inevitability, in a *dénouement*, than in savoring the experience of the moment, of a moment that must be, should be, particularly *alive* in and of itself. The Japanese investment is in the complexity and substance of individual events, with proportionately smaller commitment to the argued succession."

7. Translations from this series of interviews are all by the present author.

8. For the metaphor of dream, see, for example, Takemitsu, *Chosakushu*, 5:387-88. For the metaphor of *emaki*, see, for example, Takemitsu, *Chosakushu*, 5:425.

9. Takemitsu, *Chosakushu*, 5:38. For an alternative translation, see Takemitsu 1995, 119.

10. John Rockwell, "Two Worlds of Takemitsu, Japan's Leading Composer," *The New York Times*, February 13, 1981, quoted in (Jin 1987, 1).

11. Takemitsu once related to Roger Reynolds: "I am always analogizing [the orchestra] as a garden . . . in case of any piece. What I do is to translate an extremely specific plan of a garden into music." See (Reynolds 1996, 65).

12. Takemitsu gives another quite similar comment to Tachibana: "I first hear a mass of sound. Sometimes it comes out as a clear melody, but usually it is a more amorphous chunk of sound." See Tachibana, "Takemitsu Toru," *Bungakukai* 47 (December 1993): 375. See also Tachibana, "Takemitsu Toru," *Bungakukai* 50 (February 1996): 280.

13. See, for example, Smaldone 1989, Koozin 1988, 1990, 1991, 1993, Fukuchi 1998, Wilkins 1981, and Nuss 2002.

14. For issues regarding the segmentation, see, for example, Hasty 1981.

15. The first group of columns shows the measure number and the chord number within the measure, and the second column shows the set class of the pc set. The third groups of columns list the pitch classes contained in the set, and the fourth shows the superset/subset network or networks to which the set belongs. For example, the first four notes of the opening melody (D6, B5, C6, and A5) are

accompanied by 4-19 [10,1,2,6], 4-24 [7,9,11,3], 4-19 [4,5,8,0], and 4-24 [5,7,9,1], respectively. There is also a chord that is played by the celesta, harp I, and percussion instruments and underlies these four chords: 4-19 [9,0,1,5].

16. For the small- and middle-scale structure of these works, see Onishi 2004.

17. Personal conversation with the present author, 11 June 2004.

18. Tachibana, "Takemitsu Toru," *Bungakukai* 50 (February 1996): 280. See also Tachibana, "Takemitsu Toru," *Bungakukai* 51 (February 1997): 228.

19. Each row lists all possible supersets or subsets of certain cardinality that are obtained from the referential set (which is also listed here as "itself"). The number in square brackets next to the cardinality shows the number of different set classes obtainable. The number in parentheses after each set class shows the number of different pc sets that the set class can take in relation to a single referential pc set of this particular set class, 8-24. For example, three different nonad supersets can be obtained: 9-6, 9-8, and 9-12 from 8-24. To take the original *Dream/Window* octad [8,9,10,0,1,2,4,6] as reference, 9-6 and 9-12 can only be in one form ([8,9,10,11,0,1,2,4,6] and [0,1,2,4,5,6,8,9,10], respectively) whereas 9-8 can take two different forms ([6,7,8,9,10,0,1,2,4] and [8,9,10,0,1,2,3,4,6]) as a pc set.

20. PC represents a pitch-class field and SC represents set-class field.

References

Burt, Peter. 2001. *The Music of Toru Takemitsu*. Cambridge: Cambridge University Press.

Cook, Nicholas. 1989. Music Theory and 'Good Comparison': A Viennese Perspective. *Journal of Music Theory* 33.

Fukuchi, Hidetoshi. 1998. The Pitch Content of Selected Piano Works of Toru Takemitsu. MM Thesis, University of North Texas.

Hasty, Christopher F. 1981. Segmentation and Process in Post-Tonal Music. *MusicTheory Spectrum* 3. 54-73.

Jin, Jeong Woo. 1987. Comparative Analysis of Takemitsu's Recent Works *Rain Tree* and *Rain Spell*. Ph.D. diss., University of California at Los Angeles.

Koh, Hwee Been. 1998. East and West: The Aesthetics and Musical Time of Toru Takemitsu. Ph.D. diss., Boston University.

Koozin, Timothy V. 1988. The Solo Piano Works of Toru Takemitsu: A Linear/Set-Theoretic Analysis. Ph.D. diss., University of Cincinnati.

—. 1990. Toru Takemitsu and the Unity of Opposites. *College Music Symposium* 30/1. 34-44.

—. 1991. Octatonicism in Recent Solo Piano Works of Toru Takemitsu. *Perspectives of New Music* 29/1. 124-40.

—. 1993. Spiritual-Temporal Imagery in Music of Olivier Messiaen and Toru Takemitsu. *Contemporary Music Review* 7. 185-202

Nuss, Steven Russell. 2002. Takemitsu and the Cry of the Phoenix. Hugh

De Ferranti and Yoko Narazaki, eds, *A Way a Lone: Writings on Tôru Takemitsu*. Tokyo: Academia Press. 83-124.

Reynolds, Roger. 1992. A Jostled Silence—Contemporary Japanese Musical Thought (Part One): Introduction. *Perspectives of New Music* 30/1.

—. 1996. Roger Reynolds and Toru Takemitsu: A Conversation. *The Musical Quarterly* 80.

Smaldone, Edward. 1989. Japanese and Western Confluences in Large-Scale Pitch Organization of Toru Takemitsu's *November Steps* and *Autumn*. *Perspectives of New Music* 27/2. 216-31.

Tachibana, Takashi. 1992. Takemitsu Toru: Ongaku Souzou e no Tabi. [Toru Takemitsu: the Journey Towards Musical Creation]. *Bungakukai* 46 (August 1992). 267-68.

—. 1993. Takemitsu Toru. *Bungakukai* 47 (July 1993).

Takahashi, Belinda. 2001. Japanese Aesthetics and Musical Form: A Walk through Takemitsu's *Spirit Garden*. Ph.D. diss., the University of Rochester, Eastman School of Music.

Takemitsu, Toru. 1995. *Confronting Silence: Selected Writings*. trans. and ed. Yoshiko Kakudo and Glenn Glasow. Berkeley, California: Fallen Leaf Press.

—. 2000. *Chosakushu* [Collected Writings], 5 vols. Tokyo: Shincho-sha.

Wilkins, Blake Matthew. 1999. An Analysis of Musical Temporality in Toru Takemitsu's *Rain Tree* (1981). DMA diss., University of Oklahoma.

Wilson, Dana Richard. 1982. The Role of Texture in Selected Works of Toru Takemitsu. Ph.D. diss., University of Rochester, Eastman School of Music.

Wu, Ting-Lien. 1987. An Analysis of Toru Takemitsu's *Bryce* (1976), with an Emphasis on the Role of Articulation. Ph.D. diss., University of California, Los Angeles, 1987.

CHAPTER NINE

MUSIC IN THE BATHTUB:
READING TAKEMITSU'S MUSIC
THROUGH WESTERN CRITICISM

PETER BURT

"Considered the best-known and probably the best composer ever to emerge from Japan" – few readers will experience much difficulty guessing whom John Rockwell is alluding to in this 1981 quote (Rockwell 1981). For many Westerners indeed, Tōru Takemitsu is not simply "the best-known" but more or less *the* Japanese composer, as emblematic of his country's music as Isang Yun is of Korea's, or Tan Dun of China's. Over the years that I have been studying Takemitsu's music, it has often intrigued me how such a singular reputation could have come about. True, the quality of the music speaks for itself, but it seemed there must be other factors involved in the construction of such an egregious pre-eminence which would prove an interesting field for research.

The opportunity to engage in such research unexpectedly came my way a few years ago, when the editor of the *Complete Takemitsu Edition* – a CD collection of the composer's music published in Tōkyō – asked me to trawl through criticism on Takemitsu from around the "Western" world to find materials for the supporting programme booklets.[1] Kindly placed at my disposal for this purpose was the vast archive of press cuttings meticulously assembled over the years by Takemitsu's publisher, Schott Japan, and it is (for the most part) on these that the following article is based. Of course, this primary source material has its limitations. It is by its nature selective, representing only materials that the publishers have been able to assemble, and the omissions are particularly obvious in the earlier years. It also varies greatly in quality, ranging from informed pronouncements by experts like Rockwell to the humble hackwork of unspecialised journalists who may only have had a press release to base their copy on (and who on occasion even seem to have had difficulty spelling the composer's name!²) Nevertheless, while one must therefore approach this material with a certain caution, I believe that it can reveal a number of aspects of the manner in which Takemitsu's reception in the West developed over the years, and the rest of this brief article will be devoted to a summary of what I consider some of the more important of them.

An initial point that emerges clearly enough is that, as the years progress, the source publications from which the archive materials are taken come from an ever-widening circle of countries. This may, of course, simply have been due to the increasing efficiency of the publisher's collecting mechanisms, but–especially when one considers other historical data–it also seems reasonable to assume from this that what one critic referred to as "Takemitsu's crescendo" (Winters 1969) was not simply historical but geographical too–that his star did not rise evenly over all parts of "the West" at the same rate. At the risk of oversimplification, indeed, it is almost possible to visualise the spread of his reputation as a kind of series of concentric circles, spreading further and further around the globe with each succeeding decade.

In the 1950s and 1960s, for instance, it would appear that Western awareness of Takemitsu was largely confined to the "new world." The very earliest document in the Schott archive comes from the United States (Anon. 1959), and it is still a few years before contributions from this country are joined, during the 1960s, by examples from Canada and, in 1969, Australia, where Takemitsu was composer-in-residence at the Canberra Spring Festival of *Musica Viva*. Examples of European criticism do not appear until the 1970s, and here it is France that seems to have taken the lead – though while Takemitsu had been present at the Paris International Rostrum of Composers in both 1963 and 1965, it is not until his residency at the 1971 *Journées de Musique Contemporaine* of the *Semaines Musicales Internationales de Paris* that much notice of him seems to have been taken by the French press. Elsewhere in Europe, while a pioneer monographic evening at the London Music Digest in 1973 received passing critical notice, the United Kingdom still appears to have remained *das Land ohne Takemitsu* until the following decade, when Takemitsu finally established a permanent foothold in that country, from his 1984 residency at the Aldeburgh Festival onwards. And by this time – the 1980s and 1990s – the press reports on Takemitsu seemed to be coming from all quarters of the globe: not just the rest of Western Europe, including the Austro-German symphonic heartlands, but also former *Ostbloc* countries such as Poland, Czechoslovakia and Hungary – even Russia and South America.

This incremental proliferation of Takemitsu's music in turn suggests a second observation: namely, that it often seems to have been associated with the presence of certain enthusiastic advocates – what I have elsewhere dubbed "Takemitsu ambassadors" – who were "flying the flag" for him in different countries.[3] It is not too surprising, for instance, that the first examples of criticism come from the USA, where Stravinsky – and, through his influence, Aaron Copland – were instrumental in promoting Takemitsu after the former famously heard the *Requiem for strings* "by accident" in 1959. Nor is it exactly inexplicable that his name starts appearing in the Toronto press around the mid-1960s, after his colleague Seiji Ozawa became conductor of the symphony orchestra there.

Ozawa in fact demonstrates a recurrent quality of these "ambassadorial" figures, namely that so many of them seemed to combine musical affection with deep personal loyalty. As one critic put it after a posthumous tribute concert (Kozinn 1997), "the musicians who play [his music] clearly do so out of affection rather than duty." To this category of personal friends belong such figures as: the pianist Peter Serkin and his ensemble Tashi; the cellist Florian Kitt, dedicatee of *Orion*, who organised a pioneer all-Takemitsu recital in Vienna in 1984; Sir Simon Rattle, a stalwart advocate first in the US (e.g. with the New York première of *riverrun*) and then in the UK; Michael Vyner, artistic director of the London Sinfonietta, who commissioned *Rain Coming* in 1982; Oliver Knussen, who conducted the first performance of the above, and was the "prime mover and shaker" of the *Spirit Garden* festival held in London in 1998 (Murray 1998); the flautist Aurèle Nicolet, for whom *Eucalypts*, *Voice* and *Air* were written; the pianist Roger Woodward and composer Barry Conyngham – Takemitsu's "ambassadors" down under; and the American critic Heuwell Tircuit, consistently and effusively complimentary about Takemitsu's music.

In addition to these powerful individuals, one should not underestimate the importance of the fact that – after a few years with the domestic publisher *Ongaku no Tomo* – Takemitsu was promoted by a succession of prestigious Western publishing houses. Interestingly, indeed, the countries in which these were located map onto key centres in the global spread of Takemitsu's reputation described above: beginning in the 1960s with New York (Peters Edition), then (after a brief interlude involving UE in Vienna) moving to Paris in the 1970s (Editions Salabert) and, in the 1980s, to a publisher with an office in London (Schott). And finally, no list of "Takemitsu ambassadors" would be complete without including the composer himself: frequently out of Japan to attend performances or accept residencies, he was often "physically present" in the West to an extent that few (if any) other Japanese composers had been – and there is no doubt (as the examples below show) that the West, in its turn, found his appearance and manners striking and endlessly engaging.

Perhaps the most obvious point that emerges from these archive materials, however, is that the sample of Western reception it represents is dominated by a number of recurrent themes which must surely have played their role in constructing perceptions of Takemitsu in the West. The first of these has already been hinted at in the opening words of this article: Takemitsu's pre-eminence on the Japanese contemporary music scene. Rockwell's assessment here (even if he distances himself from it somewhat) actually has a long history. As early as 1959 Takemitsu was being introduced to the American public as "foremost among avant-garde composers" (Anon. 1959), and such assertions of his premier status are legion in Western criticism right up to the death of "Japan's leading composer" in 1996 and beyond (Littler 1996). Even the specific wording of these assessments is often strikingly similar. When Takemitsu appeared at the Paris *Journées* in 1971, for instance, he was hailed as "*chef de file de la jeune école japonaise*" (Cadieu 1971), and variants of this phrase of Martine Cadieu's can be found in French criticism right up to Fousnaquer's "*chef de file de la musique contemporaine japonaise*" in the composer's *Le Monde* obituary (1996). It can hardly have done Takemitsu much harm to have been introduced, right from the beginning, as "Japan's No. 1" in this fashion; while the subsequent repetition of such pronouncements, by this kind of "memetic" replication, surely helped guarantee that they ended up becoming a self-fulfilling prophecy.

A second facet of Takemitsu's early Western reputation is suggested by the 1959 quote just alluded to: he was "foremost among *avant-garde* composers." But, as critics were quick to discover, this was the *nice* avant-garde – as a later writer expressed it, "contemporary music for people who don't like the stuff" (Hughes 1977), "non-violent modernism," "serene, pretty, instantly accessible" (Murray 1998). Writers often underscored its accessibility by using the composer's film music as an entry point for their readership: if you enjoyed the soundtrack to *Suna no Onna*, so the implicit argument went, you'll love this. And there were, of course, the inevitable invidious comparisons with various representatives of the not-so-nice avant-garde: e.g by Jean Cotte (1971), who compared the "sanity" of Takemitsu's approach with that of the other 1971 *Journées* participants (Stravinsky, Eloy – and Karlheinz Stockhausen).

This "avant-garde" label seems to have stuck to Takemitsu so tenaciously that critics were still attempting to apply it even after the massive stylistic change he underwent during the later 1970s had seriously degraded its adhesive properties. "Has TT forfeited his avant garde standing amongst his peers?" asked Allen Hughes (1977) after *Quatrain*'s New York première: "If not we have to revise our notions of what constitutes avant gardism in music in the mid-1970s." Subsequent events, however, suggested that it would be better to abandon the term altogether – but if Takemitsu wasn't "avant-garde," what was he? As early as 1971 the composer himself had given his own preferred answer (Cadieu 1971) – "*Je suis romantique*" – but "romantic" is not an accepted stylistic category in contemporary music circles, and critics tended to ignore it in favour of their own assessments. One German obituarist (Koch 1996), for example, summed up Takemitsu's "late style" as "Japanese-toned New Simplicity."[4]

The most virulently contagious cliché of all in Western criticism of Takemitsu, however, was some sort of variation on the idea that in his music "East meets West" (Cairns 1984) – often with implicit (as here) or explicit reference to Kipling's famous dictum that "never the twain shall meet."[5] Almost certainly the early success of *November Steps* played a vital role here in perpetuating the myth that he continued to be interested in "a fusion between East and West," and in this connection it is salutary to read a later interview in *Libération* (Leblé 1990) where he dismisses this idea as "a gigantic misunderstanding." This interview, moreover, describes him as a "Euronippon," an identification which – like similar references in the French press (Doucelin 1990) to "un Debussy Nippon" or even "le 'Pierre Boulez' japonais" (Anon. (F.V.) 1996) – defines one extreme of the spectrum of positions allocated to Takemitsu on this map of East and West. The opposite extreme can be found – unsurprisingly – in Japan itself, where the English-language *Yomiuri* called him "the most Japanese of our composers" (Wilkes 1968), and in the German-speaking world, where writers tended to locate Takemitsu in a more specifically Japanese milieu – often (as we shall see) explicitly highlighting the antitheses between his music and the European symphonic tradition.[6]

As suggested earlier, Takemitsu clearly represented a fascinating interview subject for several journalists, and there are frequent references to his physical appearance and presence. "Fragile in physical size, but big in personality" (Prerauer 1969), the "five-foot-five" composer (Hertelendy 1977), "elegant, diminutive" (Hertelendy 1977) and "paper-thin" (Prerauer 1969; Morrison 1991) was nevertheless "a man of singular self-composure" (Dettmer 1969), "a reef unmoved by turbulence" (Tircuit 1968) who, though "a quiet man," "highly poetic" and "shy" (Hertelendy 1977) was able to say "much in little" (Oakes 1969) and, as such, seemed to "epitomize the Westerner's notion of the Japanese" with his "quiet, reserved and delicate manner" (Rockwell 1981). For many Westerners, of course, the archetypal emblem of such qualities is the Buddhist monk (preferably Zen), and commentators on Takemitsu did indeed sometimes take the extreme step of comparing him to one. Particularly priceless in this respect is a *Figaro* article of 1990 depicting the composer squatting in a Zen garden (Doucelin 1990), with the unforgettable headline: "Toru Takemitsu, le gourou."

Figure 9-1

TōruTakemitsu as «guru» © Jacques Doucelin/*Le Figaro*, 1990

But not all criticism was so benign, of course, and recurrent themes also feature in the more negative responses to Takemitsu's music. "The almost total lack of form and development" was, for some, a "problem for the Western ear" (Kenyon 1984), as was the lack of goal-directed motion: *riverrun*, for some German critics, was a "river of stagnant water" (Dümling 1985) or even a "river in the bathtub" (Geitel 1985). Various critics implied that Takemitsu's music was somehow commercialised, "a brand in its own right" (Driver 1994), with such associated negative characteristics as the modishness of "a dandy let loose in a tailor's shop" (Henehan 1981) or the cloying sentimentality of "swooningly beautiful voicing of chords and textures" (Driver 1998). Some transalpine critics in particular, perhaps unsurprisingly, found it "insufficiently deep, too pretty, too meaningless" (Weber 1993) for their tastes. In such contexts, comparisons with film soundtracks now acquired negative connotations, with the inevitable ironic references to "Hollywood's great musical moments" (Geitel 1985).

Takemitsu also came under attack for producing "his scores by strolling in the great garden of twentieth-century orchestral composition, picking and choosing, a flower of Messiaen harmony here, a Debussyan melodic tendril there" (Driver 1998). Other critics were bothered by the music's lack of differentiation: he "seemed to have been all too ready to cultivate the same garden over and over again, never extending its boundaries" (Clements 1998). While for others still–particularly, again, the Germans and Austrians–his "non-European" qualities made him "at first hearing incomprehensible for an audience schooled in Western music" (Breuer 1977).

It would be unwise for me to try and challenge all these negative criticisms, but I would like to conclude by suggesting that many of them, at least, unwittingly enhance our perceptions of the composer. By pointing to what is *absent* in Takemitsu's music, such critics inadvertently alert us to what is actually present. Take, for example, another section of one of the German *riverrun* reviews already cited (Dümling 1985):

"I admit that the expectation of a goal-directed process is a typically European listening attitude ... A piece should not simply break off, but, like a conclusion in logic, express a result."

I am irresistibly reminded by this of the following (Adorno 1978, 171-2):

"Anyone educated in German and Austrian music can rely on experiencing disappointed expectation with Debussy. All through the piece the innocent ear tensely asks if 'it is coming'; everything appears to be a prelude, a preparation for musical satisfactions, for an '*Abgesang*,' which then fails to appear. The ear must be re-educated in order to perceive Debussy correctly: not as a process of accumulation and release, but as a juxtaposition of colours and surfaces as in a painting. The succession merely exposes what, in terms of its significance, is simultaneous: this is how the eye wanders over the canvas."

Substitute "Takemitsu" for "Debussy," "colours and forms in a garden" for "colours and surfaces in a painting" and "a stroller in a garden" for "an eye wandering over a canvas," and I think one begins to see the point. As a more enlightened writer from the German-speaking world put it: "Takemitsu's music demands that Western ears surrender themselves to unaccustomed ways of listening. His works pursue no dramaturgy of tension and release" (Kurz 1984). What critics such as Dümling have identified as problematic in Takemitsu's music thus, viewed from another angle, in fact constitutes one of its great strengths – its refreshingly alternative approach to form to that of the great central European traditions. And, while one would not wish to counter every single negative criticism of Takemitsu, much the same could be said of many of the other features which critics have identified as "weaknesses." In so identifying them, such writers unintentionally perform a most valuable service. Their misunderstandings clarify our own understanding of this much-misunderstood composer.

Notes

1. *Takemitsu Tōru Zenshū*, 5-volume CD set, STZ1-58 (Tōkyō: Shōgakukan, 2002-4)
2. Cf. references, *inter alia* to: 'Mr Takamatsu' (Schafer 1978) and the rather inappropriately bovine 'Toro Takemitsu' (Buell 1984; Falck 1986). In an article by Wes Blomster the composer's name even becomes conflated with that of a major Japanese electronics giant: 'Takemitsui' (Blomster 1984). My apologies, by the way, to any of the above whose errors were the fault of typesetters or proofreaders rather than their own.
3. In *Takemitsu Through the Eyes of the World*, a series of articles written for the *Complete Takemitsu Edition* and included in the supporting materials (cf. note 2)
4. Koch 1996. Interestingly, Takemitsu's obituary in the Vienna *Standard* also spoke of the 'Japan-oriented "new simplicity"' of his later work (Tošic 1996)
5. Rudyard Kipling, *The Ballad of East and West* (1892). Cf. for example (*inter alia*): Commanday 1967; Stadlen 1984; Chism 1988; Gardner 1989; Drillon 1990; McLennan n.d.; Chatelin 1992; Zimmerlin 1996
6. Cf. for example the following obituaries in the German-speaking press: Zimmerlin 1996; Brembeck 1996; Koch 1996.

References

Adorno, Theodor W. 1978. *Philosophie der neuen Musik*. Frankfurt: Suhrkamp.

Anon. 1959. Programme notes for *Le Son-calligraphie No. 2*. Chicago Pro Musica. 10/20/1959.

—. ('F.V.'). 1996. L'esthétique de la dualité. *Liberté dimanche*. 10/6/1996.

Blomster, Wes. 1984. CMF concert embraces a century of development. *Daily Camera*. 7/2/84.

Brembeck, Richard J. 1996. Träume, Wellen, Winter, Nichts. *Süddeutsche Zeitung*. 2/23/96.

Breuer, Robert. 1977. Neues bei den New Yorker Philharmonikern. *Österreichische Musikzeitschrift* 32/5-6 (May-June 1977). 277-8

Buell, Richard. 1984. An enclave of peace and quiet at Symphony. *Boston Globe*. 11/23/84.

Cadieu, Martine. 1971. Journées internationales de musique contemporaine: Toru Takemitsu. *Les Lettres françaises*. 11/10/71.

Cairns, David. 1984. East meets West in Takemitsu. *Sunday Times*. 6/24/84.

Chatelin, Ray. 1992. Takemitsu mixes East and West. *The Province*. 4/23/92.

Chism, Olin. 1988. Beauty and the East meet in Japanese composer's music. *Dallas Times Herald*. 4/27/88

Clements, Andrew. 1998. Cultivating the musical garden. *Guardian*. 10/30/98.

Commanday, Robert. 1967. Japan, western music marriage. *San Francisco Chronicle*. 11/13/67.

Cotte, Jean. 1971. Enfin Takemitsu vint aux Journées de Musique Contemporaine. *France-Soir*. 10/29/71.

Dettmer, Roger. 1969. Takemitsu – a master. *Chicago's American*. 1/26/69.

Doucelin, Jacques. 1990. Toru Takemitsu, le gourou. *Le Figaro* 7/13/90.

Drillon, Jacques. 1990. Toru Takemitsu, entre l'Orient et l'Occident. *Nouvel Observateur*. 7/5/90.

Driver, Paul. 1994. Contemporary composers: Toru Takemitsu. *Sunday Times*. 7/10/94.

—. 1998. Empty Spirits. *Sunday Times*. 10/25/98.

Dümling Albrecht. 1985. Ein Fluß als stehendes Gewässer. *Der Taggesspiegel*. 12/20/85.

Falck, Jørgen. 1986. Naturens toner. *Politiken*. 5/16/86.

Fousnaquer, Jacques-Emmanuel. 1996. Le chef de file de la musique contemporaine japonaise. *Le Monde.* 2/22/96.

Gardner, William O. 1989. An East-West music mix. *Columbia Daily Spectator.* 11/9/89.

Geitel, Klaus. 1985. Fluß in der Badewanne. *Die Welt.* 12/20/85.

Henehan, Donald. 1981. Strings: Tokyo Quartet. *New York Times.* 2/24/81.

Hertelendy, Paul. 1977. A man in harmony with nature. *Oakland Tribune.* 12/2/77.

Hughes, Allen. 1977. Concert: Takemitsu, Tashi and Ozawa. *New York Times.* 3/25/77.

Kenyon, Nicholas. 1984. Aldeburgh Festival. *The Times.* 6/20/84.

Koch, Gerhard R. 1996. Zauber sanften Klangs. *Frankfurter Allgemeine Zeitung.* 2/22/96.

Kozinn, Allan. 1997. Tribute to Takemitsu evokes a private world. *New York Times* 2/11/97.

Kurz, Ernst. 1984. Toru Takemitsu. *Falter.* 8/84

Leblé, Christian. 1990. Takemitsu, Euronippon. *Libération.* 7/21-2/90.

Littler, William. 1996. Japanese composer Toru Takemitsu, 65 won Gould prize. *Toronto Star.* 2/21/96.

McLennan, Douglas. n.d. A mixed musical marriage. *Seattle Weekly.* n.d.

Morrison, Richard. 1991. Doing what comes naturally. *The Times.* 10/10/91.

Oakes, Meredith. 1969. *Daily Telegraph* (Australia). 10/8/69.

Murray, David. 1998. Takemitsu festival closes with honours. *Financial Times.* 11/3/98.

Prerauer, Maria. 1969. Banquet of fine music. *The Sun* (Canberra). 10/9/69.

Rockwell, John. 1981. 2 worlds of Takemitsu, Japan's leading composer. *New York Times.* 2/13/81.

Shafer, Milton. 1978. New York. *Music Journal.* December 1978.

Stadlen, Peter. 1984. East meets West at Aldeburgh. *Daily Telegraph.* 6/20/84.

Tircuit, Heuwell. 1968. A reef unmoved by turbulence. *San Francisco Examiner and Chronicle.* 8/12/68.

Tošic, Ljubiša. 1996. Toru Takemitsu 1930-1996. *Der Standard.* 2/23/96.

Weber, Derek. 1993. Die Leichtigkeit des Seins durch Töne. *Salzburger Nachrichten.* 11/6/93.

Wilkes, Edmund C. 1968. Orchestral space. *The Yomiuri.* 6/13/68.

Winters, Kenneth. 1969. Takemitsu's crescendo. *The Telegram* (Toronto). 1/15/69.

Zimmerlin, Alfred. 1996. Vermittler zwischen Ost und West. *Neue Zürcher Zeitung* (Internationale Ausgabe). 2/23/96.

SECTION THREE

CROSS-CULTURAL USES OF JAPANESE
AND WESTERN INSTRUMENTS

Japanese society today supports a tremendous and continuously increasing number of musical events and variety of music, including those works that display cross-cultural confluence according to their compositional strategies (Itoh 2007).[1] The rapidly changing cultural milieu in Japan and among Japanese (especially in Tokyo) suggests a number of processes of musical transculturation and cross-fertilization.

Yayoi Uno Everett (Everett & Lau 2004, 15) has drawn taxonomic categories for cross-cultural (East Asian and Western) art-music "observable in the repertoire spanning roughly between 1945 and 1998." These categories include transference, syncretism, and synthesis. Transference is described as music where cultural resources (music, philosophy, etc.) of Japan are "borrowed or appropriated within a predominantly Western musical context." Syncretism is defined as music that either transplants specific timbral or scalar attributes of Japanese *hogaku* instruments onto their Western counterparts, or works that juxtapose musical instruments of Asian and Western musical ensembles. Synthesis in music transforms cultural idioms into a new entity where they are no longer identifiable as separate elements. The last two of these descriptions seem especially relevant for the music discussed in these pages.

The essays of Section Three examine innovative uses of instruments from common families (voice, flutes, strings and piano) found in traditional Japanese music and Western art-music, by contemporary Japanese composers. These uses demonstrate various approaches to cultural and musical cross-fertilization. Direct collaborations and investigations between composers and performers of these instruments, are also uncovered.

The growth in importance of texture and tone color in Western art-music composition during the twentieth century and into the twenty-first is indisputable. In addition to exploring almost every conceivable combination of traditional European instruments, composers and performers have invented new acoustic instruments (especially percussion instruments), imitated or used traditional instruments of non-Western cultures (as part of a migration towards a globally eclectic music), created "synthetic" instruments controlled by computers and tape music of manipulated "concrète" sounds, and expanded the resources of traditional instruments through "extended techniques." It is relevant to note that many of these new sonic resources have been a part of Japanese *hogaku* and its aesthetic for hundreds of years – an aesthetic where the instruments personify and assimilate nature. Nuances and transformations of pitch and timbre, as well as natural noise elements, carry important musical meaning in this tradition – a tradition where instruments are learned by ear through rote imitation of a master teacher, rather than through a notation system with its many limitations that concern detail. The interest and sensitivity which many Japanese composers have shown for new sonic resources (extended techniques) for Western instruments often parallel their interest in the natural sounds found in the world of *hogaku* instruments.

From the mid-nineteenth century, the improvements in design of European instruments developed to support/create the evenness of pitch and timbre throughout all registers, the fashion in conventional performance practice (especially in orchestral playing) to the present day. Rather than exploit the inherent acoustical qualities of a particular instrument (which do not promote "homogenized" timbre, for example), most players have been satisfied with refining the sound and technique necessary for the performance of music from past musical epochs. However, along the paths towards new sounds for European instruments (including voice), composers have discovered that innovative performers can not only produce registers of different colors on their instruments, but that (to mention only a few examples) significant color contrasts are possible within each register – and that vibrato depth and shape can be widely varied – and that *portamenti* can take on a variety of shapes - all through actions by the player. As a result, these performers are now asked to deliberately create sounds that were formerly considered unorthodox and generally unacceptable in performance of music from the common practice period: "breathy tone," sounds of indefinite pitch, intervals smaller than half-steps, more than two pitches sounded simultaneously (multiphonics), etc. Reginald Smith Brindle (1975, 156) has aptly described the fascinating consequences:

"players can 'sculpture' sounds in an extraordinary way, varying timbre, attack, and speed or depth of vibrato from moment to moment, so that their instruments have a rich variety of expression hitherto undreamt of."

Beginning in the 1960s, a period of experimentation with these extended techniques produced mixed outcomes. Fears by performers of damaging one's conventional technique or instrument eliminated some of these techniques from further development, as did the unpredictability of the sounds (which, in other cases, was a desired outcome). Vocalist Karen Jensen (1979, 13) articulates a common response among performers:

"The musician's instrument which to some extent is a known entity to its owner, becomes unfamiliar and unpredictable - a situation not unlike determining to cross an unlit room in one's house at night: potentially treacherous!"

A number of catalogs, written by performers in Europe and America, began to appear from the late 1960s – some attempted to explain how to produce the new sounds (Bartolozzi 1969; Rehfeldt 1977).[2] Most were collections of effects drawn from empirical methods. It was not until the 1980s that studies were undertaken based on the acoustical principles of particular instruments (woodwinds), combined with a basic theory of traditional technique, in order to systematically discover and organize new sounds: to expand the sonic resources of instruments based on peculiarities of their acoustical designs (Richards 1984; Veale 1995). All of these materials and more eventually became available to composers in Japan (especially with the increased popularity and speed of the internet) – Takemitsu referred to Bartolozzi's book during composition of *Voice* for solo flute (1971), and a number of other Japanese composers, discussed in this book and elsewhere, referred to these catalogs in addition to willing instrumental collaborators.

As extended techniques have become more prevalent, a consolidation has taken place within the last twenty years. Rather than using these sounds for their novel effect or stereotypical reference, more composers have successfully integrated them within their own musical language.

Also during the last twenty years, sounds and scholarly information about the systems and ideas surrounding Japanese *hogaku* have become more commonly available to European and American performers and composers. This wealth of information, carried through the internet and more traditional methods, include recordings, research publications and translations of work previously only available in Japanese, and personal encounters with ethnomusicologists at universities, immigration of artists, and international exchanges of students and touring/resident artists (just to name a few avenues!). A number of Westerners who have researched/lived for extended periods in Japan have also made analytical material available through their first hand experiences – material that is practiced, but not written about in detail, by Japanese artists (Blasdel 1988, Regan 2006). This way of thinking stems from *hogaku* as an aural culture – one learns by doing (through the body), not through analysis, discussion, or reading about it.

In addition, an increasing number of *hogaku* performers in Japan have broken away from the guild system in the last thirty years, in order to play new music. This, in turn, has encouraged mixed ensembles (*hogaku* and Western instruments), supported by commissioning projects, reconstruction of ancient instruments through the National Theater of Japan, and other initiatives. Finally, it is significant for the future of cross-cultural ensembles that a new wave movement in *hogaku* (combining rock, pop, world music) has led more young people to study *hogaku* instruments in Japan, which has also been assisted by a dictate from the Ministry of Education (2002) to include instruction of *hogaku* instruments in public junior high schools (Everett 2006, 141). The special challenge facing composers of music for *hogaku* instruments has become to move beyond the derivative stereotypical gestures, related to constraints of these instruments, that has evolved during their long history.

Voice

Among pioneers in developing new expressive possibilities for the voice in Western art-music after the Second World War were composer Luciano Berio and the extraordinary singer Cathy Berberian. Through their work with vocal improvisations in the electronic music studio in Milan during the early 1950s, they discovered timbre as the single most malleable and exciting area for exploration (Halfyard 2004). The sounds/techniques of the extended voice were later classified by Trevor Wishart (1980) as *exhaled* and *inhaled* sounds; *voiced* (speech) and *unvoiced* (whispered speech) sounds; and *lunged* (no breathing during sound), *unlunged* (phonetic clicks produced while breathing normally), and *pseudo unlunged* sounds (not breathing normally: sources = larynx, tongue, lips, cheeks, whistling). Later groups, such as the Extended Vocal Techniques Ensemble, in San Diego, added additional resources in their catalog (Higginbotham 1994) -*monophonics* (reinforced harmonics, whistle stop, ululation, fry [dry, click-like pulses], shake, flutters, voiced whistle); and *multiphonics* (Chant, forced blown exhaling, force blown ingressive, glottal overpressure, buzzes and squeaks).

It was two musicians from this group (Edwin Harkins, Philip Larson) who later formed [THE] – an experimental theatrical/musical duo. Joji Yuasa wrote his work *Observations on Weather Forecasts* (1983) for [THE], which is discussed by Colin Holter (*Structural Integration of Television Phenomena in Joji Yuasa's "Observations on Weather Forecasts"*) in the first of a pair of essays that center on works that use the human voice outside of the bel canto tradition. Holter looks at the large palette of "voices" and theatrical gestures used in *Observations* within the context of how the work is characterized by both Yuasa's perspective on popular media (television) and by concepts of temporality from *Noh* that are manifested in the varied means of coordination between the performers (*ashirai* and *mihakarai*).

Born in 1929 in Koriyama, Japan, Joji Yuasa is a self-taught composer. He first became interested in music as a child. Yuasa made the acquaintance of Toru Takemitsu (composer), Kuniharu Akiyama (musicologist) and others while a pre-medical student at Keio University in Tokyo. He joined them in forming the *Jikken Kobo* (Experimental Workshop) in 1952, and turned to devote himself to music. Since then, Yuasa has been actively engaged in a wide range of musical composition, including orchestral, choral and chamber music, music for theatre, and intermedia, electronic and computer music. Yuasa has won numerous commissions for his works from such institutions as the Koussevitzky Music Foundation, Saarland Radio Symphony Orchestra, Helsinki Philharmonic Orchestra, Japan Philharmonic Orchestra, NHK Symphony Orchestra, Canada Council, Suntory Music Foundation, IRCAM and National Endowment for the Arts of the U.S.A.. From 1981 through 1994 Yuasa was actively engaged in music research and education at the University of California, San Diego (currently he is a Professor Emeritus). He has also been a guest professor at Tokyo College of Music since 1981 and a professor for the postgraduate course of the College of Arts at Nihon University since 1993.

Stacey Fraser examines a work by Koji Nakano (a young composer currently living in Boston) - *Time Song II: Howling through Time*, for female voice, flute, and percussion (2006), which utilizes Western and non-Western vocal techniques (the voice part is comprised of a wordless text). Nakano combines multicultural elements in his music through three approaches he describes as *essence, coexistence*, and *fusion*. This work is written in five large sections, which Nakano has labeled "stages."

"The word 'stage' reflects the spiritual and emotional development through the piece. Stage I, "Incantation," is an opening ceremony for calling spirits, where all performers sit on the floor as in a meditation of Zen Buddhism. Stage II, "Trance Dance," not only functions as a transition between Stage I and III, but is also the beginning of vocalizations, entering a spirit into each player. Stage III, "Song of Offering," is the "real" beginning of the piece, where the female singer slowly stands up and delivers messages in a trance. Stage IV, "From the Ancient Voices...," starts with a short quotation from *Kaibairaku* of *gagaku* music which becomes a point of departure to the deeper trance. The last part, Stage V, "Transformation of Souls," is the closing ritual that sends back all spirits."

Koji Nakano earned degrees in composition at the New England Conservatory where he studied with Lee Hyla and John Harbison, and the University of California, San Diego, where he studied with Chinary Ung. The recipient of a number of awards in Japan and the US, he has also studied with Louis Andriessen in Amsterdam and at the Royal Conservatory of the Hague.

Notes

1. every day in Tokyo there are 30-40 concerts of Western art-music – Tokyo currently has seven full-time orchestras.
2. both the Bartolozzi 1969 (Ediziono Suivini Zerboni) and Rehfeldt 1974 (U. of California) texts are part of a series for specific instruments.

References

Anhalt, Istvan. 1984. *Alternative voices: essays on contemporary vocal and choral composition.* London, Toronto: University of Toronto Press.
Bartolozzi, Bruno. 1969. *New Sounds for Woodwind.* Trans. by Reginald Smith Brindle. Oxford U. Press.
Blasdel, Christopher Yohmei. 1988. *The Shakuhachi: A Manual for Learning.* Tokyo: Ongaku No Tomo Sha Corp.
Brindle, Reginald Smith. 1975. *The New Music: The Avant-garde since 1945.* London, Oxford U. Press.
Dame, Joke. 1998. Voices Within the Voice: Geno-text and Pheno-text in Berio's *Sequenza III.* Adam Krims (ed.), *Music/ideology: resisting the aesthetic.* London: Routledge. 233-246.
Everett, Yayoi Uno and Frederick Lau. 2004. *Locating East Asia in Western Art Music.* Wesleyan U. Press.

Everett, Yayoi Uno. 2006. Review of *Yogaku: Japanese Music in the Twentieth Century*, by Luciana Galliano. *Asian Music*, Winter/Spring 2006. 136-42.

Halfyard, Janet K. 2004. A few words for a woman to sing: the extended vocal repertoire of Cathy Berberian.
http://www.sequenza.me.uk/ Berberian_web.htm

Higginbotham, Diane. 1994. Performance Problems in Contemporary Vocal Music and Some Suggested Solutions. Ed.D. diss., Columbia U. Teachers College.

Itoh, Hiroyuki. 2007. Transcription of Panel Discussion, Music of Japan Today 2007, Baltimore, MD (March 31, 2007).

Jensen, Karen. 1979. Extensions of Mind and Voice. *The Composer* 66. 13-14.

Osmond-Smith, David. 1991. *Berio*. Oxford, New York: Oxford University Press (2004)

—. The Tenth Oscillator: the work of Cathy Berberian, 1958-1966." *Tempo* 58, 2-13.

Regan, Martin P. 2006. *Concerto for Shakuhachi and 21-String Koto*: A Composition, Analysis, and Discussion of Issues Encountered in Cross-Cultural Approaches to Composition. Ph.D. diss., University of Hawai'i, Manoa.

Rehfeldt, Phillip. 1977. *New Directions for Clarinet*. U. of California Press.

Richards, E. Michael. 1984. Microtonal Systems for Clarinet: A Manual for Composers and Performers. Ph.D. diss. University of California, San Diego.

Veale, Peter, et al. 1995. *The Techniques of Oboe Playing: A Compendium with Additional Remarks on the Oboe D'Amore and the Cor Anglais*. New York: Barenreiter.

Wishart, Trevor. 1980. The Composer's View of Extended Vocal Techniques. *The Musical Times* 121:1647, 313-4.

CHAPTER TEN

STRUCTURAL INTEGRATION OF TELEVISION PHENOMENA IN JOJI YUASA'S *OBSERVATIONS ON WEATHER FORECASTS*

COLIN HOLTER

The sonic vocabulary of Joji Yuasa's music varies widely from piece to piece, but its conceptual terrain is comparatively circumscribed. The composer cites two broad *topoi* from which his more specific musical concerns are drawn: First, a "universal domain founded on the commonality of sensory capability to be found throughout humanity;" second, a "domain tightly linked to [his] own identity, that of one who was born into and grew up within the cultural zone of Japan" (1993, 216). Each of these realms contributes a cluster of thematic particulars to Yuasa's work, but one idea from each "domain" is perhaps most apparent throughout it.

Of the possibilities presented by the first area of exploration, Yuasa seems most fascinated by the study of metacommunication - the sub-linguistic, "nonverbal communication" that exists in a stratum separate from ordinary verbal articulation (Yuasa 1989, 194). His 1973 piece *Calling Together* is a theatrical survey of vocal inflections on improvised texts based on distance (intimate, social, apostrophic, etc.). Yuasa's approach to metacommunication also includes purely physical, non-sounding gestures: In *Inter-posi-play-tion II* (1973), Yuasa instructs the performers to make motions with their heads to suggest inquisitiveness; in *Interpenetration for Two Percussionists* (1983), the players make eye contact at prescribed moments and raise their mallets as if to signal to one another (Yuasa 1989, 180-182). The latter two pieces incorporate metacommunicative impulses into a musical environment that also includes traditional instrumental performance. This juxtaposition of discourse is critical to Yuasa's music.

Of the areas of creative potential provided by the second "domain," Yuasa's lifelong interest in *Noh* has propelled him toward the investigation of different ways to experience time. Having studied and internalized the music of *Noh* theatre since childhood, Yuasa has developed an unparalleled understanding of the stratification of temporalities in *Noh* – the coexistence of unrelated but complementary layers of rhythm. Mari Kushida (1998, 39-51) makes specific connections between the temporal construction of Yuasa's *Cosmos Haptic II* (1986) and the layering of time in *Noh*; the composer himself (1989, 178) explains the two coeval and constantly shifting tempi of *Interpenetration for Two Flutes I* (1963) in terms of their *Noh* analogues. Significantly, this complex conception of time is found in Yuasa's music both between (as in *Cosmos Haptic II*) and within (as in *Interpenetration for Two Flutes I*) passages of music – in other words, both horizontally and vertically.

Given the commitment with which Yuasa explores these issues in his work, it is unsurprising that they figure heavily in his piece *Observations on Weather Forecasts* (1983, for baritone voice and trumpet). Appropriately, they are broached in ways that seem to mimic the dynamics and imagery of television. *Observations* is clearly a piece "about" television, but Yuasa's adaptation of television phenomena in this particular work is especially striking not only in that it evidences complex interactions between these phenomena and Yuasa's preexisting aesthetic interests, but also in that these interactions are integrated into every level of the piece's compositional design, beginning with its text.

Obviously, Yuasa's text is an imitation of a television weather forecast transcript. Beyond this given, however, several important details emerge. The piece is introduced by both performers "in character"- this unusual device establishes a presentational frame for the piece, emphasizing the "pieceness" of *Observations* much as the opening titles of a new program emphasize its "showness." The performers are directed to make this introduction in a "cool, objective and steady manner," a mode external to their expressive roles within the body of the piece (Yuasa 1986, 3).

After the introduction, Yuasa elucidates these roles by attaching expressive modalities to the weather prognostications in the text. The first "recitational" passage in *Observations* is to be spoken "in appropriate low pitches. . . in the manner of objective statement, however with somewhat depressed feeling," setting as the starting point of the piece's "affective transformation of forecast readings" arc the neutral delivery that an actual weather reporter might use (Yuasa 1986:5). At this stage, Yuasa only hints (i.e. "with a somewhat depressed feeling") at the potential for affective development.

The second reading represents a sudden flowering of these possibilities: Yuasa requests that the baritone "burst into articulation with restrained passion," describing the incoming weather systems "with heart swelling [*sic*] sympathy." By the bottom of the page, this outpouring of emotion intensifies to visible "sobbing" and "crying" on the part of the speaker; meanwhile, the trumpeter is to "gaze at [the] Baritone wonderingly," perhaps amazed that the baritone's yearning for self-expression has been so unabashedly indulged (Yuasa 1986:7).

The third and final reading takes the baritone to the other extreme of emotion. Yuasa indicates that the baritone should begin by "suppressing a laugh"–ultimately, a lost cause (Yuasa 1986:10). The end of the section finds both the baritone and the trumpeter consumed with uncontrollable hilarity. The teleology presented by this affective transformation begins with the speculation that the desire to emote lurks inside a weatherman whose function is to dispassionately read meteorological forecasts; it ends with that weatherman liberated, paying lip service to his professional obligation but finding in the metacommunication of hysterical laughter the opportunity to transcend the mundaneness of his job.

Figure 10-1

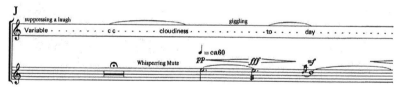

Yuasa OBSERVATIONS ON WEATHER FORECASTS
© 1986 Schott Music Co. Ltd., Tokyo
All Rights Reserved
Used by permission of European American Music Distributors LLC,
sole U.S. and Canadian agent for Schott Music

Yuasa's staging of *Observations* is noteworthy as well. Both performers are to be seated on the stage facing the audience directly, four feet apart, with "glaring spot lights" from stage right. This seating arrangement is reminiscent not only of a news broadcast, in which several anchors may be seated at a desk facing the camera, but also of traditional Japanese music (for instance, a *Noh hayashi* ensemble), in which the performers face the audience and are unable to look at each other for cues.

Furthermore, Yuasa costumes the performers with ski goggles in order to "depersonalize their personalities," preventing the performers from achieving meaningful eye contact with one another or with the audience (Yuasa 1986, 3). In news programs, eye contact is conventionally used to "establish an I/you axis between newsreader and viewer, without, apparently, any unwanted editorializing interventions" - in Western chamber music, however, the performers' eyes are often used to convey expressive information beyond what the music proper provides (Hartley 1992, 76). Yuasa eliminates the performers' capability to communicate with their eyes and severs the "I/you axis" between them and their audience, cleverly allowing only the metacommunication *in the score* to take place.

By casting the baritone as an anchor, Yuasa draws an interesting parallel between the anchor's role as an "all-seeing, all-knowing mouth" and the musician's role in much of his chamber music – to actuate pieces that expose some cosmic truth or supply some perspective on matters of a "universal domain" (Morse 1998, 42). The trumpeter, meanwhile, acts as both a foil for the baritone and as the accompaniment to the weather forecast, furnishing musical cues that show a more-than-passing resemblance to the smooth jazz favored by weather stations.

In addition to these local details, *Observations'* large-scale formal construction calls to mind the shape of a television news broadcast. John Hartley (1992, 79) explains that news programs "frame, focus, realize, [and] close" their content. *Observations* is very clearly "framed" and "closed" by the aforementioned introduction and a similar "sign-off" in which both performers say, in unison and "in normal voice and manner," "See you tomorrow" to the audience (Yuasa 1986, 11). The dramatic arcs of the piece are "focused" early on, including the first recitational passage that establishes the "affective transformation of forecast readings" arc, the rapid flurry of sitting and standing that introduces a "physical gesture coordination" arc, and the first trumpet solo that initiates an "instrumental commentary" arc. These arcs are realized to varying degrees of completeness during the second half of the piece as the readings become increasingly expressive, the sitting and standing reaches a frenzy, and the trumpet's material is played ever more explosively. Note, however, that while Yuasa maintains these news-program formal categories, he repurposes them to fit the piece: Jonathan Bignell (1997, 121) explains that their function in the context of television news is to offer content to the viewer in the most persuasive manner for the advancement of a "discursive position." Yuasa, on the other hand, uses them to establish and elaborate upon the materials of the piece on a structural level and to suggest a news broadcast itself on an associative level.

These television news segments and their smaller subdivisions often shift from one to the next without fluid transitions; such juxtapositions are not uncommon in Yuasa's music, but *Observations* is particularly full of such "jump cuts," and they are put to a distinctly different use in that piece than in many of Yuasa's others. In *Projection Esemplastic for White Noise*, for example, Yuasa places an unexpected silence after a roaring crescendo for dramatic effect, but in *Observations* such dislocations "change the channel" among the aforementioned dramatic arcs and a handful of smaller segments (analogous, perhaps, to commercial breaks).

Many of these local and global features evoke television through metaphor or direct reference *a priori* – they only occasionally happen to intersect with Yuasa's overarching musical interests. It is the piece's middle-ground construction, its connective tissue, that represents most substantially the confluence of television phenomena and the composer's creative preoccupations. Specifically, this connective tissue comprises shifts in the temporal relationship between the performers and among sections of the piece and changes in the individual performers' modes of communication.

In reference to the influence of *Noh* in his music, Yuasa (1989, 180) mentions *mihakarai* and *ashirai*. The composer defines *mihakarai* as a "process from the performer's point of view" of playing in an ensemble but without deliberate synchronization thereto. *Ashirai* is "any given result of the act of *mihakarai*." Yuasa asserts that the seventh page of *Observations* (the second recitational passage, as I have been labeling it) exemplifies his adaptation of *mihakarai* because "the dotted lines designate only approximate vertical synchronization." This manner of loose coordination is quite common in *Observations*, found on five of the score's eight pages.

Another type of asynchronization is found in *Observations* - one that occurs when the performers are playing or singing in the same precisely notated time-space but are unable to attune their gestures. This quality is apparent at rehearsal letter I, when the phrase "San Diego area" is spoken disjointedly and out-of-sync by both performers; in the following measures, Yuasa (1986, 10) applies this sort of asynchronization to the "physical gesture coordination" arc as the performers frenetically attempt to sit or stand in tandem.

Figure 10-2

Finally, at significant moments in the piece, the performers synchronize their actions normally. These coordinations tend to punctuate the ends of periods, as on the word "forecasts" immediately before rehearsal letter B or the coordinated seating at rehearsal letter H.

Figure 10-3

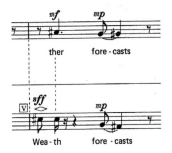

Because the latter two timings are notated in a compatible manner, they may coexist at different levels of communication. This stratification can be seen at rehearsal letter G, for instance, when the performers sing and play out of sync but execute a series of arm gestures simultaneously.

Figure 10-4

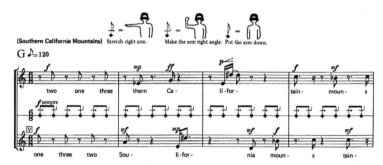

Yuasa OBSERVATIONS ON WEATHER FORECASTS
© 1986 Schott Music Co. Ltd., Tokyo
All Rights Reserved
Used by permission of European American Music Distributors LLC,
sole U.S. and Canadian agent for Schott Music

Multi-layered asynchronization, an outgrowth of Yuasa's understanding of comparable phenomena in *Noh*, is reminiscent of the co-presence of several time-spaces in a weather forecast: the anchor explicates the report in one stratum - in another, the map behind him shows in a matter of seconds meteorological changes that take place over days. Unless the filming is being broadcast live, we watch the program at home several hours displaced from its actual occurrence. Such asynchronization is also analogous to the "several layers in the same visual field simultaneously" identified by Margaret Morse as a defining concept of televisuality. Where a weather forecast might offer the viewer a seated or standing anchor, a computer-generated map of the country, and a stock quote crawl at the bottom of the screen, *Observations* offers the listener multiple strata of time-space.[1]

The investigation of televisual elements as analogues for musical layers is especially relevant to *Observations*: Morse (1998, 95-114) cites their "seamlessness," their paradoxical quality of artificial verisimilitude (a computer-generated network logo that reacts to light as would bronze, for example, but floats weightlessly in a corner of the screen). Whenever the baritone and trumpeter sit in their chairs or speak "in natural voice and manner," to use Yuasa's expression, they are in a way behaving "seamlessly;" the audience knows that they are not simply speaking conversationally, that their actions are prescribed by a score, but the substance of their actions is – context aside – perfectly verisimilar.

Rearrangements of the "hierarchy of discourse" as described by Morse occur both between and within news segments; similarly, Yuasa moves freely between modes and levels of communication in *Observations*. Like a news broadcast, *Observations* makes use of verbal, musical, and (physical) gestural signifiers. The piece includes instructions to speak, sing, play an instrument, sit down, stand up, gesture with one's arm, cry, laugh, and breathe audibly. The trumpeter's sudden abandonment of his instrument to "gaze at [the] Baritone wonderingly" constitutes a reshuffling in the hierarchy of discourse within the second recitation; before this shift, the trumpet is playing an *animato* passage with wah-wah mute, in *mihakarai*, with no acknowledgment of the baritone whatsoever (Yuasa 1986, 7). The trumpeter's gaze implies that, although they remain in different temporalities, they occupy the same communicative wavelength. The sharp transition from the levity of the third recitational passage to the concluding "sign-off" in which the performers' "natural" laughter becomes synchronized, precisely notated "HA's" exemplifies a quick change in discursive character between sections.

The composer uses the term "cosmology" to denote "both [one's] cultural identity and the collective consciousness of the society which shares [one's] language" (1989, 197); television is the filter through which this cosmology is regarded in *Observations*. The filter emphasizes certain features of Yuasa's cosmology and obscures others, sometimes mapping neatly onto it, sometimes generating ambiguous interference, but always providing textured results with which Yuasa is able to build a compelling piece of music.

Notes

1. These televisual features are of course not contemporaneous with the piece's composition in 1983, but they necessarily inform the author's twenty-first-century reading of *Observations*.

References

Baggaley, Jon, and Steve Duck. 1976. *Dynamics of Television*. Westmead: Saxon House.

Bignell, Jonathan. 1997. *Media Semiotics: An Introduction*. Manchester: Manchester University Press.

Hartley, John. 1992. *Tele-ology: Studies in Television*. London: Routledge.

Kushida, Mari. 1998. *Noh Influences in the Piano Music of Joji Yuasa*. DMA diss., University of Illinois at Urbana-Champaign.

Morse, Margaret. 1998. *Virtualities: Television, Media Art, and Cyberculture*. Bloomington: Indiana University Press.

Yuasa, Joji. 1986. *Observations on Weather Forecasts*. Tokyo: Schott Japan.

—. 1989. Music as a Reflection of a Composer's Cosmology. *Perspectives of New Music* 27. 176-197.

—. 1993. Temporality and I: From the Composer's Workshop. *Perspectives of New Music* 31. 216-228.

CHAPTER ELEVEN

CONFLUENCES OF VOCAL TECHNIQUES IN KOJI NAKANO'S *TIME SONG II: HOWLING THROUGH TIME*

STACEY FRASER

Japanese composer Koji Nakano, like many young Asian composers, left his native country to continue his study of music composition techniques in the Western art tradition. Although he was exposed to various kinds of Japanese traditional music throughout his childhood in Japan, it was not until much later in his studies in the United States that he began to consciously incorporate non-Western elements into his music. Nakano explains his own personal rediscovery of his native culture and how it has affected him as a composer.

> "When I finished my study with Louis Andriessen as the Japanese Government Overseas Study Program Artist in 2003, I went back to the University of California, San Diego to complete my Ph.D. degree. My mentor Chinary Ung told me "you seem to master one of two cups, the Western compositional techniques, but you forgot to fulfill another cup, your Asian musical heritage, to complete your total vision. What Chinary told me was an eye opening experience. I realized that I had to start understanding and researching my own original culture and other musical cultures to fulfill the missing cup."[1]

Nakano realizes that many questions that concern cross-cultural borrowing must be seriously considered before integrating non-Western aesthetics into the Western art tradition. It is also not only necessary to study the music of a specific culture, but attempt to find a deeper understanding of the music by studying the various customs and spiritual meanings behind the music. Nakano believes that some elements from different musical cultures blend well, and some do not. In *Time Song II*, he juxtaposes culturally distinct elements with three different intentions:

- *Essence* of musical cultures – loosely interpreted and abstract adaptation of traditional Japanese instruments to a Western compositional language
- *Coexistence* of musical cultures – a layering of musical elements in a kind of counterpoint to one another, letting them interlock without losing their separate identities.
- *Fusion* of Musical cultures – joining two or more things together to form a new, single, and distinct entity.[2]

Vocal techniques and aesthetics in *Time Song II*

As a singer who has been trained in the *bel canto* tradition, I have invested many years to establish a reliable technique that not only corresponds to the aesthetic that is expected in Western opera and concert music, but also allows me to maintain healthy vocal cords. Although I am a performer of standard repertoire, I have an interest in singing music that goes beyond the traditional techniques of the Western art-music tradition. I have become interested in music that integrates these different aesthetics because of my attraction to the unconventional use of vocal timbre to produce emotional and dramatic effects. This means that I must find a way to interpret extended techniques in a way that is not harmful to my voice. I believe that with a firm technical foundation, one can explore these expressive vocal timbres. .

One of the biggest challenges in this piece for me is accessing the very low notes that Nakano incorporates in the vocal part. I do train the lower register of my voice every day as I believe it is the foundation for the entire instrument. Many of Mozart's arias, for example demand an easy chest register as well as an easy top. One may look at the role of Fiordiligi in *Cosi fan tutte* to discover that Mozart uses abrupt changes in registers, sometimes jumping an interval of a twelfth. One must have a secure vocal technique to be able to master this type of writing in performance.

The first phrase that I sing in *Time Song II* is at measure 113 in the second movement. Nakano asks for a low G below middle C, moving up to the middle register A4, and then returning to the low G. My voice does not particularly shine in the low chest area. However, I believe the composer is looking for a vocal gesture or an effect rather than a beautiful resonating tone. Nakano also asks for some *sprechstimme* at the end of the phrase, an example of a vocal gesture where one must be careful to execute the *sprechstimme* with proper breath support to avoid any excess tension on the vocal cords.

Figure 11-1

One of Nakano's primary inspirations for the vocal parts of all three performers is from the vocal and instrumental techniques of the traditional *Satsuma-Biwa* player, as well as various folk singings and vocalisms heard in Japanese traditional music.[3] Nakano describes his intent to use the *essence* of some of the *Satsuma-Biwa* techniques in which there are high and low intervallic leaps and sudden changes in vocal registers. He states that "for the very low vocal parts in particular, he was especially thinking about some characteristics from traditional singings which have various pitch inflections and ornamentations with deep and melancholic sounds from one's chest/throat voice."[4]

Nakano describes measures 129-134 in Stage III as another example of his use of *essence* as a compositional technique. The melody in the vocal line is based on a *gagaku* tuning piece but is given a new musical syntax through its primitive and guttural treatment of the voice. In addition to the essence of the *gagaku* melody, the bongos and conga played in these same measures give the *essence* of *kotsutsumi* drumming in Japanese *Noh* theatre. The *essence* of the *gagaku* melody and the *essence* of *kotsutsumi* create a *co-existence* of musical cultures that creates a kind of layering whereby each element retains its own identity. *Fusion* of musical cultures also plays a role in this particular example as the flute part presents a new layer of *shakuhachi*-like vibrato and pitch bends to the entire ensemble and becomes a kind of glue that binds these materials together.[5]

Figure 11-2

Stage III contains many dramatic contrasts for the voice as the composer often incorporates large intervallic leaps from the low chest register up into the second passaggio and high voice. The singer must be able to execute these leaps with ease and precision while moving between percussive inflections in the middle and chest register to legato melodies in the top. Nakano challenges the singer by asking her to sing a low A in chest voice, jump up to G#5, and then move to a B5 on a hum at measure 153. The singer must then return into chest voice on a low A in the same bar.

Figure 11-3

In addition to the specific references to the *gagaku* melodies and traditional narrative style of singing, Nakano asks for vocal inflections that are inspired by various types of traditional Japanese instruments. The singer is required to bend pitches and sing microtones in a style similar to what may be played on the *shakuhachi* or *ryuuteki*. In addition to these various pitch inflections, Nakano asks for sliding glissandi that often occur between large intervals. Percussive accents, as well as howling gestures that are inspired by *Taiko* drumming and the composer's image of society during the *Joomon* period in Japan, are also incorporated into the vocal lines. The challenge for the singer is to be able to execute these contrasts of percussive accents and legato singing in a relatively short amount of time.

Figure 11-4

Nakano asks for an even more dramatic type of howling beginning at measure 210: he requires the singer to do hand trills through the second passaggio. These hand trills are similar to what Luciano Berio asks for in *Sequenza III* - the tapping of one hand against the mouth to create a sound that mimics a traditional vocal trill by producing a rapid oscillation between two notes, and an alternation between a normal and muted sound.

Figure 11-5

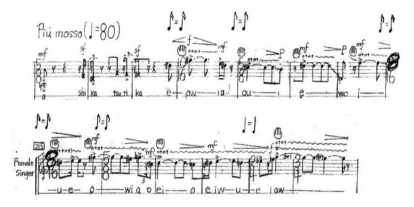

The most difficult part of the piece for the singer begins at measure 301 and continues through the end of the movement. The singer begins here on a low F3 and is required to execute a type of coloratura gesture up to G5. These next moments of the piece are very reminiscent of Western opera, as the singer is required to display a kind of vocal virtuosity that one might find in an operatic cadenza. Nakano however, asks for molto vibrato on the trills, perhaps almost to the point of an intended wobble. These vocal gestures are mirrored by the flutist, who must alternate between a frenzied character and one with a calm and lyrical disposition.

Figure 11-6

The movement concludes with a final coloratura passage from the extreme bottom of the voice up to a tongue trill on high C#6. The tongue trill on such a high note presents a difficult challenge to find a way to successfully execute the effect, yet maintain an open throat in order to sing the C#. The tongue is connected to the larynx and thus must typically be in a relaxed and low position in order to sing a high note: A high larynx position is simply not conducive for singing at the top of one's range. In order to perform a tongue trill, the tongue must vibrate on the hard palette thus the larynx is pulled to a higher position. I have found a solution to phonate on the high C# with the tongue trill, but it takes a certain amount of coordination!

Figure 11-7

Spirituality and Ritual

The composer's intention to express the spiritual side of Japanese traditional music is an essential element of this work. Performers are asked to progress through various emotional and spiritual states throughout the piece that are reminiscent of rituals associated with Japanese ceremonies. Nakano was inspired by ritual ceremonies found in 1) *Shintoism*, and its music that originated from ancient native music, as well as 2) Buddhism, 3) *bugaku*, and 4) the ritual aspect of music for *taiko* drum ensemble.[6] It is through his experience in observing a variety of Asian traditional music that he has learned that the origin of the music has always been rooted as part of ceremonies and rituals. In addition to these spiritual influences, Nakano's decision to use only syllables for a text rather than a text in a recognized language gives the piece a raw kind of primitivism. *Time Song II* was composed as Nakano's own imaginative ritual or ceremony.

I believe that this piece has been carefully planned with regard to a confluence of Japanese and Western aesthetics. The composer has considered each musical element and how it should be incorporated through three different compositional approaches. He has also gone beyond the music and composed something that is motivated by a deeper spiritual meaning, similar to what he has experienced when observing various forms of traditional Japanese music. The piece not only contains direct quotations from this music but combines a variety of aesthetics to create something that is expressive, musical, highly evocative, and most importantly, new and innovative. It is a pleasure to perform a work that not only challenges the technical prowess of the performer, but also envelopes a truly spiritual experience and understanding towards a universal culture.

Notes

1. Nakano, Koji. An interview conducted by Dr. Stacey Fraser via e-mail in February of 2007.

2. Dr. Nakano attributes these three compositional techniques to his teacher and mentor, Professor Chinary Ung.

3. All three players in *Time Song II* are required to sing and to play percussion in addition to their conventional roles on their respective instruments. One of Nakano's reasons for having the percussionist and flutist sing was inspired by an analogy he draws from various forms of Japanese traditional music. "In my initial sketches of the vocalizations, I was especially focused on exploring various vocal techniques heard in traditional Japanese instrumental performance. For example, one of musical inspirations came from the *Satsuma*-style *Biwa* player who sings and plays to tell a tragic story. I was amazed how his singing and playing interplayed continuously, intermingling, blending, and often contrasting each other. Another musical inspiration came from a recording of an *Ondeko* ensemble, in which several *Taiko* drummers play different sized *Taiko* drums with different rhythmic ratios. *Ondeko* is especially famous for its strong, energetic and virtuosic drumming with the use of thick wooden sticks. I was particularly attracted to how *Taiko* drummers communicate to each other by shouting random words or phrases; which functions doubly as a cue to play together as an ensemble, as well as being in the same direction and emotional stage in the music."

4. Nakano, Koji. An interview conducted by Dr. Stacey Fraser via e-mail in February of 2007.

5. It is necessary to mention that there might be varying degrees of *essence, coexistence* and *fusion* and each listener may perceive these three techniques differently depending on how they hear the different layers of multiculturalism. The lines between these three compositional techniques can perhaps become blurred.

6. All over Japan, different sizes and kinds of *Taiko* drums are played outside as part of ritual ceremonies and festivals to swipe away evil sprits, to call for rain or to pray for a good harvest year.

FLUTES

Even though the *shakuhachi* can be considered a member of the flute family, it is necessary to understand that the instrument varies greatly from the Western flute (Lependorf 1989). The modern *shakuhachi* itself is a simple bamboo tube (held vertically) with an angular cut at the mouthpiece. Four holes are bored in the front, with one in the back that is played by the top (left) hand – the instrument is held/balanced by the thumbs and middle fingers. Resting the instrument on the chin beneath the lower lip, the performer blows into the tube to create sound. Several aspects of traditional performance practice on the *shakuhachi* differ from the Western flute: the tongue is not used to reiterate a pitch (a system of grace note articulations is used instead); the diaphragm is not used for vibrato (a variety of vibrati are obtaining by shaking the head); the open tone holes (no keys) allow techniques such as half-holing (alternate timbre fingerings) or finger sliding (various types of *portamenti*) to become idiomatic. These constraints allow very subtle gradations of color and pitch, including timbre and microtonal trills, which require extraordinary sensitivity and careful listening to oneself from the player. Christopher Yohmei Blasdel (American *shakuhachi* player who has lived in Japan 30 years) comments on this sensitivity (Blasdel 1988, 66):

"Instruments like the *shakuhachi* provide us with a living, vital connection with natural tones. Performance techniques such as *muraiki* and *tamane* have their origins in natural sounds: wind and bird cries. A performer cannot execute such techniques if these sounds have not been thoroughly experienced in nature, and their tonal richness will not come across unless the performer maintains a corresponding inner richness......Mastering the *shakuhachi* is a time-consuming experience, but at each stage there are many things to learn about the instrument, its sound, the sounds of nature, and the sounds within yourself."

The *shakuhachi* has been a part of Japanese music in one form or another since the seventh century when it was imported from China as part of *gagaku* music (Blasdel 1988, 72). Since the end of the Second World War, it has expanded to an international arena as part of jazz, fusion, electronic music, rock, and "new age" music, and is even taught at some universities in Europe and America (Blasdel,132).

Composer and *hogaku* performer Marty Regan (*Composing for the Shakuhachi*) offers an explanation of the idiomaticities of the *shakuhachi*, and also discusses notation and problems encountered when combining *hogaku* and Western instruments. Other topics that he explores, in the form of a primer for composers, include distinctions between fundamental and derived pitches, effective scales and runs, grace notes and ornaments, special breath techniques, and pitch inflection.

With regard to the Western flute, Antares Boyle (*Beyond Imitation: Extended Techniques in the Solo Flute Works of Toshio Hosokawa*) identifies and explores three recurring themes in the solo flute works of Toshio Hosokawa: 1) the relationship between silence and sound in a way that Hosokawa has compared to the art of Japanese calligraphy; 2) the slow transformation of different tone colors on a particular pitch; and, 3) the relationship between breath and sound, and between breath and time, which shows Hosokawa's deep relationship with the sounds of nature.

In preparing these works for performance, Boyle recounts that:

"the idea of ambiguity of meaning that permeates Hosokawa's thinking became especially relevant. This enabled me to view passages that seemed highly complex from a performance perspective as a layering of many unique sonic possibilities. When I learned these passages, what seemed a dense and difficult thing could then be transformed into an expansive moment in which I was aware of, yet unhindered by, the passage of time."[1]

In addition to passages that imitate the sounds of the *shakuhachi* or the style of its *honkyoku* (original solo works in the *shakuhachi* repertoire) in Hosokawa's flute works, Boyle notes that:

"the *kakegoe* used in *Sen I* comes directly from traditional *nagauta* and folk music. A flutist learning these works should also expect to become comfortable integrating extended techniques fluidly into his or her normal playing. The specific techniques Hosokawa uses are an essential part of his language when writing for the flute and should not sound like special effects."[2]

Toshio Hosokawa (b.1955, Hiroshima) studied composition in Berlin with Isang Yun, and in Frieburg with Klaus Huber. In 1980, his music was performed at the Internationale Ferienkurse für Neue Musik in Darmstadt, and since then has been heard at major venues throughout Europe and Japan. Hosokawa has won numerous awards and prizes, especially in Germany, and has been invited to nearly all of the major contemporary music festivals in Europe as composer in residence, guest composer or lecturer. At the Münchener Biennale in 1998, his first opera, *Vision of*

Lear, was premiered, and highly acclaimed as "a work inspired by the encounter of East and West which has opened up a new musical world." In 2004, Hosokawa's second opera *Hanjo*, was commissioned by the Festival d'Aix-en-Provence, and in August 2005, his orchestral work, *Circulating Ocean*, commissioned by the Salzburg Festival, was premiered by the Vienna Philharmonic. Hosokawa has served as Composer-in-Residence at the Tokyo Symphony Orchestra (1998-), as Music Director for the Takefu International Music Festival (2001-), and as guest professor at the Tokyo College of Music (2004-).[3]

Notes

1. personal correspondence with the Editor, 1/15/08
2. ibid.
3. see http://www.schott-music.com/

References

Blasdel, Christopher Yohmei. 1988. *The Shakuhachi: A Manual for Learning*. Tokyo: Ongaku No Tomo Sha Corp.
Lependorf, Jeffrey. 1989. Contemporary Notation for the Shakuhachi: A Primer for Composers. *Perspectives of New Music* 27:2. 232-251.

CHAPTER TWELVE

COMPOSING FOR THE SHAKUHACHI

MARTY REGAN

Growing interest among Western composers in composing for non-Western instruments is but one manifestation of the increasingly global nature of recent musical developments, reflecting the phenomenon of multiculturalism that characterizes our lives in the twenty-first century. Advances in technology and growth in institutional resources have resulted in the blurring, and in some instances, the disintegration of national, geographic, cultural, and linguistic boundaries while the circulation of ideas, people, and material culture across the planet has accelerated to an extent unprecedented in the history of humankind.[1] One can say that the current conditions of the field of music composition are fertile for cross-cultural music encounters – whether or not a composer consciously seeks to appropriate elements of non-Western music – and that the numbers of composers who are interested in non-Western music and instruments is a reflection of this fertility.

Composers who write for the *shakuhachi* in particular have a formidable and daunting task in front of them. Despite the widespread globalization of the *shakuhachi* and the hundreds of non-Japanese performers who reside throughout the world, information specifically geared to composing for this instrument is still relatively scarce (Casano 2001). The purpose of this essay is to provide practical information about the instrument by focusing on its fundamental and unique qualities. At the same time, there is a more challenging issue at stake. One could argue that works for non-Western instruments composed by Westerners run the risk of (Bellman 1998, xiii):

"being invariably castigated as artistically or culturally objectionable, as resulting in artworks that are somehow not as authentic as those free of exotic stimuli of a particular land or alien culture, and – following from all these objections – as inhabiting a lower plane than other varieties of music."

Taking advantage of the instrument's unique idiomatic capabilities without exclusively resorting to gestures found in traditional Japanese music is extremely difficult. Another challenge is in finding ways to overcome the instrument's natural limitations, especially in regards to modulation. At what point does stretching the instrument result in the piece not really requiring a non-Western instrument at all, but instead merely become a superficial exploration of exotic timbres and technical exploration? And on the other end of the spectrum, at what point does composing idiomatically for the instrument result in derivative music?

The *shakuhachi* is constructed from the root of timber bamboo using a stalk that has seven nodes. Four holes line the front of the instrument and one hole is drilled in the back. While seven and nine-holed *shakuhachi* exist, this essay will focus on the standard five-holed *shakuhachi*, which is considered standard. The name of this instrument is derived from its length of one *shaku* and eight – in Japanese, *hachi – sun,* which equals approximately 54.5 centimeters.[2] At the same time, *shakuhachi* come in different lengths that correspond to different keys. A more specific name for each length is derived from the pitch that is produced when all of the holes are covered and the instrument is blown in a normal position. The standard *shakuhachi*, which produces the nuclear pitch d^1 under these conditions, is called the *d-kan*, or 1.8 (*isshaku-hassun*), while the most common *chô-kan*, or long *shakuhachi,* produces the pitch a and is called the *a-kan*, or 2.3 (*ni-shaku-san-sun*).[3]

From the standard 1.8 *d-kan shakuhachi*, each increase in length by one *sun* lowers the pitch by approximately a minor second. Similarly, each decrease in length by one *sun* raises the pitch by a minor second. Figure 12-1 indicates various length *shakuhachi* and their corresponding nuclear tones. Most professional *shakuhachi* players own a 1.8 *d-kan*, 2.3 *a-kan*, 1.6 *e-kan*, and 2.1 *b-kan*, but it is best to consult with the performer in advance and confirm which lengths are available.

Figure 12-1: Name of length and nuclear pitch for each size *shakuhachi*

Length	Nuclear tone
1.1	a^1
1.2	$g^{\#1}$
1.3	g^1
1.4	$f^{\#1}$
1.5	f^1
1.6	e^1
1.7	e^{b1}
1.8	d^1
1.9	$c^{\#1}$
2.0	c1
2.1	b
2.2	b^b
2.3 (actually closer to 2.4)	a
2.5 (actually closer to 2.7)	g

Starting with the nuclear pitch of d with a 1.8 *d-kan*, which is produced by covering all of the holes and blowing in a normal position, lifting up each finger starting with the ring finger of the right hand in order from the bottom hole to the thumb hole – holes 1, 2, 3, 4, and 5, respectively – results in a minor pentatonic scale, D-F-G-A-C. In addition to these five fundamental pitches – which also repeat in the upper octaves – certain derived pitches can be produced by half-holing and adjusting the embouchure by narrowing the angle between the lips and the mouthpiece. This is referred to as *meri* technique. A lowered half-step is called *meri,* while a lowered whole-step is called *o-meri.* In contrast, by widening the angle between the lips and the mouthpiece, the pitch can be raised up to a half-step at most, and this is called *kari*. Figure 12-2 shows the easily produced fundamental (indicated by the whole note heads) pitches and derived *meri* and *kari* pitches (indicated by smaller blackened note heads) for the 1.8 *d-kan* in the three octaves/ranges of the *shakuhachi*.[4]

Figure 12-2: Fundamental and derived pitches of a 1.8 *shakuhachi*

The fundamental pitches can be produced at a rich volume throughout the range, but the volume of pitches produced by *meri* technique naturally decreases and the timbre of these pitches tends be dark, fuzzy, airy, and unfocused. *Kari* pitches on the other hand, tend to be bright and loud. When composing for the *shakuhachi* therefore, it is extremely important to know which pitches are the fundamental ones and which are derived for the particular length one is using. While fundamental pitches throughout the *otsu* and *kan* range can be produced from *pp* to a *ff* with an evenly balanced volume, one must be aware of the dynamic limitations associated with *meri* pitches in particular.

In theory, a *shakuhachi* of a given length should be in tune, but due to the large diameter of the mouthpiece which is cut obliquely outward, any increase or decrease – no matter how slight – in lip pressure or adjustment of the angle between the mouthpiece and the lower lip will result in pitch oscillation, even when playing the fundamental pitches. This is both a disadvantage and advantage for *shakuhachi* players. Producing *meri* and *kari* pitches with precise intonation throughout the range is a challenge for all but the most advanced players. On the other hand, the lack of pads or mechanical features to control pitch and intonation gives the *shakuhachi* the ability to easily produce microtonal shadings and *portamento* that would present more of a challenge for the Western flute. While the *shakuhachi* cannot compete with the Western flute in terms of agility, it is these "limitations" that impart enormous expressive potential in the hands of a well-trained performer, and since *meri* and *kari* pitches are necessary to play all but the simplest folk songs, all *shakuhachi* players must learn to work with the constraints of the instrument's physical construction. Figure 12-3 is an excerpt from my *Concerto for Shakuhachi and 21-String Koto* (2006) that illustrates effective use of *portamento*, or *suri* in Japanese. It is indicated by placing an angled line between two pitches.

Figure 12-3: m. 276

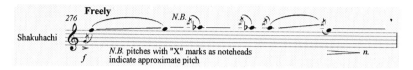

In my experience, when composing for the *shakuhachi* there are certain compositional strategies that may be utilized to help highlight the idiomatic characteristics of this instrument. First, in common with each of the Japanese transverse flutes, tonguing is not traditionally used with the *shakuhachi*. Instead, breath from the abdomen is blown through the instrument while articulations are emphasized by quickly opening and closing the holes. This results in rapid grace note figures that can be used to turn what would otherwise be a simple melodic line into what is perceived to be dazzling finger work. When decorating a melodic line with idiomatic grace note figures, it is important to remember that while grace notes can be executed in a moment, they do take up a certain degree of time for preparation and recovery. Hence, it is best to add them in moderation, and only to pitches in the passage that need to be emphasized for one reason or another. As a general rule, if the composer calls for a dynamic accent, grace notes should fundamental pitches and not derived pitches. Figure 12-4 is an excerpt from my *Concerto for Shakuhachi and 21-String Koto* (2006) that illustrates extensive use of grace note figures to decorate a passage.

Well-trained *shakuhachi* performers can accurately play rapid scale-like melodic passages on the five-holed *shakuhachi*. Normally, precise intonation and an even balance of volume can easily be obtained when playing the fundamental pitches on any of the various lengths, although the longer *shakuhachi* instruments tend to be sluggish. Since *meri* pitches in particular tend to make the intonation unstable and reduces the volume, rapid flourishes must be constructed carefully. A basic rule is to use fundamental pitches as often as possible and to avoid rapid chromatic passages where the performer must alternate between fundamental and derived pitches. As Jeffrey Lependorf writes (1989, 245):

"The *shakuhachi* seems best suited for playing sustained passages, but various scales and runs are certainly possible. However, because the *shakuhachi* lacks keys or valves some care must be taken in constructing them. For example, a chromatic scale, though possible on the *shakuhachi*, is difficult to perform without it sounding like a glissando."

Figure 12-4: m.18-44

Figure 12-5 is an excerpt from the score of the original version of my *Concerto for Shakuhachi and 21-String Koto*, which was composed for two soloists and Western orchestra. It is a flourish divided among the woodwinds.

Figure 12-5: m. 65-66

When I arranged *Concerto for Shakuhachi and 21-String Koto* for an ensemble of Japanese instruments, with the woodwind section of the ensemble now comprised of three *shakuhachi* and a *shinobue,* this particular passage became problematic. Since I was more interested in the gesture of the rising flourish rather than exact pitches, I made necessary adjustments to the lines in order to assure that it could be executed cleanly. Figure 12-6 is an excerpt of the same passage as above taken from the Japanese instrument version of *Concerto for Shakuhachi and 21-String Koto.*

Figure 12-6: m. 65-66

Even though playing the *shakuhachi* does not traditionally involve tonguing, composers have been making more and more technical demands on *shakuhachi* players since the 1960s, including passages where double, triple, and even flutter-tonguing is needed. Double-tonguing on the *shakuhachi* leaves a strong impression on the listener because most lines on the *shakuhachi* are naturally played *legato.* Like grace notes, it is best used in moderation. Figure 12-7 is an excerpt from my *Concerto for Shakuhachi and 21-String Koto* (2006) that illustrates effective use of double-tonguing. Staccato marks are written above the notes to be double-tongued. Without such articulations, *shakuhachi* performers will generally play legato.

Figure 12-7: m.254-261

One is also capable of producing a wide range of timbral nuances on the *shakuhachi* by adjusting the airflow inside the throat. The hallmark technique of the *shakuhachi* is called *muraiki,* produced by blowing aggressively into the mouthpiece to "dirty" the tone with the breath. It is most effective when used with pitches in the lower *otsu* octave, which often results in audible overtones above. This technique is best used in moderation and is indicated with the symbol "*m.*" for *muraiki* followed by a wavy line which gives a visual approximation of the intensity of the airflow (see Figure 12-8, m. 282). A similar technique, called *sorane* is used for pitches of shorter duration, indicated by placing an "X" mark through the stem (see Figure 12-8, m. 281).

The *shakuhachi* can effectively produce tremolo and trills between any two fundamental pitches. However, similar to other Western woodwinds, playing tremolo between pitches in different ranges (i.e. *otsu* and *kan*) is difficult. *Koro-koro* is a kind of multiphonic trill executed between two microtonal variations on the pitch c^2 using alternate *meri* fingerings between the dynamic levels of *pp* and *mp*. In addition to the microtonal difference in pitch between the two fingering, there is also a subtle difference in timbre. Needless to say, *koro-koro* is a remarkable technique, characterized by a whirlwind of subtle timbre and pitch variation executed in an instant. In traditional *honkyoku* repertoire, *koro-koro* is usually followed by a final trill-like flourish ascent to d^1, which creates a sense of timbral and pitch resolution. It is indicated by writing "*koro-koro*" or in katakana, "□ □ □" above the pitch.[5] Figure 12-8 is an excerpt from the *shakuhachi* cadenza of my *Concerto for Shakuhachi and 21-String Koto* (2006) that illustrates *muraiki, sorane,* and *koro-koro* in one passage.

Figure 12-8: m.280-283

Since the *shakuhachi* has certain limitations when it comes to modulation, one has to be extremely careful in finding ways to incorporate it into chromatic progressions. One of my solutions is to find common pitches between the harmony or pitch collection being used and the non-*meri* pitches of the *shakuhachi* and in turn emphasize those pitches. This means that when the *shakuhachi* plays along with an ensemble in a modulating passage, the solo line has a sustained, lyrical character rather than rapid scale-like gestures or intricate fingerwork. For example, in my *Concerto for Shakuhachi and 21-String Koto* (2006), in m. 129-130 the strings outline G Phrygian (G-A^b- B^b-C-D-E^b-F-G), a pitch collection that perfectly matches the tuning of the a 1.8 *shakuhachi.* Suddenly, in m. 131 there is a direct modulation to G^b Lydian (G^b-A^b-B^b-C-D^b-E^b-F-G^b).

While this harmonic change is not particularly difficult for the strings, it presents a problem for the *shakuhachi*. Among the pitches in the new pitch collection at m. 131, the only ones that the *shakuhachi* can produce *without* resorting to *meri-kari* techniques are F and C. Hence, these two pitches play a prominent role from m. 131-134.

Figure 12-9: m.129-134

I am not implying that the *only* pitches available during modulations like this are the fundamental pitches of the *shakuhachi* that are found in the mode of G^b Lydian. Rather, I am suggesting that the new pitch collection can help the composer determine which pitches can be emphasized and what types of melodic lines can be constructed in order to prevent the *shakuhachi* from sounding strained. *Meri-kari* pitches can easily be produced on the *shakuhachi* to add a certain character, providing timbral relief from a melodic line that would otherwise contain nothing but fundamental pitches. In fact, with half-step inflections up to g^{b1} in m. 131 and d^{b1} in m. 132, this is precisely what I do in this example. However, it is important to realize that due to the difficulty that the *shakuhachi* has with modulation, there are certain gestures that are impractical - for example, ascending or descending diatonic scales or runs. Since chromatic modulation is used extensively in this piece, this compositional technique allows the soloists to continue playing over remote chromatic modulations, despite the fact that in most cases, the types of gestures and pitches I can assign to the *shakuhachi* become somewhat limited. I would like to suggest that this kind of approach seeks to stretch Japanese instruments westward to a point where they can assume their place as global instruments and overcome their harmonic limitations. Combining Japanese instruments with Western instruments creates a kind of *aural illusion* that gives the impression that Japanese instruments are more chromatic than they really are, opening up new possibilities for stimulating musical exchange and cross-cultural expression.

Notes

1. For a detailed historical account of the cross-fertilization of Western and Asian musical aesthetics since World War II, see Everett 2004.
2. One *shaku* equals approximately 30.3 centimeters, and one *sun* equals approximately 3.03 centimeters.
3. In this essay, pitches are designated by the Helmholtz octave designation system. Middle c is referred to as c^1 and higher octaves are indicated with a corresponding superscript, the "small" octave is indicated by lower case letters, and the "great" octave is indicated with capital letters. Depending on the school, there is disagreement as to whether the longer length *shakuhachi* should be referred to in terms of their theoretical length or actual length. In particular, many players refer to the *a-kan* as a 2.4 (*ni-shaku-yon-sun*). When in doubt, it is best to reference the nuclear tone of the *shakuhachi* in question.
4. The five-holed *shakuhachi* cannot produce the pitches f^3 or b^3.
5. The repertoire of 'original pieces' for the *shakuhachi* that have been orally transmitted over the past 500 years within the context of Zen Buddhism – sacred pieces that are considered a kind of "blowing meditation."

References

Bellman, Jonathan. 1998. *The Exotic in Western Music*. ed. Jonathan Bellman. Boston: Northeastern University Press.

Casano, Steven. 2001. *From Fuke Shu to Oduboo: Zen and the Transnational Flow of the Shakuhachi Tradition from East to West*. Masters thesis. University of Hawai'i, Manoa.

Cronin, Tania. 1994. On Writing for the *Shakuhachi*: A Western Perspective." *Contemporary Music Review* 8:2. 77-81.

Everett, Yayoi Uno. 2004. Intercultural Synthesis in Postwar Western Art Music: Historical Contexts, Perspectives, and Taxonomy. *Locating*

East Asia in Western Art Music. Everett, Yayoi Uno and Frederick Lau. eds. Middletown: Wesleyan University Press.

Lependorf, Jeffrey. 1989. Contemporary Notation for the *Shakuhachi*: A Primer for Composers. *Perspectives of New Music* 27:2. 232-251.

Miki, Minoru. 1998. *Nihongakkihô* (Composing for Japanese Instruments). 3rd ed. Tokyo: Ongaku no Tomo-sha.

Nakamata, Nobukio. 1994. Ways of the *Shakuhachi*: Exploitation or Creation?" *Contemporary Music Review* 8:2. 95-101.

Regan, Martin P. 2006. *Concerto for Shakuhachi and 21-String Koto*: A Composition, Analysis, and Discussion of Issues Encountered in Cross-Cultural Approaches to Composition. Ph.D. diss., University of Hawai'i, Manoa.

Samuelson, Ralph. 1994. *Shakuhachi* and the American Composer. *Contemporary Music Review* 8:2. 83-94.

CHAPTER THIRTEEN

BEYOND IMITATION: EXTENDED TECHNIQUES IN THE SOLO FLUTE WORKS OF TOSHIO HOSOKAWA

ANTARES BOYLE

Solo pieces by Japanese composers make up a significant body of repertoire for the contemporary flutist. Two of the most frequently performed twentieth-century flute works are Kazuo Fukushima's *Mei* (1962) and Toru Takemitsu's *Voice* (1971). Fukushima (b. 1930) and Takemitsu (1930–1996) have each written several other works for solo flute, as have many other important Japanese composers, including Yoritsune Matsudaira (1907–2001), Joji Yuasa (b. 1929), and Toshi Ichiyanagi (b. 1933). These artists are all members of the first generation of internationally active and recognized Japanese composers. The next generation, including figures such as Toshio Hosokawa (b. 1955), has continued to compose for the solo flute.

One may wonder why so many Japanese composers have chosen to write for solo flute. An obvious reason would seem the importance of flutes in traditional Japanese music. The *Noh* Theater employs a transverse flute called the *nohkan*. It is the only melody instrument in the ensemble and often plays an independent line against the singer to intensify the emotional affect. Three kinds of flutes are used in *gagaku*, often to play an embellished version of the melody. And of course *honkyoku*, traditional solo pieces for the *shakuhachi*, are one of the most obvious sources of inspiration to contemporary composers.

The importance of the *nohkan* and *shakuhachi* in traditional music as purely melodic instruments, free from any harmonic obligation, may be part of the inspiration for the many solo Japanese flute pieces. However, Western composers also embraced the solo flute idiom after World War II. The flute plays an important role in such twentieth-century landmarks as Schoenberg's *Pierrot Lunaire* and Boulez's *Le Marteau sans Maître*. It was not a far jump from pieces such as these to composers writing substantial works for solo flute. The precedent had already been established by the twin miniatures of pre-war modernism, Debussy's *Syrinx* (1913) and Varèse's *Density 21.5* (1936). It was the acclaimed reception of these works and their eventual entry into the twentieth-century canon that indicated that the world was ready to accept a composition for solo flute as a significant piece of music. Examples of important post-World War II solo works include Luciano Berio's first *Sequenza* and Brian Ferneyhough's *Unity Capsule*.

These pieces are evidence of what Paul Griffiths (1995, 191) labels a "revolution in performance practice." Composers had already begun to write extended techniques into their pieces when Bruno Bartolozzi's landmark *New Sounds for Woodwind* appeared in 1967. This "revolution" impacted strongly on the Japanese compositions for solo flute— Takemitsu's *Voice* directly references Bartolozzi's book in the performance instructions. Soloists who could play these new sounds became an important part of the new music scene, both enabling and inspiring composers. Berio and Fukushima's flute works were written for Severino Gazzelloni; later, Ferneyhough and Hosokawa would both compose for Pierre-Yves Artaud.

Despite the vastly different compositional styles of composers such as Takemitsu and Fukushima, their flute works are often discussed together. Certain qualities have become associated with these pieces, perhaps most importantly a conscious musical involvement with the Japanese heritage of the composers. The nature of this involvement is highly individual, but the composers are all assisted by an innovative and sensitive use of extended techniques. Takemitsu and Fukushima were early pioneers in this field. *Mei* uses *glissandi* and quarter-tones to imitate the sound of the *shakuhachi*. *Voice* employs a wide variety of highly original and somewhat ambiguously-notated effects, including speaking, grunting, and whispering into the instrument. Some notes call for a special attack to imitate the sound of the *nohkan*. It is certainly the effectiveness of Fukushima's delicate *portamenti* and the lasting freshness of *Voice*'s theatrics that have helped these works enter into the standard flute repertoire.

In later compositions, extended techniques reach a new level of sophistication and often allow the composer to explore traditional Japanese aesthetics in ways that go beyond simple imitation. Exemplary of this is Toshio Hosokawa, who has written three solo flute works: *Sen I* (composed 1984–6), *Vertical Song I* (1995), and *Atem-Lied* for solo bass flute (1997). These three pieces display a progressively more advanced integration of extended techniques. The techniques are not only an essential part of Hosokawa's flute language, but become indispensable to illustrating his musical philosophy.

Even in Hosokawa's first solo flute work, *Sen I,* the variety of techniques used and the extent to which these sounds are incorporated into Hosokawa's language is remarkable. In some twentieth-century works, extended techniques are used infrequently and exist merely as effects, in stark contrast to the "normal" instrumental color. In others, such as Ferneyhough's flute works, the focus of the composition is on the process of producing these sounds, and the effects' tests on the limitations of the instrument transform extended techniques into a sort of battleground on which the flutist fights with the flute. In *Sen I*, however, these sounds are part of the basic language of the piece, seemingly an obvious extension of traditional flute playing.

Among the many techniques used, perhaps the most original is Hosokawa's notation for varying degrees of air noise in the sound. This continuum between airy and clear tones offers a new parameter of sonic possibility, comparable to carefully notated dynamics. New layers of possibility such as this add to the multi-dimensionality of Hosokawa's work and tie in with his philosophy about layers of meaning in music. He describes this philosophy using the metaphor of "the pattern and the fabric," the concept of a foreground and background which are permeable and inseparable (Hosokawa 1994). As Takemitsu's *Voice* was heavily influenced by Bartolozzi's manual, *Sen I* was inspired by contemporary flutist Pierre-Yves Artaud's *Present-Day Flutes*, a compendium of extended techniques published in 1980. The following example (Figure 13-1) from the opening of *Sen I* illustrates Hosokawa's skillful use of extended techniques. In measures 6–8, note how the variation in air noise (represented by square and triangular note-heads) is used in conjunction with an extreme variation in dynamic and a microtonal filling-in of vertical pitch space around the central note, A.

Figure 13-1

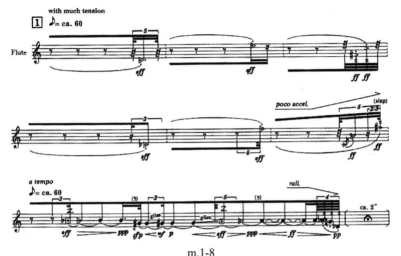

m.1-8
Hosokawa SEN I
© 1993 Schott Music Co. Ltd., Tokyo
All Rights Reserved
Used by permission of European American Music Distributors LLC,
sole U.S. and Canadian agent for Schott Music

Vertical Song I, Hosokawa's second solo flute work, is quite different in impact. It is a shorter work and more economical in its use of material. Writing about the piece, Hosokawa says, "I believe that the language of music is born not from a superficial place but from deeper places unnoticed in our daily lives…. I want to sing songs which are born from those depths and come rising up vertically to the place of our singing" (1997c). In *Vertical Song,* Hosokawa's wide catalogue of flute techniques is introduced slowly and deliberately, leading to a feeling of trepidatious, awed discovery and of tension below surface level. The opening of the work moves slowly from one sound to another in an exploratory fashion. The emphasis rests on each sound as a unique and complete entity rather than on the relationship between those sounds, but this simplicity is deceptive. Different levels of air noise and other contemporary techniques subtly inflect or vary each pitch, creating a surface of seemingly infinite variety. Many notes emerge from and return to unpitched noise or silence. Later in the work, various techniques are used to explore the many facets of a single pitch in a passage that lasts over a minute.

Figure 13-2

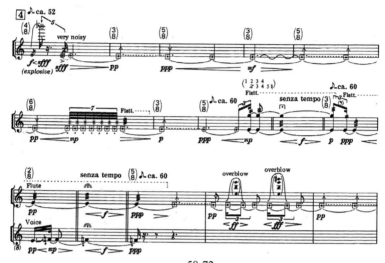

m.58-72
Hosokawa VERTICAL SONG I
© 1994 Schott Music Co. Ltd., Tokyo
All Rights Reserved
Used by permission of European American Music Distributors LLC,
sole U.S. and Canadian agent for Schott Music

Extended techniques in *Vertical Song* also function to create contrasting musical textures. One example appears only near the end of the work and is defined by its characteristic use of quarter-tones and the breathiest of Hosokawa's airy sounds (see final measure of Figure 13-3). These soft microtones frame and suggest pitches of an octatonic set not yet heard in the piece. The effect is a slippery, fuzzy octatonic language, almost as if the pitch set is being heard through some kind of distorted lens. In the closing bars of the piece, Hosokawa introduces another technique not yet used: whistle tones. These ethereal sounds, heard at the top of the flute's range, combine with the new low-register texture and new pitch language to form an eerie conclusion that resembles nothing heard thus far (Figure 13-3). This move to something completely new at the very end happens in all Hosokawa's flute works, often assisted by the introduction of a new flute sound. The technique of ending a work just as it opens up a new area for exploration creates a sense of spontaneity, a quality Hosokawa values in nature. Hosokawa explains that, "the Japanese word for nature—*shizen*—can also be read as *jinen*, with the meaning: nature, spontaneity" (1995, 53).

Figure 13-3

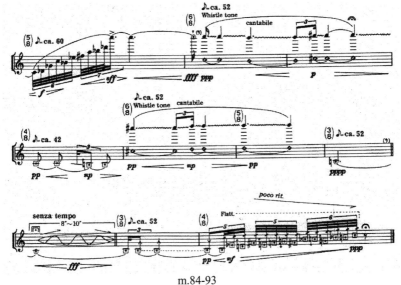

m.84-93
Hosokawa VERTICAL SONG I
© 1994 Schott Music Co. Ltd., Tokyo
All Rights Reserved
Used by permission of European American Music Distributors LLC,
sole U.S. and Canadian agent for Schott Music

Unlike *Sen* and *Vertical Song*, the sonic landscape of *Atem-Lied* is dependent on a single kind of extended flute technique: manipulation of breathing sounds and air noise in the flute tone. Much of the work consists of airy pitches produced by both exhalation and inhalation. The relationship between breath and sound becomes the perfect realization of Hosokawa's "pattern and fabric" metaphor. In his notes to Eberhard Blum's recording of *Atem-Lied*, Hosokawa explains, "Breath is the very foundation of music" (1998). Breath allows the music to be born; it creates the canvas on which the music may be drawn. In *Atem-Lied*, the sound of breathing is a backdrop that is established at the beginning (Figure 13-4) and constantly re-emerges. By constructing breath as the background (or fabric) and music as the foreground (or pattern), an ambiguity is created between breathing and music. Since breathing always exists in the same moment as sound, it becomes impossible to say when the flutist is playing and when he or she is merely breathing. These ambiguities are captured in the title, "Breath Song."

Figure 13-4[1]

m.1-9
Hosokawa ATEM-LIED
© 1997 Schott Music Co. Ltd., Tokyo
All Rights Reserved
Used by permission of European American Music Distributors LLC,
sole U.S. and Canadian agent for Schott Music

Shortly after composing *Vertical Song*, Hosokawa wrote, "I am now interested in trying to… change and to rebuild different tonal materials from Western music. I am thinking of a method of rebuilding new music without the use of special playing techniques and without "alienation" of the sounds, but rather aiming to discover a new meaning in something already in existence" (1995, 52). The last comment may lead us to believe Hosokawa intended to discontinue his use of extended techniques. This clearly has not happened in *Atem-Lied;* however, one can hear a move away from the "alienation" of unusual sounds. There is no longer any need to combine these sounds with more familiar ones. By allowing them to stand on their own, Hosokawa has indeed moved these sounds beyond the realm of "special playing techniques" and they can now take on new meaning. Through this liberation, Hosokawa has opened up new dimensions of expression for flutists and composers.

Note

1. Square note-heads represent the airiest possible sound; stems with upward arrows represent inhalation.

References

Artaud, Pierre-Yves, and Gérard Geay. 1980. *Flûtes au présent: Traité des techniques contemporaines sur les flûtes traversières, à l'usage des compositeurs et des flutists* [Present-day flutes: Treatise on contemporary techniques of transverse flutes for the use of composers and performers]. Paris: Éditions Jobert/Musicales Transatlantiques.

Fukushima, Kazuo. 1966. *Mei for solo flute*. Milan: Zerboni.

Griffiths, Paul. 1995. *Modern music and after*. Oxford: Oxford University Press.

Hosokawa, Toshio. 1994. The pattern and the fabric: In search of a music, profound and meaningful. In *Ästhetik und Komposition: Zur Aktualität der Darmstädter Ferienkursarbeit*, ed. by Gianmario Borio and Ulrich Mosch, 74-78. Mainz: Schott.

—. 1995. Aus der Tiefe der Erde: Musik und Natur. Trans. Ilse Reuter, unpub. English trans. by Megan Lang. *MusikTexte: Zeitschrift für neue musik*, no. 60: 49-54.

—. 1997a. *Atem-lied for solo bass flute*. Mainz: Schott Japan.

—. 1997b. *Vertical song I for solo flute*. Mainz: Schott Japan.

—. 1997c. Notes to *Works by Toshio Hosokawa V*, various artists. Fontec, FOCD3406 (compact disc).

—. 1998. Notes to *Japan flute*, Eberhard Blum. Hat Hut, hat[now]ART 106 (compact disc).

—. 2003. *Sen I for solo flute*. Mainz: Schott Japan.

Takemitsu, Toru. 1971. *Voice pour flûte solo*. Paris: Salabert.

STRINGS AND PIANO

The music for particular instruments investigated in the essays that follow (works by Mayuzumi, Hosokawa, Tanaka, Ishii, and Yuasa) places great importance on the subtleties of color transformation, including the similar vocabulary of percussive sounds that the *koto*, piano, violin, and cello can all create. Examples of diverse concepts of temporality borrowed from *hogaku* and employed in these works of art-music, are also discussed.

Marty Regan (*Composing for 21-string Koto*) presents the basic possibilities and constraints of the 21-string *koto* (a "new" *koto*, invented by Minoru Miki and *koto* performer Keiko Nosaka in 1969), through topics that include basic tuning and tuning modifications, left hand pressing techniques, and timbral modification techniques for the right hand. He includes a number of musical examples from his own compositions.

Cellist Hugh Livingston (*Adaptation of Performance Style from Early Modern Japan to the Contemporary Cello*) describes his development and use of many new cello techniques, some of which he applies to his performance interpretation of Toshiro Mayuzumi's *Bunraku*. Livingston has researched and categorized over 100 types of pizzicato for cellists, which apply in realizing Asian music, as well as other techniques and sounds for the modern cello (an instrument with infinite pitch flexibility, a wide range, a substantial relative volume, and the ability to be bowed, plucked, and played percussively) connected to traditional Asian instruments.

Toshiro Mayuzumi (1929-97) studied with Ikenouchi and Ifukube at the Tokyo National University of Fine Arts and Music shortly after the war. He went to Paris in 1951 to study at the Conservatoire with Aubin, and had the opportunity to learn of the new developments of Messiaen, Boulez, and musique concrète. Returning to Tokyo in 1953, Mayuzumi founded (with Akutagawa and Dan) the *Sannin no Kai* (Group of Three), and wrote the first musique concrète work ("X, Y, Z" [1955]) and first electronic piece ("*Shusaku* I" [1955]) in Japan. His experimentations also included the use of prepared piano, serial and aleatory methods, and unusual instrumentations. From the late '50s on, Mayuzumi's music was increasingly influenced by traditional Japanese music and Buddhism – in his work *Nehan kokyokyoku* (*Nirvana Symphony*), he analyzed the sonorities of temple bells acoustically and tried to reproduce their profound sensation by means of tone qualities, volumes and the use of space in his music. At the same time he developed interests in traditional Japanese music, such as *gagaku* and *shomyo* (Buddhist chants), the *Noh* drama, and the *gidayu* singing which accompanies *bunraku*. Mayuzumi also composed much music for films (including *The Bible* in 1965), and two operas (*Kinkakuji* and *Kojiki*), which expressed his nationalistic politics.[1]

Airi Yoshioka ("*Ma" (sense of time) as Compositional Tool*) discusses different definitions and performance realizations of Japanese "*ma*" in violin works by Hosokawa (*Vertical Time Study III*), Karen Tanaka (*Wave Mechanics II*), and Maki Ishii (*A Time of Afterglow*).[2] Previous definitions for *ma* include "structural down-silence" vs. structural down-beat (Kazuko Tanosaki), as research continues in an attempt to differentiate it from "the rest" in Western music.

Maki Ishii (1936-2003) studied composition and conducting in Tokyo before moving to Berlin where he continued his studies at the *Hochschule für Musik*. From 1969, when he was invited back to Berlin by the German Academic Exchange Service (DAAD) to take part in their "Berliner Künstlerprogramm," he was active in Germany as well as in Japan as a composer and conductor. Ishii's early music was influenced by serialism and the European avant-garde of the 1950s and 60s, but from the late 1960s his interest turned to Japanese traditional music. He wrote a number of works combining Western instruments and Japanese instruments such as the *shakuhachi*, *gagaku* orchestra, and various Japanese drums. Ishii's compositions have been performed all over the world, and he conducted many leading orchestras in Europe and Asia.[3]

Looking closely at Joji Yuasa's work for solo piano, *Cosmos Haptic II*, Kazuko Tanosaki (*Cosmos and Temporality within Joji Yuasa's Cosmos Haptic II: Transfiguration*) considers Yuasa's concepts of temporality (uncountable time, compressed time, polychronicity among layers of music, elastic time, shrinking time, and floating time), and their relationships to *Noh*, within this masterpiece.[4]

Notes

1. see "Toshiro Mayuzumi," Joslyn Layne (naxos.com) and Masakata Kanazawa, from the *New Grove Dictionary of Music and Musicians* online (grovemusic.com).
2. see bio of Hosokawa on page 132-3, and bio of KarenTanaka on page 227.
3. see http://ishii.de/maki/en/profile/
4. see Yuasa bio on page 111.

CHAPTER FOURTEEN

COMPOSING FOR THE 21-STRING KOTO

MARTY REGAN

The basic construction of the *koto* has hardly changed since it was introduced from China along with *gagaku* in the seventh and eighth centuries.[1] It is fundamentally a zither, an instrument that consists of a sound body laid on its side with strings stretched across the front.

The *koto* that most people are familiar with has thirteen strings. However, in 1921 the 17-string bass *koto* was invented by Michio Miyagi, and in 1969 the 21-string *koto* was invented by composer Minoru Miki and *koto* performer Keiko Nosaka. Some performers have also experimented with 25 and 30-string instruments, but they have not yet become standard. In Japanese, the 21-string *koto* refers to an instrument called the *ni-jû-gen* (□□□), which literally means "twenty strings"- an abbreviation for "twenty-string *koto*." Why is an instrument with twenty-one strings literally called a twenty-string koto? In 1971, an extra string was added to the bottom of the register of the 20-string *koto* in order to more effectively execute a rapid tremolo-like gesture, otherwise known as *sukui* or *sukuizume* (see Figure 14-7 below) on the lowest string in Minoru Miki's composition *Tatsuta no Kyoku* ('*The Venus in Autumn'*). In order to execute this technique, the performer rapidly plucks downwards with the thumb, strikes and stops briefly on the next string, and then plucks backwards with an upstroke. Before the addition of the extra string, in order to play a *sukuizume* pattern on the lowest string, without an adjacent string to support the downstroke one had to strike the body of the *koto* instead.[2] One string was therefore added to the bottom part of the range for the exclusive purpose of allowing the thumb to strike an adjacent surface (Miki 1996: 171). Despite the addition of the extra string, for some reason the name *ni-jû-gen* stuck. Since 2004, Mr. Miki has referred to this instrument as the *nii-goto* (新箏), whose Chinese characters literally mean "new *koto*." This term is slowly gaining common usage in Japan, especially among Mr. Miki's closest colleagues, although there are some people who still call it the 21-string *koto*, including myself when I am among native English speakers. As the number of pieces for 21-string *koto* continues to grow, the original function of the "zero string" has been forgotten, and composers can feel free to use this string as equally as any of the others.

Many of the techniques discussed below are common to all *koto*. However, the purpose of this essay is to promote the version of the *koto* that, in my opinion, has yet to be "discovered" outside of Japan. In addition, through my experience in composing for all three versions of the *koto*, I believe that the addition of the extra strings to create a 21-string *koto* imparts significant advantages in terms of range, flexibility of tunings, volume, and expressive potential for the contemporary composer. At the same time, since the 21-string *koto* was designed to incorporate traditional pentatonic tunings used with the 13-string *koto,* it sacrifices nothing in terms of aesthetics or timbre. Lastly, zithers from all over Asia now have their own version of the 21-string *koto*, and 21-string zithers are gradually becoming standard. As a result, repertoire can circulate freely between different cultures, leading to precious opportunities for collaborations and stimulating musical exchange.

The *koto* is played with the fingers or three ivory *tsume* (picks or plectrums) attached to the index, middle, and ring fingers of the right hand. *Koto* tunings are set in advance by placing ivory bridges – called *ji* in Japanese – underneath the strings. These bridges are adjusted to set each of the strings to one specific pitch. The basic range of the 21-string *koto* is illustrated in Figure 14-1. Theoretically, this range may be extended by a third in either direction, but reverberation is poor and the timbre is thin and metallic-sounding.

Figure 14-1: General range of the 21-string *koto*

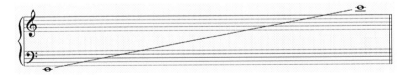

The basic tuning of the 21-string *koto* is indicated in Figure 14-2 below. This is not meant to give the impression that pieces for the 21-string *koto* should be based on a diatonic scale. Rather, as Minoru Miki writes (1998, 153):

".....One intent in creating the 21-string *koto* was to establish as much of a fixed relationship as possible between Western staff notation and the actual sounds produced on the instrument in order to make sight-reading easier. Placing a few strings in the extreme registers aside, the 21-string *koto* was designed in hopes that its middle range would use the basic tuning as much as possible, with free application of sharps and flats."[3]

Figure 14-2: General tuning of the 21-string *koto*

In my experience composing for the 21-string *koto*, I have found that most performers can practically sight-read most simple pieces that adhere to Mr. Miki's recommendation above. In other words, as long as you tune string one (notated 一 in the tuning in Figure 14-2 above) to the *alphabetical* pitch C (i.e. it could be C, C♭, C♭♭ or C, C#, C× etc.) and string two (notated 二 in the tuning in Figure 14-2 above) to the *alphabetical* pitch D, the performer will be able to orient themselves to the music more quickly without having to notate string numbers or transcribe the Western staff notation into tablature notation.

The harmonic limitations imposed by the fixed tuning of the 21-string *koto* present a unique problem for composers who wish to compose for this instrument in combination with Western instruments. Of course, tunings may be changed in the middle of a piece by moving the bridges. Most bridges can be adjusted and moved back to the original position within a few seconds and well-trained performers can do this so elegantly it is hardly noticeable. However, there are several things to keep in mind regarding tuning changes.

First, since the left hand is not available when a bridge is being adjusted, the performer is unable to manipulate sustained pitches or execute any left hand techniques that give the *koto* its particular character. Second, the strings take some time to stretch or loosen into the new tuning, so one always takes a risk that the instrument will be out of tune. Third, extensive bridge adjustments in the middle of the piece often result in the player losing concentration on his or her playing. Fourth, the bridges at the lower end of the range cannot be moved unless the performer gets up and walks over to the left hand side of the instrument. This is not to suggest that one should be hesitant to move the bridges in order to access a different tuning if the music demands it. Rather, I am simply trying to make the reader aware that there are other ways to enrich one's harmonic and melodic palette when composing for the *koto*, in particular the left hand, which is in many ways one of the secrets of learning how to compose idiomatically for this instrument.

Pitches outside of a fixed tuning can be obtained without having to resort to changing the bridges. This is easily achieved by pressing down on the string on the left side of the bridge before plucking with the right hand, a technique referred to as *oshide*. By adjusting the pressure of the left hand, the pitch can be raised by either a half-step or whole-step. Figure 14-3 illustrates the symbols used to indicate this technique.

Figure 14-3: Left hand pressing (*oshide*) techniques

Utilizing the basic principal of *oshide*, one of the most effective ways to impart a certain grace and elegance to a melodic line is to use a combination of four techniques called *oshi-biki, oshi-hanashi, ato-oshi,* and *tsuki-iro,* respectively. With these techniques, a composer can turn an ordinary passage into one of distinctive character, decorated with ornaments that are unique and idiomatic to the *koto*.

Figure 14-4: Notation for various *oshide*-based techniques

a) *Oshi-biki* – plucking with the right hand *before* pressing down on the string with the left hand, resulting in an upward glissando-like gesture.

b) (variation on *oshi-biki) oshi-hanashi* – pressing down on the string with the left hand *before* plucking with the right hand and then releasing the string to create a downward glissando-like gesture.

c) *Ato-oshi* – plucking with the right hand *before* pressing down on the string with the left hand, but instead of ascending up to higher pre-determined pitch, the left-hand presses down on the string more quickly and a lower-pitched string is immediately plucked. Sometimes this pattern can be repeated on the same string, but it is less common for the plucked string to be higher than the ornament.

d) *Tsuki-iro* – plucking with the right hand and immediately pressing the string with the left hand in a quick, jab-like motion.

e) *Hiki-iro* – lowering a pitch by pulling a string towards the right with the left hand from the left side of the bridges after being plucked. This technique is indicated by using a graphic line in combination with the character ヒ or ひきいろ - it is ineffective in the higher register and difficult to execute in the lower register. In the middle register, the pitch can theoretically be lowered about a half-step, but it is better not to consider this technique as a method for lowering a pitch. Rather, *hiki-iro* should be considered as a type of delicate ornamentation.

Just as importantly, left hand *oshide*-based techniques give the right hand an opportunity to rest, – if even for a moment – allowing for wide intervallic jumps that would otherwise be impossible if the right hand had to pluck every single note. Figure 14-5, from my *Concerto for Shakuhachi and 21-String Koto* (2006), demonstrates extensive use of *oshide*-based techniques. What is important to notice in this example is that all of the pitches *could* be played without any left hand pressing techniques with the particular tuning used in the passage. However, the passage is vastly changed (improved) by allowing the left hand to play an important role in the subtle details of the line. When composing for the *koto* therefore, it is crucial to go through the part and find places to add these characteristic ornaments. The most obvious places would include intervals of a half-step or whole-step in either direction. Like the *shakuhachi*, *koto* ornaments are best used in moderation, otherwise they tend to lose their effectiveness as the left hand becomes too busy.

Oshide-based techniques also allow the composer to access pitches that are outside of the tuning, and when used in combination with Western instruments, can create an aural illusion giving the impression that the *koto* is more chromatic than it really is.

For example, in Figure 14-6, from my *Concerto for Shakuhachi and 21-String Koto* (2006), the pitch collection drops a half-step from f-dorian to a hexatonic scale based on e-minor (i.e. the 6th scale degree is absent) in mm. 67-68. Since the only pitches in common between the tuning of the 21-string *koto* (E^b, F, G, A^b, B^b, C, D) and the new pitch collection at m. 68 (E, $F^{\#}$, G, A, B, D) are d and g, I deliberately avoid the other strings. Instead, the common tones are emphasized, while I use *oshi-biki* to access pitches that are outside the *koto* tuning but contained in the new pitch collection at m. 68 (such as A). This gives the aural impression that the 21-string *koto* is modulating along with the ensemble. The stretching of the harmonic capabilities of the two solo Japanese instruments is one of the most distinguishing characteristics of this work, and it represents a possible solution to problems that composers always face when composing for Japanese and Western instruments in combination.

Figure 14-5: m. 43-66

Figure 14-6: m. 67-71

In addition to the extensive use of left hand pressing techniques that provide ornaments, right hand techniques are indispensable to the character of the *koto* because they make possible a broad range of timbral expression. Figure 14-7 illustrates several of the most common right hand techniques and their corresponding notation.

Figure 14-7: Notation for various right hand timbral modification techniques

a) *Awasezume* – plucking two or more strings more or less at the same time with the thumb and middle finger. It can be executed in three distinct ways; at the exact same time (indicated by a bracket), as an upward arpeggio, or as a downward arpeggio.

b) *Sukui*, or *sukuizume* – plucking backwards with the backside of the *tsume* attached to the thumb. It is most commonly seen in repeated sixteenth-note gestures, where the thumb alternates between downstroke and *sukui* upstrokes, but since *sukui* has a lighter, delicate sound quality it is also used for timbre variation with single pitches. A stronger, more distinctive variation of *sukui* can be produced by scraping the strings in the direction of the bridges while plucking backwards. One should add an accent to give a more accurate visual representation of the resulting sound.

c) *Tremolo* – placing the *tsume* of the thumb and index finger close together and making a rapid cutting-like gesture over the top of the string. Similar to the notation for Western string instruments, it is indicated with an unmeasured tremolo symbol. It is effective to use tremolo in combination with *oshibiki* or *oshi-hanashi*.

d) *Chirashizume* – placing the index and middle finger together as if you were making the shape of a pair of scissors and quickly swiping two adjacent strings from right to left in one broad scooping motion. Since this gesture is more for timbral modification than melodic emphasis, it is easier to play and simply sounds more effective and convincing as a gesture, when swiping two strings (although one-string *chirashizume* is possible at softer dynamic levels).

e) *Uchizume* – striking the strings with the part of the plectrum that wraps around the performer's fingers. At soft dynamic levels pitch can be heard quite clearly. It is possible to tap up to three adjacent strings at a time, but tapping two adjacent strings is more common.

Figure 14-8, from my *Concerto for Shakuhachi and 21-String Koto* (2006), illustrates extensive use of right-hand timbral modification techniques a through f, while Figure 14-9 illustrates *uchizume*.

Figure 14-8: mm. 72-86

Figure 14-9: m. 447-449

Left hand pizzicato can be used to differentiate timbres in a contrapuntal line and to play over a wide range, since it allows the right hand to move while the left hand is plucking. It is indicated by the symbol "+." It is also useful in producing up to six-note chords and playing arpeggios in combination with the right hand. Figure 14-10 is an excerpt from my composition *Seven Values of the Warrior Code* (2006) that illustrates several different uses of left-hand pizzicato.

Subtle timbral variations can be produced by varying the playing position: near the *ryûkaku* (N.R), off the *ryûkaku* (Off. R.), and ordinary position (pos. ord). The *ryûkaku* is the farthest right edge of the instrument, and playing off the *ryûkaku* produces a hard and brittle timbre analogous to *sul ponticello*. Playing off the *ryûkaku*, or closer to the bridges, results a soft, delicate, and somewhat muted timbre analogous to *sul tasto*.

Figure 14-10: m. 34-40

One of the problems that plague composers who attempt to combine Western instruments with Japanese instruments like the 21-string *koto* is balance. Emphasizing transparent textures is one effective solution. However, in my work I also seek to "pair up" the 21-string *koto* with instruments in the orchestra, searching for timbres that can take the form of imitative gestures. For example, in my *Concerto for Shakuhachi and 21-String Koto* (2006) mm. 55-57 (see Figure 14-11), the 21-string *koto* plays a virtuosic passage that requires extensive use of left hand pressing techniques. In imitation of the specific techniques *oshi-biki* and *oshi-hanashi*, from mm. 55-66, the strings play an interlocked ascending pyramid. As each family passes the ascending line up through the string section, they are requested to either slide up or down the string at the end of their pattern. The effect is subtle but effective for establishing a certain degree of interplay with the 21-string *koto*.

Highlighting potential similarities and correspondences between two musical cultures by virtue of imitative techniques results in a work where it is difficult to locate the divisions between what we stereotypically associate with the "East" and "West," and where imagined boundaries are blurred and transcended.

Figure 14-11: m. 55-57

In the same piece, from m. 290 through m. 341 there is extensive interplay between the *koto* and harp. This entire section is orchestrated quite delicately with softly sustained strings and percussion, allowing the subtle ornaments of the 21-string *koto* and the gentle timbre of the harp to come to the foreground (see Figure 14-12).

Figure 14-12: m. 338-340

Non-western musical instruments like the 21-string *koto* offer an alternative to the sounds of Western instruments, and with the coordinated effort of ethnomusicologists and composers, a transnational flow of non-Western musical cultures to the West has already begun to complement the flow of Western musical culture to the East. To deepen and enrich our relationship with non-Western musical cultures takes time and patience, but it is an effort that carries great aesthetic rewards. I believe that composers should remain aware of the idiomatic capabilities and limitations of non-Western instruments as well as the subtle differences in aesthetics between traditional musical cultures that are often confused, or mistakenly fused together (i.e. Japan, Korea, and China) as if they were one geo-musical entity. I hope that this essay encourages composers to promote the 21-string *koto* as a vital medium for art-music in the twenty-first century and contributes to the emerging discourse of surrounding cross-cultural approaches to composition.

Notes

1. The terms *gakusô*, *chikusô*, and *zokusô* refer to historical instrument types. The *gakusô* refers to the *koto* used in *gagaku*. The *chikusô* refers to the *koto* used in *Tsukushigoto* (songs derived from vocal court music) founded by the priest Kenjun in the sixteenth-century and named after Tsukushi, a province in northern Kyûshû where he lived. The *zokusô* refers to the modern day *koto*. Kengyô Yatsuhashi (1614-1685) invented the *hirajôshi* tuning based on the *in* scale and adapted it into *Tsukushigoto* compositions. The *koto* that Yatsuhashi used became known as the *zokusô* because of its use in *zokugaku* ('common music'). These terms, therefore, developed as a result of the instrument being used in new genres, and not because of any major structural differences between them. See Johnson 1996-7.
2. This "extra string" at the bottom of the range is now referred to as the "zero string." See Figure 14-3.
3. translation by the author.

References

Johnson, Henry M. 1996-7. A "Koto" by Any Other Name: Exploring Japanese Systems of Musical Instrument Classification. *Asian Music* Vol. 28:1. 43-59.

Miki, Minoru. *Nihongakkihô* (Composing for Japanese Instruments). 3rd ed. Tokyo: Ongaku no Tomo-sha, 1998.

Regan, Martin P. 2006. *Concerto for Shakuhachi and 21-String Koto*: A Composition, Analysis, and Discussion of Issues Encountered in Cross-Cultural Approaches to Composition. Ph.D. diss., University of Hawai'i, Manoa.

CHAPTER FIFTEEN

ADAPTATION OF PERFORMANCE STYLE FROM EARLY MODERN JAPAN TO THE CONTEMPORARY CELLO

HUGH LIVINGSTON

Toshiro Mayuzumi's solo for cello *Bunraku* (1964), takes its name and sound world from the Japanese puppet theater. A product of the growing cities of the seventeenth century, the dramas of *bunraku* were portraits of the issues of the time – honest looks at the shaping forces of contemporary culture. Historian Mary Elizabeth Berry (2007) describes these as sex, violence and money. Their dramatic arcs almost always end in tragedy, with lovers committing suicide together. The plays deal with "people unable to make the necessary compromises of society."[1]

Mayuzumi composed *Bunraku* for performance at the opening of a new museum, and consequently in its evocation of a formalized tradition may have intended a statement about preserving older works. The composition is painted heavily with the tone colors of the *bunraku* theater, superimposed on Western harmonies and pyrotechnics.[2] Mayuzumi's composition is not merely a transcription, but a synthesis of the sonic elements of the *shamisen* and the narrator's voice designed to give longer life to musical ideas facing extinction. It is clearly not depicting a particular play from the traditional canon, nor, at nine minutes long, truly representing the hour-long performances of puppet plays. Nevertheless, it follows a trajectory from introductory bells to fiery conclusion that constructs a valuable vignette, and one that I find seminal in a composer's dynamic integration of East and West.

In the years since this composition, many Asian composers have synthesized distant traditions with the technical potential of the new cello as a vessel for representing diverse sound worlds. Obvious materials such as pentatonic scales and a variety of pizzicato are the beginning, but one finds the tradition expressed more intimately through the Japanese openness to sound that includes noise. Whereas the Western flute is a metal, idealized pure sonority, the *shakuhachi* evokes the wind in the very bamboo groves that gave the instrument its body. The approach to elements of nature and expressive variation in tone production are equally part of Japanese string sound. There is a strong practical component to the adaptation of traditional musical ideas to the cello and Western flute— both frequently linked to the human voice—versatile, loud instruments that are the parallel funnels of synthesis efforts from numerous composers. The large dynamic range, pitch range and versatile playing techniques of the cello placed it, in the latter third of the twentieth century, at an important nexus in the evolution of composition and instrumental style.[3]

The Asian composer speaks to the West through screens of temporal and geographical displacement. The filter of instrumental performance practice, tempered by limitations of musical notation, serves to further modulate the result. The performer who seeks to understand this music clearly has a broad freedom of interpretation.[4] Mayuzumi's composition moves well beyond exotica to a rich evocation of the spirit of another time and place. He employs sounds of the *shamisen* buzzing and sliding, giant handfuls of ninth chords, dramatic cadenzas covering the whole range of the instrument, gentle passages where the expressive art of *ma* can define foreground and background to heighten the expression, and quadruple stops and pizzicato strums, each serving as a thread from either the East or West.

While Mayuzumi's score is practical and readable for the Western cellist in terms of its notation, there is one element to address from the start. This is probably the most overlooked element in proper notation of techniques by the Asian synthesis composer: the glissando. It is too often assumed that the modern interpreter will understand what to do, or that any interpretation will be acceptable. In fact, there are quite a few different ways to approach the melodic connecting or ornamentation of notes, and traditional notation is sadly lacking. I encourage composers to strictly employ a graphic notation that is exactly proportionate to the time divisions of the space between notes and exactly proportionate to the distance the hand has to travel. In the simplest terms, the relevant questions are: how long is the starting note sustained before the slide starts? What is the curve (constant or accelerating) of the upward motion? And, is the arrival note articulated precisely at its notated point? A simple curve proportional in two dimensions provides a necessary supplement to this missing element in Western notation. This is true whether it is an ornamental filigree to the end of a note, or a connecting melodic figure in a larger line.

Figure 15-1

Looking deeper into the score, it is instructive to consider the sound environment of the *shamisen* in all aspects, even if some elements may be impractical to reproduce on the cello. The major characteristics include: *sawari* (the typical buzzing sound), percussive sounds, nearly silent "shadow playing," use of the large plectrum, glissandi, dryness of the sound, rhythmic patterns divided into rigorously march-like or wild acceleration, with no middle ground. Lesser elements to be cognizant of include player vocalizations to support the narrator at key moments.[5]

Bowed technique is obviously absent from *shamisen* practice, yet Mayuzumi alternates bowed and plucked passages, evoking the shaking, intensely characterized vocalizations of the narrator. I advocate a playing style opposed to the *bel canto* cello tradition in order to convey the often guttural stylizations of the narrator's voicings (Adachi 1985).[6] This would include rocking the left hand contact point (even in the midst of the expressive molto vibrato indication) so that the varying pressure produces noise colorations surrounding the pitches rather than a pure core of lush string sound. I extend this technique further with varied bow pressure and speed, sometimes almost grinding the string, and often choking up on the C-string towards the fingerboard to hit the really fat vibrational points of the string. By moving away from the bridge, the bow can track directly on nodes, and its normally smooth idealized stick-slip motion runs into interference with the very tones it is activating, producing a sound very much like the throat-sticking oscillations of the human voice. Any accents in the bowed line are best executed with vibrato width or speed intensification and some increase in bow speed as *sul tasto* playing limits conventional pressure accents.

Plucked string technique in Western cello practice differs considerably from the techniques (and resultant sounds) of the large ivory plectrum in *shamisen* practice. This is the principal starting point for my research into adaptation of Asian music that eventually resulted in the codification of over 100 cello pizzicato techniques. The sounds or techniques to be emulated in *Bunraku* are *sawari*, left-hand pizzicato and the sharp striking nature of the *bachi* (plectrum), including the percussive element added as it follows through to strike the taut catskin head of the instrument.

I propose a noisy pizzicato effect which takes some effort to acquire but can be exceedingly versatile when mastered. This effect is like the *sawari* buzzing of the *shamisen*, where the buzz develops even after the note is struck. [Figure 15-2] In the example (all pizzicato) from m.18-20 (Mayuzumi 1965), the cellist should begin the note with the finger flat across the string, practically stopping it with the first knuckle.[7] The finger is held solidly through the glissando, and when the A—definitely the focal point—has sounded, the hand is rocked bit-by-bit to produce a buzzing against the fingerboard. On the lowest strings, it is also possible to use only the fingertip (but very much the end, not the pad which normally stops the string) to produce this same effect. Again, it should start very firmly, to prevent dissipation of the energy of the string, and after the glissando is concluded, the pressure can be released just slightly to allow the string to come off the fingerboard and vibrate against it. The symbols shown in Figure 15-2 are well-accepted notation, first for snap pizzicato and second for open string on the upper D.

Figure 15-2

mm18-20

The low pair of cello strings is remarkably susceptible to buzzing (the upper strings less so), which is a product of the angle of the fingerboard, the height of the bridge and the normal density of the individual strings. In general, an upward glissando is easier to maintain with this partial pressure than a downward glissando, and slow one easier than fast. On a downward glissando, the lengthening string absorbs more energy. On an upward slide, the ever-shortening string takes less energy to continue vibrating, increasing the resonance time, just as when an ice skater pulls in her arms she suddenly rotates faster.

The snap pizzicato, also known as the Bartok pizzicato from its frequent deployment in his string quartets, is a percussive slap which Mayuzumi takes advantage of to suggest the sound of the *shamisen*. One problem is its tendency to die away quickly, and to concentrate all its noise at the beginning of the impulse. The string has to be pulled straight up away from the fingerboard, and it rebounds to its opposite displacement. The more this displacement exceeds the available space under the string,

the louder the snap sound, and the more rapid the decay, as much of the
string's energy is used up. As a result, a ringing sound, glissando
ornamentation, or vibrato afterwards can not be well executed.

In measures 74-76 [Figure 15-3], the best results for ringing can be
produced with what I call a 'vertical' pizzicato. This sound, useful for the
C-string and a long-ringing note, is one which is quite nearly vertical, but
is pulled down to the fingerboard (grabbing the string right at the end of
the fingerboard) and released up instead of the reverse for a snap pizz.
Since the string's maximum displacement before release is defined by the
location of the fingerboard, and the string loses vibrational energy as it
returns, it is safe from ever 'snapping.' Meanwhile, one can still add noise
to the note through variable pressure with the left hand, and there is plenty
of room for glissando up and down, as well as a good dynamic range from
the start. This is the longest-ringing pizzicato I have learned to produce,
and will be useful in any contemporary performance. If this is used in
m.76 [Figure 15-3], along with a gently feathered bowstroke on the
harmonic (played on the G-string, so the glissando moves roughly a minor
seventh before the thumb reaches its destination) the glissando will give
the illusion of continuing indefinitely. An additional performance tip is to
set the bow on the G-string early, even while the glissando is still
approaching the point where it will stop. Draw the bow cleanly and gently,
letting it ring free and mix with the decaying pizzicato sound, never letting
up on the contact with the pizzicato note.

Figure 15-3

mm73-76

The *shamisen* player uses the left-hand fingernail (Adachi 1985, 61), as
opposed to the fleshy pads of his fingers, to stop the upper string and
perform many glissandi (and never lets this finger touch water in the
course of daily life). The playing style is very much characterized by
ornamental glissandi in this manner, either shortly before, or drawn out
after, the note. The technique changes the overtone properties, tending to
evoke a thin sound with stronger fundamental and brassier overtones, but
also enables quicker slides and longer resonance from a single stroke. This
is possible to execute on the cello, although it takes some strength and an

adjustment of the hand position to execute. In general, it should be requested only when there is time to prepare the hand angle. The hand is turned out and the other fingers are no longer in line with the string, and consequently cannot be used, so the gesture is all played by sliding with the index finger from note to note. The left hand must also learn to account for the extreme precision of pitch required with such a narrow contact point, whereas the fleshy normal stopping is more forgiving. In general the nail produces predominant fundamentals with less resonant overtones compared to the flesh, a brassier sound. It is recommended for the upper (thinnest) cello string only.

Measures 46-49 [Figure 15-4] are an excellent place to use the nail instead of the flesh of the left hand to stop the strings. This sound will be more intense, especially in the fundamental. This technique can be difficult to utilize because the hand needs time to approach the rotated position (taking the other fingers out of line with the string), but with resonant lifted bow-strokes or pizzicati as appropriate on the low fifths, the space will not be noticeable.

Figure 15-4

The gestures at the end of measures 46 and 48 should be suddenly different, and especially brittle. Use the thumb to stop the notes and the third nail of the left hand to strike them as loudly as possible. I add the additional color variation of stopping the string with the left-hand thumb nail, either by rolling the thumb back to catch the rounded portion of the top of the nail, or by turning the whole hand in so that the end of the nail stops the string. Either way, a considerably increased hand pressure will be necessary to fully stop the string, and the glissando must likewise have continuously firm contact. The asterisk in measure 49 is a footnote indicating that a single finger be used for the grace note gesture, which of course is the ideal evocation of *shamisen* technique.

Measure 52 is where I strive to produce the most accurate simulation of the *shamisen bachi*, accomplished by letting the right hand thumbnail grow quite long so I can forcefully strike the strings [Figure 15-5]. It is trimmed on the inside edge to avoid damaging the wood of the bow where I grip it, and is not so long that I cannot play a conventional Western fleshy strummed sound, but by tailoring it precisely like a guitar pick I can instantly have another sound at my disposal. This solution has been reached after trying all the possibilities of holding a plectrum simultaneously with the bow or wearing a *koto* or *pipa* pick on one finger, none of which proved practical.

Figure 15-5

The secret to executing the last pizzicato of page 5 [Figure 15-6] with a snap pizz, and also *piano* as indicated, is to bring the left hand down on the string at the same moment as the upward pizzicato. This slaps the string against the fingerboard: when the stroke begins, there is only partial pressure from the left hand, so a noise is heard, and then the finger fully comes down, sounding the pitch. This is a very effective technique, producing quite nearly the same effect, sounding much like sawari, and very delicate. Although it would seem counterintuitive to the hard edge required on a note's articulation, the soft snap pizzicato is useful throughout contemporary cello literature.

Figure 15-6

In the frenzied section of page 6 [Figure 15-7], the main focus should be on voicing the chords so there is a convincing suggestion of an upper melodic instrument supported by a drone or percussive instrument. In measure 124, the strumming pizzicato is effective, but I use flesh of the finger for the D-string and nail for the A-string. From measure 128 there are several solutions, but I would always strum the three-note chords up (thumb) and the melody notes down (second finger). The repeated D-string can be executed with the thumb (thus using two fingers for the chords) or as a consequent part of the downward stroke with the second finger, which I prefer. The open D has plenty of presence, and the melody is the focus. The melodic notes simultaneous with the lower three open strings can also be played as a consequence of the upward strum, or in unison with the first or second finger. I prefer the latter solution as it maintains the prominence of the upper voice, which is then always executed with the second finger. I maintain these rules through measure 130 (simple alternation of up and down strokes, a moment of calm) and measure 131 (many consecutive down strokes with the first finger).

Figure 15-7

The *shamisen* player frequently utilizes pizzicato with the left-hand, and this is also an everyday technique for the contemporary cellist. The short string length provides a steely, twangy sound. Mayuzumi uses this to both free the right hand for other activity, and as a contrasting tone color to other pizzicato materials. It can be executed with both the flesh of the third and fourth fingers, and their respective nails, if one allows them to grow. The notation used is the conventional + over the note, with the initial abbreviations *m.s.* and *m.d.* where necessary (*mano sinistra*, left hand; *mano destra*, right hand).

The lighter touch required in the left hand for *shamisen* playing (lower bridge, lighter strings, silk or modern synthetic string in contrast to the cello's higher friction steel, less restrictive core sound requirement, use of nail instead of flesh to stop the string) allows for a considerably more expressive use of glissando than is possible on the cello. But wherever possible, the player should attempt to adjust the striking technique of the right hand and the stopping technique of the left hand to achieve a clearly ringing tone. Western practice overlooks what happens as the note tails off, but the Japanese aesthetic requires thought to these micro variations shading the sound as one leads nearly imperceptibly to the next.

Bunraku gives the interpreter an excellent opportunity for exploration of "the instrument within," to go beyond the surface of the notation to find maximal colors and shadings for the composer's expressive purposes, whether modifying one's native technique to match a different instrument or finding alternate ways to replicate the original sound. In this way, rich new performance practices are built.

Notes

1. Mary Elizabeth Berry. History, Culture & Aesthetics of Bunraku. Lecture at Wheeler Hall, UC Berkeley. Conference presented by UC Berkeley Institute for East Asian Studies and Center for Japanese Studies, and the Japanese American Cultural & Community Center, in conjunction with US tour of The National Puppet Theatre of Japan. October 11, 2007.
2. To make clear what would otherwise be a continual confusion, I will refer to the cello composition as Bunraku and the traditions of the puppet theater as *bunraku*. Also, Mayuzumi adopted the first name-last name conventions of the West.
3. See Livingston 1997, available through the library of the University of California, San Diego. Detailed discussion of work with Asian composers and bar-by-bar performance guides for several compositions.
4. I did not have the chance to work directly with Toshiro Mayuzumi, who died the weekend we were supposed to meet at *Music of Japan Today: Tradition and Innovation III* (1997), so I offer only my own ideas for this composition.

5. Based on discussions with shamisen players John Welsh and Toyozawa Tomisuke.
6. This wonderful insiders' book has a discussion of the narrator's chanting style, p. 60.
7. As the Peters score is not numbered, I count the partial first measure as 1 in all my references.

References

Adachi, Barbara. 1985. *Backstage at Bunraku*. New York: Tokyo: Weatherhill.
Livingston, Hugh. 1997. The Modern Performer and the Asian Composer. Unpublished manuscript as part of DMA Qualifying Examinations, bound and available at the University of California, San Diego Library.
Mayuzumi, Toshiro. 1965. *Bunraku*. New York: C.F. Peters.

CHAPTER SIXTEEN

MA (SENSE OF TIME) AS COMPOSITIONAL TOOL

AIRI YOSHIOKA

The Japanese concept of *ma* can be found in any form of art, be it music, dance, theater, painting, architecture or in any entity that involves two parts that create a visual or temporal space. Many Japanese composers incorporate this sensibility into their works and have actively embraced it as a critical tool for their musical expression. This article investigates the use of *ma* in works of Maki Ishii, Toshio Hosokawa and Karen Tanaka - works that all involve a popular Western instrument, the violin.

Rarely does one encounter a work that is not concerned about arriving somewhere, exposing us to the art of being reflective, mindful and yet passionately expressive at the same time. In *Vertical Time Study III*, Toshio Hosokawa (b. 1955) boldly challenges the listeners to awaken another dimension of musical time by the prevalent use of unison, and the neighboring pitches, unschematic phrase structure, and silence.

Silence placed between sounds may be the most obvious way to represent a space, or *ma*. However, what is expected to occur during the silence is what gives Hosokawa's sense of time a more complex flavor. In Figure 16-1, he intermittently places empty measures marked "without any action." The enforced silences in which the performers are requested to be physically immobile are a tall order since the played measures are often wrought with vigor and splendor, resulting in large musical as well as physical gestures. Within about a minute of music, a third of the score calls for the performers to remain still.

Though no sound comes through, a lot happens in these non-active measures. The performer regains physical composure after the declamatory measures, which requires a readjustment of physical alignment. The added time allows the visual and aural gestures to resonate fully and follow through their full curve. The request of "no action" placed before the commencement of the passage in m. 72 suggests that in addition to its role as a follow-up, the space functions as a preparatory agent. As in the case of a dancer gathering momentum for a pirouette, *ma* recognizes the mechanism of tapping into the resources that lie deeply within and letting them blossom in strength and shape.

This work exemplifies the use of silence as *ma*, silence that not only connects the sounding entities but lets the sound settle down between each note. Furthermore, it is during this silence that the ideas gestate and gain prominence. The effective use of this tenuous moment by the performer leads to a successful rendering of the piece. For Hosokawa the *ma*, embodied in this moment of no movement and sound, is where the power of expressivity lies.

Figure 16-1

Hosokawa VERTICAL TIME STUDY III
© 1994 Schott Music Co. Ltd, Tokyo
Used by permission of European American Music Distributors LLC,
sole U.S. and Canadian agent for Schott Music.

One of the definitions of *ma*, given by Japanese dictionaries, translates as "free time." Such freedom of pacing may seem incongruous with the rigidity of pre-recorded sounds, but not for composer Karen Tanaka (b.1961), who specializes in electro-acoustic music. For her, *ma* is: "Sense of space. The best timing and the best measuring that a sound comes in."[1] She is able to let the performer make a choice on what is the best timing for a particular note when there exists an unbending structure.

Indeed for Tanaka, the pre-recorded sounds provide the necessary structure for the piece, encouraging the performer to be even more creative in aleatoric and cadential passages. She sets up the score so that a section that is meticulously timed is followed by a large section in which the performer is left to his/her own device to improvise with given material.

Shifting back and forth between one's inner pulse and an unalterable framework is essential to grasping and internalizing a complex unveiling of time. Tanaka challenges the performer to experience freedom within a structure and to find the "best timing and measuring." Here, the performer can perceive *ma* as a tool that opens up interpretive choices.

Figure 16-2

WAVE MECHANICS II
Music by Karen Tanaka
Copyright © Chester Music Limited.
International Copyright Secured. All Rights Reserved.
Reprinted by Permission.

In *A Time of Afterglow* for violin and *koto*, composer Maki Ishii (1936-2003) uses non-metric writing and allows the players to exist in two temporal spaces. The idea of giving a unique time frame to each section or each part highlights Ishii's desire for the listener to experience a non-traditional conception of time. In traditional Western music, the progression of time is most often linear, measured by a build-up, arrival and resolution of a climax and each voice is engaged in a specific role that is a part of the general movement of the music. In this example, however, Ishii introduces an undirected temporal space in which violin and *koto* do not share the unified directional path and ignore each other's existence.

In Figure 16-3, the two instruments move in a parallel space, without a regard for each other's developing lines. The *koto*'s growing intensity in the previous section spills into the next as it catalyzes a sequence of chordal and arpeggiated eruptions. Defiantly and assertively, the *koto* commences its monologue of disjunct and angular melodramas. The content of the line displays various emotional qualities such as confusion, hysteria, resolution and restlessness, all achieved by the carefully spaced and placed notes.

On the other hand, the buzzing and mesmerizing tremolo of the violin is achieved by keeping and playing fleeting sequences of closely packed intervals on the adjacent string. The harmonic clash is created not only by the inherent dissonance in the melodic line but also by its juxtapositions against the drones of the open strings. The violin remains textural and ambient throughout this section except when it steps into the foreground with the arpeggiated exclamations.

The contrasting materials of the two instruments do not intersect. Both are equal in importance and neither part dominates or accompanies. Ishii's observation takes this a step further: "As two varied musical times unfold simultaneously, a certain layering is produced, and a quality of space is felt in the distances between one layer and another."[2] By calling attention to this simultaneous existence of lines, Ishii points to an existence of *ma*, a by-product of these two independent lines.

Figure 16-3

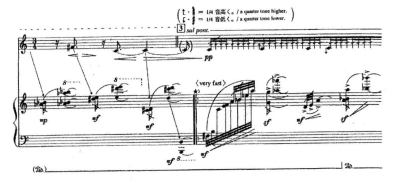

Japanese dictionaries define *ma* as "between, space, room, free time, passing, distanced", as preposition, noun, verb and adjective. These dictionary definitions leave room for the word to be interpreted somewhat freely and as now seen, the above composers incorporate this sensibility according to their creative forces. For these composers, *ma* is how they perceive time and space and how they illustrate this perception in the music.

Notes

1. Karen Tanaka, interview conducted by the author over e-mail, November, 2001.
2. Maki Ishii, lecture (San Francisco, CA.), Feb. 18, 1989. Translator unknown.

CHAPTER SEVENTEEN

CONCEPTS OF COSMOS AND TEMPORALITY WITHIN JOJI YUASA'S *COSMOS HAPTIC II* FOR PIANO

KAZUKO TANOSAKI

Cosmos Haptic II (1986) is the second of five works by Joji Yuasa under this title and aesthetic premise, spanning almost fifty years (1957-2003).[1] The formulation and development of Yuasa's ideas concerning the cosmos, human beings, and art, as well as his reflections on temporality (many of which are drawn from Japanese *Noh* theater), have their roots during his collaboration with other musicians/artists as a member of the *Jikken Kobo* from 1951-7 (Galliano 2003, 150-4).[2] One of the concerns of this group was to find new artistic directions, separate from elements of Japanese culture that had been exploited by radical nationalism during the war, and Western methods that were not compatible with the aesthetics of Japanese art and culture (Galliano, 154). Composers in this group (including Yuasa) sought to design music that had not been heard before, by creating a new musical narrative that did not follow the expressive pattern of conventional music.

For Yuasa (1992), this meant going back "archaeologically to the real genesis of music – that is, genesis of culture, genesis of human beings….and to think at that point what music is, what role music plays for human beings." In his program note for *Cosmos Haptic V* (Yuasa 2007), he recounts "Since my twenties, I have coined the image of the birth of music with the genesis of humankind and civilization….music unbound by the past but with the understanding of musical evolution and history." During the process of developing his views, Yuasa adopted what was to become one of his fundamental ideologies from Daisetz Suzuki. Yuasa's resulting artistic concept did not place human beings at the center of things (Galliano 154) – "their existence reflects a far greater mirror and resonator, the cosmos that Suzuki defines as the Cosmic Unconsciousness." The term "haptic" (in cosmos haptic) is taken from the book *Icon and Idea* by Sir Herbert Read – another important influence on Yuasa beginning in the 1950s. Read states that (Yuasa 2007):

> "in the Neolithic era, the concept of symmetry had emerged and would later become the measurement of beauty in Europe. However, in Roscoe and the cave painting of Altamira, the arts were not ruled by such aesthetics and people perceived the cosmos with an internal antenna or in 'haptic.'"

In other words, haptic describes art forms whose structures are results of internal sensations rather than external observations. In his works entitled cosmos haptic, Yuasa attempts to recreate the experience by which humans discover themselves in the cosmos, not by observing it from outside (Kushida 1998) but by being in it and becoming part of it (this idea is also a tenet of Zen). In *Cosmos Haptic II*, he creates a sense of surrounding space, a kind of sonic cosmos, that emanates from his image of this religious world. In his program notes for *Cosmos Haptic* (1957) Yuasa writes "This piece inhabits the space where human beings and the cosmos intersect. It is an attempt to express a primordial, vitalistic religious belief," and in other notes (2007), describes *Cosmos Haptic V* as "the expression of origin and genesis which could be exemplified by such occurrences as the birth of religion."

In his look into the genesis of music, Yuasa also calls attention to the fact that music has no fixed meaning – it changes with humans and societies – and the activity of composing (Yuasa 1989a, 177) not only "challenges the very nature of music," but asks us to "redefine ourselves as human beings." He has identified two aspects of human universality that clarify the essential nature of human beings, and significance of composing music: 1) a universal sensory capability to be found throughout humanity, transcending racial and cultural differences; and, 2) a local domain tightly linked to one's own identity (Yuasa 1993b) – for Yuasa, it is the cultural zone of Japan, which adheres to tradition as a structure that frames thought. Embracing (from Suzuki) the Zen concept of non-duality of opposing ideas, Yuasa (1993b, 217) states "the individuality and universality in my work are positioned as opposed polarities across a circle." He elaborates in more specific detail (1989b, 177) how this belief shapes his artistic process:

"Not long after I chose to become a composer, I came to realize that, as a Japanese, rather than unconsciously receiving my own tradition, I wished to consciously inherit and extend it, while at the same time exploring the universal language of all human beings. However, for me, the inheritance of my tradition implied a way of thought and perception rather than simply the adoption of superficial phenomena such as the pentatonic scale, or the simple usage of traditional instruments such as the *shakuhachi*, *biwa*, and *koto*. In other words, for me, remaining within a tradition meant retaining a system of thinking."

Temporality, *Noh*, and *Cosmos Haptic II*

Yuasa's knowledge of the music and principles of *Noh* (beginning, as a child, with his study of *utai* singing, and participation in *Noh* performances with his father) have had a profound effect on his music (1989b, 186) – "it does not even seem excessive to say that all the issues arising in my musical creation exist in the world of *Noh*." The influence includes not only sounds and methods, but aesthetic values, as well.

Among the important temporal concepts of *Noh* are the use of non-linear time, and of time and space conceived as a single entity (*ma*). With regard to the concept of space (Yuasa 1989b), in *Noh*, space is not considered "vacant," but a "substance containing emptiness." According to Yuasa,

"Unlike the rest in Western music, a pause in *Noh bayashi* (music) is a spacing with potential of its own. The pause is not there in order that the listener grasp sounds as realities, but rather the two existences – sounds and the potential in the spacing – form a harmony at their point of contact; both have equal importance."

This perception is especially relevant in the fifth section of *Cosmos Haptic II*, discussed later in this essay.

Yuasa was also influenced by registral/pitch space in Anton Webern's music. In *Cosmos Haptic II*, pitch relationships make up vertical space, while durations become horizontal space. Yuasa (1993a, 180) also affirms that "the light and shade of timbre, density, and illusory localization can also be spatially perceived." *Cosmos Haptic II* contains many different examples of transforming densities (textures) and timbres that can be perceived spatially - some of these, from the first section, are discussed later in this essay.[3] Yuasa's program note for this piece alludes to the importance of these spatial characteristics in the music.

"I intended throughout to write a music that can come to life only on the piano, developing to the utmost the characteristics of this instrument, especially the sonority from its massive, reverberant body. In this work, the transformation of reverberation, blended by the use of pedals, rather than the arrangement of notes themselves, should be the continuous focus of attention—along with the passage of time."[4]

Continuity and discontinuity of time can also be understood with reference to *Noh*. The embodiment of time is circular or non-directional, rather than linear or directional (Galliano, 154; Kushida, 55), where "time and space is an irrational flow in which the intervention of music functions as a cut." One may experience a number of non-linear temporalities in *Noh* – vanishing time, reversed time, split time, condensed time, and others (Komparu 1983). Yuasa's music is through-composed. There is a circular quality to how elements return – they are not developed, and rarely repeated exactly, except to forecast later modifications such as contraction or expansion (Galliano 155, 159). Structure is conceived from moment to moment. As a result, the future comes unexpectedly (Yuasa 1989b, 190) – "true human vitality is created within an intense field of strain." The first and second sections of *Cosmos Haptic II* illustrate this concept very clearly.

Yuasa also models the temporal relationship of the *Noh* flute melody to the chant, in his music. The *Noh* flute has its own temporality within the ensemble, based on the uncountable continuity of breathing (Yuasa 1989a) – only the beginning and ending moment of a phrase is fixed (this technique is called *mihakarai*).[5] The effect is (Yuasa 193b, 219) "a kind of non-committal forward movement, unlike Western music which always keeps a tight vertical correspondence between two lines." A good example of this type of temporality is manifested in *Cosmos Haptic II* by the polychronic texture of the third section.

Just as *Noh* actors stand apart from their personal emotions in their own performance, it is necessary for the performer of *Cosmos Haptic II* to understand its abstract, objective, and meditative qualities. According to Yuasa (1989b, 190), in *Noh* "'Human' is, for the first time, understood in its original sense not only through human relationships but rather by employing the cosmic, the nonhuman situation....*Noh* can be comprehended within a religious world that totally transcends human individuality." With regard to his music, it is clear that Yuasa seeks to express the sensations that he receives rather than his own personal feelings.

Cosmos Haptic II: temporality and performance practice

This work is in five sections, which present different contractions and expansions of time and space. These include uncountable time, compressed time, polychronic time (strata-different tempi), elastic time, shrinking time, and floating time. All of the markings, sounds, and notes have been chosen very carefully by the composer, so the performer must be diligent to realize them.

Section	*Measures*
I	1-65
II	66-75
III	76-102
IV	103-115
V	116-144

The opening section, which contains slow moving and forceful resonances, can be divided into two parts (m.1-26; m.27-65). The second part contains a wider tessitura with longer resonances, and is generally quieter with more contrasts of volume/sound projection. It also forecasts the major/minor second sonority (m.38) that is an important element in Section II (and also used in the opening of the first *Cosmos Haptic* - 1957). The second part also uses four staves, compared to three in part 1. For the pianist, this indicates the necessity in both parts to differentiate sound/resonance from three (or four) different sources/spaces. Even though bar-lines indicate "measures" that most often contain four beats, there is no meter shown – because of the long durations and sudden entrances, there is a sense of uncountable time for the listener (the future arrives suddenly, without forecast). However, placement of entrances with relation to bar-lines *does* help the pianist imagine the type of sounds to create. For example, the first entrance occurs just before measure 2 (Figure 17-1) – usually a very weak rhythmic position – but here elevated to a fortissimo "interruption." The first part of the measure also contains a rest of fairly long duration. This is a good example of *ma* – not simple silence, but a substance containing emptiness of great tension.

With regard to pitch, Yuasa employs a custom dodecaphony. At the beginning of the work, he assigns a specific register for each pitch, and they appear as a part of block chords [m. 1 = C#/G/C/B; m.2 = Eb/D/F; m.4 = E/Bb; and m.7 = A/G#/F#]. The first chord of m.7 (A/G#/F#) serves as an elision (another circular reference) to a quick restatement of the twelve tones, now in a different chord order (m.7 – downbeat of m.8). The quick rhythmic bursts of attacks parallel abrupt movements in *Noh* dance.[6]

Figure 17-1

m.1-9
Yuasa COSMOS HAPTIC II
© 1986 Schott Music Co. Ltd., Tokyo

In Part 2 of Section I, the registral space changes, expanding another octave (the bottom stave in Figure 17-2 is in bass clef). This, in addition to longer resonances (as a result of less frequent changes of pedal) and more active composite texture within the triplets (m.27 and m.29), creates a different spatial perspective.

Figure 17-2

m.27-30
Yuasa COSMOS HAPTIC II

Section II contains two alternating motivic features (Figure 17-3) – a sustained cluster (2 notes the first time at m.66, increasing to 4 notes by the third time at m.68), followed by a two-voice contrary-motion figure of 10 notes. In the first appearance of the contrary-motion figure (m.66), the two voices form a mirror inversion. Each of the subsequent nine repetitions of this figure contain a different order of intervals in each voice, and between voices – there are 5 different 3-note cells that Yuasa uses here. Technically, this is very difficult for the pianist, and care must be taken when choosing where the thumb crosses. With regard to time, the duration of the first motivic feature (cluster) gradually becomes shorter (at the same time that its pitches change slightly) during its 10 occurrences. For the listener, there is the sense that time is compressing, though unpredictably.

Figure 17-3

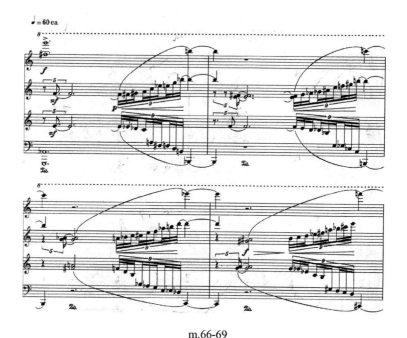

m.66-69
Yuasa COSMOS HAPTIC II

The top voice at the end of each measure continues to climb until the music is propelled into Section III (m.76-102). The texture of this section incrementally grows from two voices (m.76) to six (m.98), then reverses fairly quickly back to one (m.102). Each voice displays its own temporality (an example of polychronic time) with few, if any, attacks in common. One is referred here to the *Noh* flute, which plays between two points without any fixed relation to the chant or other instruments in tempo and rhythm (*mihakarai*). In Figure 17-4, the four polychronic voices also contain a certain elasticity of time within their own line (top stave m.85-6, for example, where the duration of pulse increases, then gradually decreases through m.87).

Figure 17-4

m.84-86
Yuasa COSMOS HAPTIC II
©1986 by Schott Music Co. Ltd., Tokyo

The complexity of Section III makes it considerably difficult to perform. This difficulty can be successfully overcome through gaining a general idea of how the voices interact by creating a time grid similar to Figure 17-5 (m.86). The next step is described by Yuasa, referring to rhythmic complexities in general in his music (1993b, 224) – "Though the situation appears to be logically constructed, it is only feasible, practically, through an intuitive, irrational rendition." Clarity of touch is important, especially in articulating the bell-like sounds and merging lines in measures 91-102.

Figure 17-5

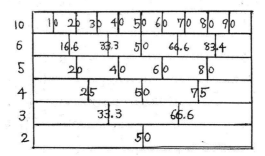

Section IV (m.103-115) can be characterized as an example of shrinking time - a two voice imitation (though not clearly heard as such) that contains two parts. The first part (m.103-110) descends sequentially, gradually moving faster (*poco a poco stringendo*). The time relationship between the two voices of the imitation remains proportionally the same (though becomes closer because of the *stringendo*, though they never share an attack), but the use of pitches in alternating 3 and 2 note cells (3 + 2 notes = 2 pulses) of several different interval combinations (minor 2nd, major 2nd, minor 3rd) is non-symmetrically organized. The second part (m.111-115) consists of a rapidly ascending, polychronic figure with imitation at the unison (m.111-112). However, because of the different temporalities of the two voices (6 = top; 5 = bottom), the unison becomes further and further displaced in time. The top voice continues to increase in speed (from 6 to 8 to 11 notes per pulse in. m.114) until the final sustained pitch (forming a tritone with the second voice) of the section. The performer needs to "spill" each note separately and clearly in this section.

The final section (m.116-144) of *Cosmos Haptic II* creates a sense of floating time (no direction of sound energy).[7] Also in this section, there is a building up of reverberant resonance in a spacious void of time. Short bursts of sound (at unexpected moments) trigger distant resonances, through use of the *sostenuto* pedal. These sounds seem like shadows. The "rests" where significant resonances occur should be thought of as negative space – not vacant. The performer can imagine them as having a similar function as haiku – suggestive (read between the lines), not descriptive.

Figure 17-6

m.108-112
Yuasa COSMOS HAPTIC II
©1986 by Schott Music Co. Ltd., Tokyo
All Rights Reserved
Used by permission of European American Music Distributors LLC,
sole U.S. and Canadian agent for Schott Music

Figure 17-7

m.120-125
Yuasa COSMOS HAPTIC II
©1986 by Schott Music Co. Ltd., Tokyo
All Rights Reserved
Used by permission of European American Music Distributors LLC,
sole U.S. and Canadian agent for Schott Music

This suggestiveness is also implied in the pitch structure of the last three measures of the work. Yuasa restates the twelve-tone field (m.142) once in its entirety, then a final time (m.142-144) as an incomplete set of 8 pitches.

As a performer, it is important to understand that *Cosmos Haptic II* is not about *Noh* itself, but the world of *Noh*. What this world is indicating is a sense of eternity. The cosmos in *Cosmos Haptic* is Yuasa's inner cosmos, and one must situate oneself in this place to perform his music.[8]

Notes

1. *Cosmos Haptic* (1957) – solo piano; *Cosmos Haptic II: Transfiguration* (1986) – solo piano; *Cosmos Haptic No.3-Kokuh* (1990) - *shakuhachi* and 20-string *koto*; *Cosmos Haptic IV* (1997) - cello and piano; *Cosmos Haptic V* (2002, revised 2003) – orchestra.
2. The *Jikken Kobo* (experimental workshop) was a group comprised of Japanese composers and artists to explore new musical and artistic trends, including multimedia. It was founded in 1951 by critic Kuniharu Akiyama, composers Yuasa, Toru Takemitsu, Kazuo Fukushima, and Hiroyoshi Suzuki, painter Katsuhiro Yamaguchi, photographer Kiyoshi Otsuji, lighting designer Naotsugu Imai, and performer Takahiro Sonoda.
3. it is interesting to note that Yuasa's concerns with the spatial perception of density and timbre are also reflected in his electronic works.
4. Joji Yuasa, program note for *Cosmos Haptic II*.
5. one phenomenal difference exists between the Japanese traditional structure of time and that of Western time – traditional Japanese time is not based on physical movement; rather, it is based on respiratory continuity.
6. personal conversation with Yuasa, April 2003.
7. this is a translation of the composer's words – "fuyuu suru jikan."
8. the accuracy of this essay has been checked by Joji Yuasa.

References

Galliano, Luciana trans. by Martin Mayes. 2003. *Yogaku: Japanese Music in the Twentieth Century*. The Scarecrow Press. Lanham, Maryland.

Komparu, Kunio. 1983. *The Noh Theater: Principles and Perspectives*. Weatherhill, NY.

Kushida, Mari. 1998. Noh Influences in the Piano Music of Joji Yuasa. DMA diss., U. of Illinois at Ubana-Champaign.

Yuasa, Joji. 2007. liner note. *Time of Orchestral Time – Works of Joji Yuasa*. CD Fontec FOCD9288

—. 1993a. Mind in Art. *Perspectives of New Music* XXXI/2. 178-185.

—. 1993b. Temporality and I: From the Composer's Workshop. *Perspectives of New Music* XXXI/2. 216-228.

—. 1992. Transcription of panel discussion at Music of Japan Today: Tradition and Innovation. March 29, 1992, Hamilton College, Clinton, NY

—. 1989a. Music as a Reflection of a Composer's Cosmology. *Perspectives of New Music* XXVII/2. 176-197.

—. 1989b. The World of *Noh* as I Perceive it, Concerning Some Problems in Music. *Perspectives of New Music* XXVII/2. 186.191.

CHAPTER EIGHTEEN

THE CLARINET OF THE TWENTY-FIRST CENTURY AND RECENT MUSIC BY JAPANESE COMPOSERS

E. MICHAEL RICHARDS

Since 1987, a number of chamber music works that include clarinet, written by Japanese composers, display a consolidation of extended traditions. This music merges late twentieth century research in extended techniques for the clarinet, derived from acoustic principles of the instrument, with aesthetics, materials, and underlying musical syntax borrowed from traditional Japanese music and culture.[1] A careful look reveals sophisticated confluences that form original musical languages which are more deeply expressive than a collection of extended technique gimmicks, introduced solely for novel effect, or mechanically incorporated Asian materials. This approach signals a new generation of work, where extended techniques are woven seamlessly into the musical fabric, so the listener's focus is centered directly on the expressive intensity of the music. The spectacle of the performer's virtuosity is of secondary importance (though mastery of the techniques by the clarinetist is clearly required!).

This essay will introduce the reader to composers and works that follow this path. Musical language found in traditional Japanese/Asian music (continuous subtle modifications in pitch [sliding/bending, microtones], rhythm [heterophony], and timbre, as well as the central importance of complex single tones) is mixed with the Western clarinet – an instrument designed for timbral homogeneity and equal tempered tuning. Composers Matsuo, Nishimura, Niimi, Itoh, and Yamamoto address this conflict in their music by transforming the clarinet into a hybrid Western/Japanese instrument through the use and development of new sonic resources, managed by basic principles of Western performance practices.

Background

In 1981, intrigued by the music of a number of progressive contemporary composers, and the clarinet/woodwind catalogues of Bruno Bartolozzi (1967) and Philip Rehfeldt (1977), I began researching new sound possibilities for the clarinet, particularly microtones.[2] The method I undertook was designed to overcome the idiosyncratic and empirical nature of earlier studies - extended techniques were systematically derived from the peculiarities of the acoustical design of the clarinet. These inherent characteristics of the clarinet, in turn, allowed the organization of extended sonic resources (multiphonics, microtones, alternate color fingerings, etc.) in ways that were logical for clarinetists to learn and execute, and thus more accurate and reliable for composers to write. In the resulting document (*The Clarinet of the Twenty-First Century*), some of these sounds were illustrated with close to 300 examples from works of almost 100 composers, in addition to original charts of particular sonic resources. The goal with these illustrations was to demonstrate possibilities while avoiding recipes for musical compositions, or suggestions of rigid limitations. Twenty-six years later (2007), after the classification (including bass and E-flat clarinets) of more than 1000 microtones, 1200 multiphonics, and 500 alternate color fingerings, this project remains a work in progress.[3]

Musical collaborations with composers, and with my duo partner Kazuko Tanosaki (pianist), shaped some of the directions of these clarinet explorations – specific musical examples referred to in this essay have been drawn from works by Japanese composers Masataka Matsuo (1987), Tokuhide Niimi (1998), Akira Nishimura (1996, 1997, 2002, 2003), Hiroyuki Itoh (2007), and Hiroyuki Yamamoto (2006). These relationships began with the purchase of a small catalogue of compositions by Japanese composers, from a Yamaha music store during my first visit to Japan in 1985, which sparked introductions through letter writing and exchange of musical scores and clarinet charts. Masataka Matsuo wrote *Distraction* for the Tanosaki-Richards Duo in 1987, which was subsequently awarded first prize in Hong Kong at the ISCM-ACL World Music Days '88. In 1990, I received a US-Japan Creative Artist Exchange Fellowship as a solo recitalist to live in Japan for 6 months. Two composers whom I met during this time, Akira Nishimura and Tokuhide Niimi, consequently wrote chamber music from 1996-2003 that utilized a number of extended clarinet techniques (Nishimura's *Madoromi III* was commissioned by the Tanosaki-Richards Duo in 2003). In 2006-7, two younger composers, Hiroyuki Itoh and Hiroyuki Yamamoto, completed commissioned works written in quarter-tones.[4]

The Composers and Music

Akira Nishimura (b.1953) –

Born in Osaka, Nishimura is widely regarded as one of the leading Japanese composers of his generation.[5] He completed undergraduate and graduate studies in composition at the Tokyo National University of Fine Arts and Music, and immediately won international recognition with awards from The Queen Elizabeth International Competition in Belgium (Grand Prix), and the Luigi Dallapiccola Competition in Milan. He has since been awarded four Otaka Prizes and four other national prizes in Japan, served as Composer in Residence (1993-4) with the Orchestra Ensemble Kanazawa, and Composer in Residence (1994-7) with the Tokyo Symphony Orchestra. Nishimura has received commissions from a number of national and international organizations, including the ULTIMA Contemporary Music Festival (Oslo), Octobre en Normandie (Rouen), the Arditti String Quartet, the Kronos String Quartet, the ELISION ensemble (Australia), Music From Japan (NY), and the Hanover Society of Contemporary Music. He has written music for traditional Japanese instruments (alone and in ensembles with Western instruments), piano, chamber groups, and more than 30 works for orchestra. More than 80 of his works have been recorded and published (many by Zen-On Music).[6]

Since his early training in Western music composition, Nishimura has also studied Asian traditional music, religion, aesthetics, and cosmology. As a result, many of his musical ideas are generated from a broad Asian perspective, in addition to his interest in ancient and medieval Japan (*gagaku* music and *Noh* theater, especially). Nishimura explains,

"One important base for me as a musician is the logic of European music composition, technique and cultural history. However, I've also been composing from an Asian point of view. For example, I don't think of the orchestra as being comprised of European instruments, because instruments of the orchestra evolved and originated in Asia. I imagine the Asian roots where orchestral instruments came from, and I often demand an approach and way of thinking different from that which led the development of instruments of the European orchestra through the common practice period."[7]

Musical qualities of the Asian/Japanese ancestry that Nishimura refers to include the importance of subtle timbre transformations over melody, the significance of small notes (grace notes) to carry musical meaning, the use of *portamento* (sliding pitches) to create (and resolve) tension both linearly and texturally (through the increase-decrease of acoustic beats), and the function of various types of heterophony to create a linear (aharmonic) structure that is asymmetric and through-composed - harmony is non-existent or accidental, and vertical sonorities are intended to be heard as overtones of a single sound (Yuasa 1989).

Nishimura has written several works of chamber music that include clarinet – examples from four, all published by Zen-On Music are included here.[8] *Aquatic Aura for clarinet and piano* was commissioned by Zen-On Music (premiered in Tokyo 1996; published 1997); *Meditation on the Melody of Gagaku "Kotoriso" for two clarinets and accordion* was commissioned by Cassals Hall, Tokyo (premiered and published 1997); *Madoromi II for oboe and two clarinets* was commissioned by Zen-On Music (premiered in Tokyo 2002; published 2003); and *Madoromi III for clarinet and piano* was commissioned and premiered by the Tanosaki-Richards Duo (premiered in Baltimore 2003; published 2005).

Tokuhide Niimi (b.1947) –

Niimi has written a number of orchestral, chamber, piano, and choral works. He has received many awards for his music, including the Geneva Grand Prix, the 18th Nakajima Kenzo Prize, 2003 Bekku Prize, Sagawa Yoshio Music Prize (2006), and 55th Otaka Prize (2007). Niimi's orchestral music has been performed by leading international orchestras such as the Suisse Romande, Netherlands Radio, BBC Scottish, Radio France, Berlin, Nurenberg, and others.[9]

Published by Zen-On Music in 2000, *Fairy Ring* (1998) for clarinet and piano was commissioned by Zen-On Music, and first performed by Yasuaki Itakura (cl) and Toshio Nakagawa (pn) in Tokyo.[10]

Masataka Matsuo (b.1959) –

Matsuo (composer and conductor) has written music for both Western and traditional Japanese instruments in various genres including solo, chamber, choral, and orchestral.[11] He has been awarded a number of prizes, including the special prize at the Japan-France Contemporary Music Composition 1985, the First Prize at ACL Young Composers Award 1988 Hong Kong, and the ISCM World Music Days 1992 in

Warsaw. Matsuo's works have been commissioned by the Tokyo Philharmonic Orchestra, the National Theater of Japan, and Pro Musica Nipponica, among other patrons of the arts, and performed internationally by the Tokyo Philharmonic, Tokyo Symphony, Lisbon Gulbenkian Orchestra, Hong Kong Philharmonic, and Music From Japan (NY) 2007.

Distraction for clarinet and piano (1987) was commissioned and premiered by the Tanosaki-Richards Duo in New Orleans. It was published by Zen-On Music in 1996 as part of *Two Pieces for clarinet* (also including *Phono III* – 1986 – for clarinet solo).[12]

Hiroyuki Itoh (b.1963) –

out of a blaze of light for clarinet and piano was commissioned and premiered by the Tanosaki-Richards Duo (2007).[13]

Hiroyuki Yamamoto (b.1967) –

The Wedge is Struck, The Fog Remains for clarinet and piano was commissioned and premiered by the Tanosaki-Richards Duo (2006; 2007).[14]

The Clarinet of the Twenty-First Century – acoustic foundations

Two basic acoustic principles of the clarinet fingering system, intertwined intimately with traditional technique, can also be applied to uncovering and organizing extended techniques. The first concerns how pitches and registers are related to the harmonic series – the second how chromatic fingerings control pitch. Most extended technique fingerings (alternate fingerings, microtones, multiphonics) differ from conventional fingerings through their common use of cross fingerings – employment of a vent, or additional vent(s), that is above the lowest tone hole (or key) covered. Cross-fingerings (often darker with fewer upper partials in the sound) present greater color contrasts with conventional fingerings than those found solely within conventional fingerings (which are designed to achieve tonal homogeneity).

1) register separation – relationship to the harmonic series

The clarinet's acoustical system consists of tones in the lowest register (chalumeau), which are all fundamentals; and higher registers (clarion, altissimo) which are derived from partials of the harmonic series of these fundamentals.[15]

Figure 18-1

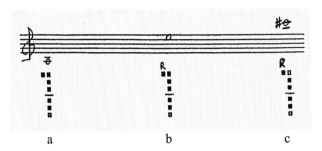

a   b   c

By adding an open register key to the A3 fingering above, E4 is produced (Figure 18-1, b – clarion register), a twelfth higher than A3, or its 3rd partial (the open register key shortens the air column to 1/3 the length of A).[16] If one alters the E fingering by lifting the first finger of the left hand, a new vent is created (shortening the air column again); this produces the pitch C-sharp5, the 5th partial of A3 (Figure 18-1, c – altissimo register). Since the pitches in the harmonic series become closer together as they move further away from the fundamental, the clarinet offers many alternate fingerings for pitches in its altissimo register, derived from the partials of several different fundamentals.

Many multiphonics draw their two main pitches from cross fingerings (two or more vents) where two simultaneous tube lengths are put in vibration – the left hand fingering determines the lowest pitch; the right hand fingering, the highest pitch (see page 214 for an example). As a result, multiphonics which are easy to connect can be organized in groups based on left hand fingering (where the lowest pitch stays virtually the same), with right hand fingerings that change chromatically.

2) longer tube length (fingers/keys covered) equals lower pitch.

One example of this relationship can be found in the ordering of practical microtonal segments; these are most successful when they involve chromatic fingerings of the right and left hands that descend from one of the conventional, twelve note per octave, pitches. In effect, the clarinetist need only learn a very few variations of the standard chromatic fingering (one, descending from an "open" G3, is below).

Figure 18-2

In Akira Nishimura's *Madoromi III*, a set of microtones below G3 (based on chromatic fingerings but not ordered), and the acoustic beats caused when they combine and "interfere" with sustained piano chords, support the image of the work as described by the composer: "..waking up for a moment among the waves of a nap....among the waves of the real and unreal, a spell and release of sleepiness, drifting among the outer layer of one's mental state."[17] Each of these microtones is produced by a cross fingering, so the colors also change – a subtle but expressive nuance.

Figure 18-3

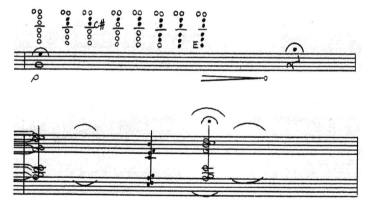

m.41
Nishimura MADOROMI III
©2005 by Zen-On Music Co., Ltd.
All Rights Reserved
Used by permission of European American Music Distributors LLC,
sole U.S. and Canadian agent for Zen-On Music Co., Ltd.

I will now further discuss the use of microtones, as well as multiphonics in the works of Nishimura, Niimi, Itoh, Yamamoto, and Matsuo, and the role they play in their musical languages.

Microtones: *Portamenti*, Trills

Aquatic Aura for clarinet and piano

All of Nishimura's writing about his clarinet music contains prose about the mysteries of life and death (conscious/unconscious), or "reincarnation" in Buddhism, which corresponds to his use of a through-composed form that defines a sort of "circular time" (non-directional form). One of his notes regarding *Aquatic Aura* talks about a "vestige of memory of the dead which is dissolved in water."[18] Both of these above images underline the Buddhist belief regarding the universe that everything that exists is constantly in transition. Musically, this is expressed here through constantly changing tone color and texture, including acoustic beats generated in a number of ways. In *Aquatic Aura*, they are generated from tone clusters between the instruments, clarinet *portamenti*, microtones, multiphonics and trills played "against" the piano, and these sounds picked up and resonated in the piano strings through the use of particular pedal techniques.

Nishimura builds tension through a sequence of ascending altissimo register microtones (one section of which is m.52-4) during which the player is asked to "slide" from one pitch to the next – a microtonal *portamento*. Once again, the sequences of right-hand fingerings move only few fingers, most often in chromatic motion.

Figure 18-4

m.52-4
Nishimura AQUATIC AURA
©1997 by Zen-On Music Co., Ltd. All Rights Reserved
Used by permission of European American Music Distributors LLC,
sole U.S. and Canadian agent for Zen-On Music Co., Ltd.

The microtonal fingerings that Nishimura draws from are among 800 chronicled in my research of clarinet microtones. Two different types of charts summarize much of this information. One (Figure 18-5), shows the relative pitch placement of microtonal fingerings within quarter-tone segments of the clarinet range (each horizontal stave equals, proportionally, a quarter-tone distance).

Figure 18-5

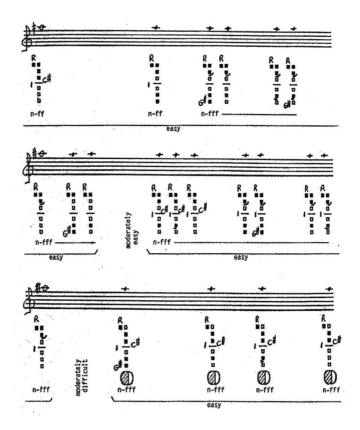

Excerpt from Table #12, p.169
Richards THE CLARINET OF THE TWENTY-FIRST CENTURY
Manuscript (2007)

Other information given for each pitch in Figure 18-5 includes a timbre indication if a particular fingering differs from surrounding fingerings (circle beneath some fingerings – examples above are "slightly dark"), the dynamic range possible to execute, and an indication of the difficulty to perform fast, legato, conjunct figures with surrounding pitches (indicated within brackets). A second type of chart (Figure 18-6) portrays fingerings for equidistant microtones in scales of quarter, eighth, twelfth, and sixteenth-tones. As can be seen from this example, equidistant microtones are not available throughout the entire range of the clarinet. Information presented, besides pitch, includes the technical feasibility of sections of these scales in performance (possibilities of legato; possibilities of fast tempo execution), as well as changes in timbre among conjunct sequences (in this example, "slightly bright" timbres).

Figure 18-6

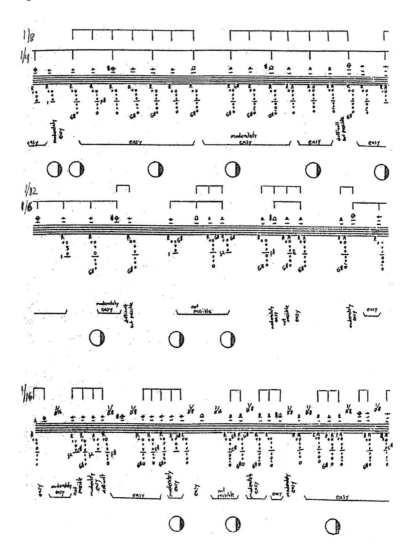

Excerpt from Table #10, p.143
Richards THE CLARINET OF THE TWENTY-FIRST CENTURY
Manuscript (2007)

Distraction for clarinet and piano

Matsuo's eight-minute work contains four large sections, excluding short introductory material, and a transition from the first to second section. The music is not metered – it depends on close synchronization of the players who either alternate phrases or short motives within a phrase, or execute ensemble silences of different lengths and tensions (leaving the precise delineations of *ma* to the players). Sometimes the sustain pedal of the piano remains down during the "silences," so previous material continues to resonate. The music has a clear direction (cresc. and accel.) during the first and third sections, but is fairly static during the second and fourth sections. The piano part is aharmonic – at no point is there more than one note played simultaneously (although pitches run together with the pedaling), and almost the entire work contains fast figures of repeated pitches. The clarinet part, on the other hand, expresses numerous characters, some through the performance of multiphonics and flutter tonguing (both used to change the color of a particular pitch). The use of subtle timbre transformations (different resonances, clarinet multiphonics), aharmonic writing, and non-directional time tie this music to elements found in some traditional Japanese music. In the five years after this work was written, Matsuo further developed these ideas in his double concerto for clarinet, piano and orchestra (*Hirai V*, 1992), and concerto for shakuhachi and orchestra (*Phonosphere I*, 1993).

In the final section of *Distraction* (*lento tranquillo*), the clarinetist plays into the piano strings (sustain pedal depressed) which creates complex resonances when the writing becomes microtonal. The penultimate gesture is a descending microtonal *portamento*, built on chromatic scale, cross-fingerings – note the eighth tones between B-flat5 and A5, and twelfth tones between A5 and G-sharp4.

Figure 18-7

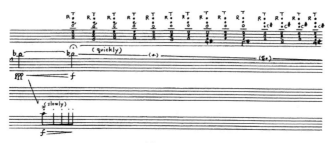

p.13 system 1
Matsuo DISTRACTION
©1996 by Zen-On Music Co., Ltd.
All Rights Reserved
Used by permission of European American Music Distributors LLC,
sole U.S. and Canadian agent for Zen-On Music Co., Ltd.

Earlier in this section, a tremolo between F4 (right hand fingering) and A quarter-tone-flat5 (left hand fingering with the third finger raised and first finger of the right hand depressed) gradually "sinks" microtonally as the right hand descends chromatically.

Figure 18-8

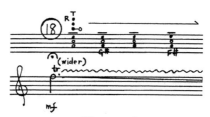

p.12 system 3
Matsuo DISTRACTION
©1996 by Zen-On Music Co., Ltd.
All Rights Reserved
Used by permission of European American Music Distributors LLC,
sole U.S. and Canadian agent for Zen-On Music Co., Ltd.

Quarter-Tones: Tremolos, *Portamenti*, Resonating Beats

The Wedge is Struck, the Fog Remains for clarinet and piano

Yamamoto describes his recent compositional interest, which runs through this work, as a "syntax of monody."

> "First, there is a sound that is the core, made from one or more pitches. The core changes/varies like a melody, and becomes ambiguous through several methods. For example, the timing and rhythm of the core is altered by the combination of instruments. In addition, the sound of a pitch that is close to the core will conflict, and the result can be a blurred core."[19]

In the opening section of *The Wedge is Struck, the Fog Remains*, a descending chromatic "core" which is close to a pitch and rhythmic unison in the composite clarinet/piano line from m.1, ultimately separates into a number of complex lines. The subtle mysteries and discrepancies of the clarinet and piano "almost unison" is heightened by the clarinet quarter-tones that Yamamoto chooses – not only are they relatively easy to execute in the conjunct figures that he writes, but their uniform timbre among themselves and with the piano contributes to the blend that is the initial core.

Figure 18-9

out of a blaze of light for clarinet and piano

Hiroyuki Itoh gathers musical inspiration from a variety of swaying and wavering images (see Chapter One for further description). These images are strengthened by his extensive use of quarter-tones in *out of a blaze of light for clarinet and piano.* "Because of the fingering and embouchure difficulties as well as the spectral complexity, a certain fragility (which constitutes the beauty of my music) inevitably remains."[20] Materials such as repeated notes, trills, and tremolos, that change their speeds constantly, are quite frequently used to realize the images Itoh mentions. In addition, the quarter-tones in the clarinet produce acoustic beats with the piano, which has its own vocabulary of pedal effects.

The descending sequence of tremolos of irregular rhythm in the following example rings in the piano strings along with the sustained piano chord, creating an additional shimmering and spatial element to the ensemble writing.

Figure 18-10

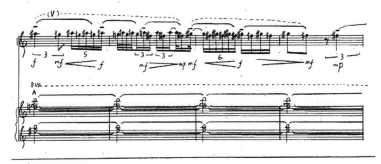

Madoromi II for oboe and two clarinets

This work is part of Nishimura's *Madoromi* series (including *Madoromi III for clarinet and piano*, mentioned earlier), where he uses extended techniques extensively, with their accompanying acoustic beating, to portray the image that the title suggests (a type of shallow sleep where dreams that one experiences take on a feeling of heightened reality). The music is through composed, and contains a number of sections. All three instruments often color sustained pitches with *portamenti*, grace note figures preceding or following, trills (quarter-tone, half-tone, double), and tremolos, or combinations of these materials.

In several instances, the oboe (top line) emerges as soloist above the two clarinets (middle and bottom lines), but there are also highly contrapuntal sections where all three instrumental voices are equal through a variety of heterophonic textures. Figure 18-11 is extracted from a lengthy heterophonic section. Note the combination of a quarter-tone trill with *portamenti* in the first clarinet part from m.225-7.

Figure 18-11

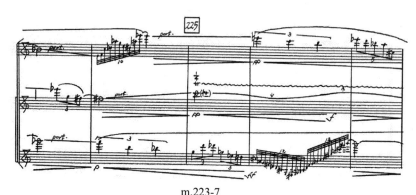

Multiphonics: Dyads, Fingered *Portamenti*, Heterophony

Meditation on the Melody of Gagagku "Kotoriso"

Written for two clarinets and accordion, this work refers to a specific
genre of traditional Japanese music – *gagaku*, which is music performed
at the imperial court and Shinto ceremonies (beginning in the 3rd century
AD). Still active today, it is the oldest extant orchestral art-music in the
world. Three wind instruments play a prominent role in this music, and
Nishimura refers to all three in his chamber piece. The *hichiriki* (a double
reed instrument with origins in central Asia and China) carries the melody
in *gagaku*, a simple collection of pitches where microtonal shadings and
note bending carries the most important musical information. Its nasal
sound is similar to both a "bass oboe," and the accordion in its middle to
low register. The *komabue* (wooden flute) simultaneously plays this same
melody, but varies it slightly, creating heterophony with the *hichiriki*. The
bending pitches and microtonal shadings of the flute and *hichiriki* surpass
the simple melody in significance. The third instrument, the *sho*, is the
only harmonic instrument in traditional Japanese music – its seventeen
reed pipes are arranged symmetrically (Malm 2000, 110), and their shape
is said to be modeled after the phoenix (a graceful mythical bird). The
sustained chords of the *sho* are played both by exhaling and inhaling, so

the shape of its sound consists of dynamic hairpins, with tones subtly added and subtracted during its *crescendi/diminuendi*. Thus, the *sho* and accordion share a similar method and characteristic of shaping sound. The constant transformation in balance among voices of the *sho* allow the chords to sound more like changing overtones of one sound, than like specific harmonies – a quality shared by clarinet multiphonics.

It is important to note that Nishimura does not imitate *gagaku* in his music, but rather models some of its principles, techniques and sounds, adding his own ideas. Often, the two clarinets (top two staves) diverge heterophonically from each other - their overlapping phrase structures do not end together until later in the work, like two parallel sliding doors that only line up at the same point when they stop moving at the same-side end of their tracks. This produces great musical tension, in the absence of harmony, to drive/color the music, and is common in *gagaku* and other Japanese indigenous music (Malm 2000).

Later in the piece, overlapping phrases among the three parts contain microtonally rising sequences of thick clarinet multiphonics of three or more voices. The unstable sustain characteristics of some of these multiphonics sound similar to the fading in and out of accordion chords in the middle to low register.[21] The ascending "chromatic" sequences of multiphonics are taken from charts found in *The Clarinet of the Twenty-First Century* (Richards 2004), where multiphonics with the same left hand fingering (lowest pitch remaining virtually constant) are grouped together (Figure 18-12 below is taken from group E) and placed in an order where chromatic-like changes in the upper voice are facilitated by chromatic changes in the right hand fingering.[22] In Figure 18-12, the unchanging left hand fingering produces a relatively stationary lowest multiphonic pitch (D-sharp or just below), while the chromatically rising right hand fingering produces a chromatically rising top multiphonic voice (from A three-quarter-tone sharp, to C sharp).[23]

Figure 18-12

In a section of building tension, Nishimura uses successions of these multiphonic groups, arranged in overlapping, ascending phrases between the two clarinets that produce a type of heterophony:

Clarinet I – m.96-8 = group D3; m.99-100 = group E1
Clarinet II – m.95-6 = group C; m.97-100 = group E

Figure 18-13

m. 95-100
Nishimura MEDITATION ON THE MELODY OF GAGAKU "KOTORISO"
©1997 by Zen-On Music Co., Ltd.
All Rights Reserved
Used by permission of European American Music Distributors LLC,
sole U.S. and Canadian agent for Zen-On Music Co., Ltd.

Nishimura employs gentle clarinet dyads in a brief cadenza for the two instruments, beginning at m.198. A descending, dyad/fingered-*portamento* idea from m.205 in the first clarinet part is combined with a microtonally ascending, three-voice multiphonic line from m.204 in the second clarinet part. The acoustic beats created within the multiphonics of each clarinet, as well as between the two parts, are striking.

Figure 18-14

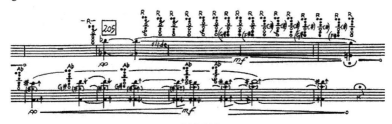

m.204-208
Nishimura MEDITATION ON THE MELODY OF GAGAKU "KOTORISO"
©1997 by Zen-On Music Co., Ltd.
All Rights Reserved
Used by permission of European American Music Distributors LLC,
sole U.S. and Canadian agent for Zen-On Music Co., Ltd.

In *Distraction*, Matsuo writes a slowly rising dyad to be played into the piano strings, towards the beginning of the final section of the piece. The lowest pitch of this multiphonic remains stationary, since changes of right hand fingerings have virtually no effect on this pitch.

Figure 18-15

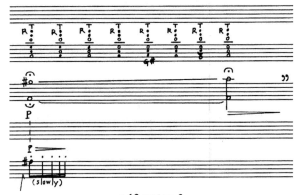

p.12 system 3
Matsuo DISTRACTION
©1996 by Zen-On Music Co., Ltd.
All Rights Reserved
Used by permission of European American Music Distributors LLC,
sole U.S. and Canadian agent for Zen-On Music Co., Ltd.

Fairy Ring for clarinet and piano

According to Niimi, "a fairy ring is the trace of their circular dance found the next morning…after a party on a moonlit night."[24] The language of the music supports this image – melodic material moves around within a mode, and the timbres of the clarinet and piano are transparent. Like Matsuo's work (although more delicate), the piano mostly plays repetitions of single tones (sometimes muted) that form a pulse, rather than harmony. The clarinet also plays repeated single tones, often varying the timbre through dynamic contrast (pp-ff *crescendo*; *subito* pp echo) or color change (different fingerings; microtonally higher; different register; flutter tongue). These single tones, as well as repetitions of these single tones in both clarinet and piano, are irregular in length, and the three voices (clarinet, piano right-hand, piano left-hand) overlap. As a result, the music (and sense of time) has no clear goals.

During the transition to the second section of the work, the clarinet plays delicate broken multiphonics that ascend from the throat tone register. These multiphonics are taken from multiphonic charts in the *Clarinet of the Twenty-First Century* (Richards 2004), and are classified as available to begin and/or end from their highest and/or lowest pitch.

Figure 18-16

m.41-2
Niimi FAIRY RING
©2000 by Zen-On Music Co., Ltd.
All Rights Reserved
Used by permission of European American Music Distributors LLC,
sole U.S. and Canadian agent for Zen-On Music Co., Ltd.

Performance Approach

Understanding the aesthetic, and faithful adherence to the musical intentions of the composers of these works is necessary to communicate the depth of the music in performance. Often, a rhythmic pulse should not be shown by the players through sound or motion – in these cases bar lines are written for visual convenience, or to show the length of the breath, rather than to indicate accents. *Portamenti*, including fingered *portamenti*, should be realized with an equally graded motion from beginning to end of the figure – this produces a desired tension since the pitch does not have a chance to settle. Silences or pauses should not be counted, but given irregular lengths depending on the level of musical tension determined by the musical context – they are equally important as the sounds to the music. Finally, the subtle details of articulations (attacks and releases) and timbre transformations during sustained pitches require a heightened sense of very careful listening to oneself and among members of a chamber ensemble. Similar to Japanese traditional music, much of the meaning of this music is carried through these elements.

Notes

1. parts of this essay are taken from sections of an article by the author - "The New Clarinet in Japan" – to appear in *Proceedings of the 2007 Clarinet and Woodwind Colloquium*, University of Edinburgh (forthcoming 2008). Since 1987, a number of works have been written for clarinet by Japanese composers, in many different styles. The composers of the works examined in this essay chose to incorporate extended technique materials (given to them by the author) in their music cited here.

2. Bartolozzi's (1967) and Garbarino's (1973) works are significant for their groundbreaking effect on other musicians, but, like many first studies, contain misinformation that has hindered real progress. One problem is that their material on clarinet focused on the Full-Boehm system; a system that very few clarinetists outside of Italy utilize. Much of the information on clarinet, therefore, is not transferable. The value of Rehfeldt's (1977) book is that it is the first for the standard Boehm-system clarinet. However, multiphonics are not categorized according to how they are produced, and microtones smaller than quarter-tones are not included. Also see the author's study of clarinet microtones (Richards 1984). My research on extended clarinet techniques (2004) is collected in several parts and formats: 1) *The Clarinet of The Twenty-First Century – B-flat clarinet* (458 pages), which includes more than 200 examples from works by almost 100 composers, and spectrograms of single and multiple sounds of unusual timbres; 2) *The Bass Clarinet of the Twenty-First Century* (141 pages); 3) *The E-flat Clarinet of the Twenty-First Century* (136 pages); 4) *Etudes and Exercises for The Clarinet of the Twenty-First Century* (175 pages) with companion CD; 5) CD-Rom of each of 1-4, with full text and more than 1000 total sound files; 6) *DVD/DVD-ROM* with companion booklet (75 pages) of selected video and audio files of etudes, exercises, examples, and charts, with html links; 7) *Website for The Clarinet of the Twenty-First Century* with composer and publisher information and links, MP3 files of some musical examples from the texts, and other information for clarinetists and composers - http://userpages.umbc.edu/~emrich/clarinet21.html

3. Composer Robert Erickson (Post 1979, 146) aptly describes the "black hole" of mining new instrumental resources: "There isn't an end to them! Extended techniques become standard techniques. There is no book on extended techniques for any instrument that can possibly end. I think that is the most fascinating part of it all. I think that what these books do is stimulate the good players. Gradually a body of attitudes grows up in relation to particular instruments...the information sort of disseminates out. So you start out with an encyclopedic view, and what you find out is that you've spurred your colleagues. What's coming up is a new virtuosity -- a step higher."

4. see http://userpages.umbc.edu/~emrich/tanosakirichards.html for further information about the Tanosaki-Richards Duo.

5. Nishimura is currently a Professor at the Tokyo College of Music, and a member of the Board to Directors for the Japan Federation of Composers.

6. Nishimura's music has been primarily recorded on Camerata (http://www.camerata.co.jp) and Fontec (http://www.fontec.co.jp) CDs.

7. interview of Nishimura by Kazuko Tanosaki and the author on April 6, 2003.

8. Nishimura also has written *River of Karuna II for clarinet and nine instruments* (premiered in 1997), published by Zen-On Music.

9. Niimi is at present a professor at the graduate school of Toho Gakuen, a guest Professor at the Tokyo College of Music, a part-time professor at the Toho Gakuen School of Music, and a member of the Board of Directors for the Japan Federation of Composers.

10. The Tanosaki-Richards Duo presented the American premiere of *Fairy Ring* in 1999 in Rochester, NY. Niimi has also written a work for two clarinets published by Zen-On Music: *Clarinet Spiral* (2002)

11. Matsuo received his education (undergraduate and graduate) in music composition at the Tokyo National University of Fine Arts and Music. He served as Executive Chairperson of ISCM World Music Days 2001 in Yokohama. At present, he is a professor at Senzoku Gakuen College of Music, and also teaches at several other music schools in Japan, including the Tokyo National University of Fine Arts and Music.

12. Matsuo has also written two other works for clarinet – *Hirai III* (1987) for clarinet and strings, and *Double Concerto for Clarinet, Piano, and Orchestra* (*Hirai V* – 1992). E. Michael Richards performed the American premiere of *Hirai III* in 1989, and the Tanosaki-Richards Duo performed the American premiere of *Hirai V* in 1992 with the Hamilton College Orchestra, and Japanese premiere in 1994 with the Shinsei Japan Philharmonic (Tokyo).

13. see bio of Itoh on pages 1-2.

14. see bio of Yamamoto on page 3.

15. chalumeau register = (written) E2-F3; clarion register = (written) B4-C5; altissimo register = (written) C-sharp5 and higher. The throat tone register (f-sharp3 to A-sharp4) functions differently acoustically - it bridges the chalumeau to clarion register through use of very short tube lengths, which raises problems with accurate intonation and stable tone color.

16. Fingering diagrams in this essay represent a standing player holding a clarinet as viewed from the front: squares = tone holes; squares above the horizontal line represent the first four fingers of the left hand (the square to the top left = left hand thumb); squares below the horizontal line represent fingers 2-4 of the right hand (the thumb supports the instrument); R = register key (played with LH thumb)

17. composer notes from score published by Zen-On Music.

18. liner notes by the composer from CD "Works by Akira Nishimura IV," Fontec FOCD2540 (Tokyo, Japan, 1997). Akira Nishimura, *Aquatic Aura* for clarinet and piano (ZWI042), ©1997 by Zen-On Music Co., Ltd. (Japan)

19. from Yamamoto's lecture "The Grey Area of Music and Hearing," presented at Music of Japan Today 2007, March 31 at the University of Maryland Baltimore County, Baltimore, MD, USA.

20. from Itoh's lecture "Swaying Time, Trembling Time," presented at Music of Japan Today 2007, March 31 at the University of Maryland Baltimore County, Baltimore, MD, USA.

21. see Richards 2004 - a recorded sound file for each multiphonic is provided, as well as a written description of its sound qualities and level of difficulty/reliability

in performance. Components that are described include stability, response, acoustic beating among voices, and dynamic range.

22. composers may select from among 463 multiphonics, separated into 73 groups.

23. pitches of the first multiphonic in Figure 18-12 can be explained as follows – A three-quarter-sharp (raised)5, from the 5th partial, from the right hand fingering, which lowers a C-sharp5 to A three-quarter-sharp (raised)5 by adding the fourth and fifth fingers (RH3 and F-sharp key); D3 from the left hand fingering F3, which is lowered with additional fingers: L2, L3, R1-3, F-sharp.

24. liner notes by the composer from CD "Lux Originis," Camerata 28CM-657 (Tokyo, Japan, 2000).

References

Bartolozzi, Bruno. 1967. *New Sounds for Woodwind*, Translated from the Italian by Reginald Smith Brindle. London: Oxford University Press.

Malm, William P. 2000. *Traditional Japanese Music and Musical Instruments.* Kodansha International: Tokyo.

Garbarino, Giuseppe. 1973. *Metodo per Clarinetto.* Milano: Ediziono Suvini Zerboni.

Post, Nora. 1979. The Development of Contemporary Oboe Technique. Ph.D. diss., New York University.

Rehfeldt, Phillip. 1977 (rev.1994). *New Directions for Clarinet.* Berkeley: University of California Press.

Richards, E. Michael. 1984. Microtonal Systems for Clarinet: A Manual for Composers and Performers. Ph.D. diss., University of California, San Diego.

—. 2004. *The Clarinet of the Twenty-First Century.* unpublished manuscript.

Yuasa, Joji. 1989. Music as a Reflection of a Composer's Cosmology. *Perspectives of New Music* 27/2. 198-214.

SECTION FOUR

MID-CAREER JAPANESE COMPOSERS AND THEIR WORK WITH COMPUTER MUSIC

CHAPTER NINETEEN

RECENT COMPUTER MUSIC BY JAPANESE COMPOSERS IN JAPAN, AMERICA, AND EUROPE

E. MICHAEL RICHARDS

Even though Japan has emerged as a leader in producing high-quality computer hardware, computer music studios for research and serious music creation were not launched until the 1990s (Rai 2004). One event that stimulated the evolution of computer music in Japan, partially through the import of music and ideas, was the hosting of the International Computer Music Conference (ICMC) in Tokyo (1993), which received significant attention from both the scientific and music fields.

The documented history of electronic music in Japan began with the establishment of the NHK Studio in the 1950s (Loubet 1997), as well as among members of the *Jikken Kobo* ("experimental workshop"). The earliest work at NHK, by Toshiro Mayuzumi and Makoto Moroi, was modeled on the sine-tone, serial etudes of Stockhausen. Also, performances of multimedia and musique concrète were organized as early as 1952 by the *Jikken Kobo*, and Mayuzumi introduced his work in musique concrète (which he came in contact with during his time attending the Paris Conservatory from 1951-2) in 1953. At NHK, electronic radiophonic music was introduced in the work of Minao Shibata in 1955 – listeners were supposed to have two radios, adjusted to two different frequencies (a simulated stereophonic image). In the late 1950's, Mayuzumi produced a work (*Campanology*) drawn from the resources of Japanese music (bells recorded in Buddhist temples), which was followed by *Shosange* (instruments from a traditional Buddhist ceremony) by Moroi in the 1960s. The approach to traditional Japanese material by Moroi was significant – rather than building sound through sine-tones, he began with rich natural material (sounds from the *shakuhachi*, for example), and sculptured it. Contrary to European studios, a number of music formats and aesthetics existed side-by-side at NHK. – no ideological barriers were present. However, the lack of visiting or resident international composers slowed stimulation from outside ideas.

Three events had profound impact on Japanese electronic music in the 1960s: Toshi Ichiyanagi's return to Japan from his work with John Cage in New York (and Cage's subsequent visit to Japan); the visit by Iannis Xenakis to Tokyo (his ideas of musician-machine interaction, and use of computers in music); and Stockhausen's work at the NHK Studio, where he introduced ideas of feedback and spatial distribution of sound. Stockhausen's influence continued during his performances at the Universal Exposition at Osaka in 1970. The Osaka festival and Cross Talk Intermedia (organized by Kuniharu Akiyama, Joji Yuasa, and American composer Roger Reynolds) opened activities in Japan to the outside world. Cross Talk Intermedia explored the relationship between multimedia, art, and technology (Loubet 1998).

Since the 1990s, sound installation and multimedia work (video, computer animation, and multimedia were very popular among the young generation in Japan) has become more familiar in Japan. One branch of this field, detached from art-music, that exploded in the 90s was "digital performers" – most had no musical background (they were graphic designers, programmers, rock musicians, etc.). These performers can be separated into general categories such as live laptop performers or sound artists (including Sachiko M who is discussed by Yann Leblanc in Chapter Twenty-One), audio CD designers, and techno artists (Loubet 2000).

With regards to serious music, one composer who stands at the front edge is Atau Tanaka.[1] After his work with sensors began in the 1990s, Tanaka produced network performances, followed by public space installations, works for web browsers, and hybrid pieces (Tanaka 2006). In his network performances, musicians from different locations interacted in live performances through video and audio conferencing systems, in front of live audiences at all of these locations. Instead of fighting the visual and time delays that faced the musicians, Tanaka chose to respect and exploit the limitations of the network transmission (2006, 278), "just as one does when composing for specific physical spaces." Subsequently, through investigation of musical qualities found within the spatial dimension of the internet, he created web-site based installations (rather than concert works). Tanaka explains that he (2006, 278) "sought to situate the listener in network space and acoustical space at once."

In 2002, Tanaka worked with Kasper Toeplitz on the *Global String*, a musical instrument wherein the network is the resonating body of the

instrument, through the use of a real-time sound-synthesis server. He
describes the instrument (2006, 280) as:

> "....a steel cable, 16mm diameter, 15 meters long. Although this seems big
> already, it's only part of the string as the concept was to use the network
> (internet) to make an instrument that connects two cities...By building a
> single 'string,' it was a use of the network not as a medium to collapse
> distance, but a resonant medium to span distance."

The instrument was not only a concert instrument for virtuosos, but a
public-space installation – museum visitors could "play" it (2006, 280).
"The goal was to make a single musical instrument that could adapt to
different levels of playing."

Tanaka has continued to explore the social dynamics of interactive
music, in the last several years, by including active listener participation in
the musical process; one project he calls *Malleable Mobile Music* is (2006,
281) "deployed on mobile systems and takes urban dynamic and listener
gestures as input...the system places communities of listeners together in a
shared musical experience." This extends Tanaka's earlier goal of
applying the notions of "idiomatic" that are part of the performance
practice of acoustic instruments, to the "utilitarian conceptions of
computers."

Computer music presented at Music of Japan Today 2007 focused on
mid-career composers from three general backgrounds: 1) those trained at
the Sonology Department at the Kunitachi College of Music (Tokyo),
under the tutelage of Takayuki Rai and visiting American professor Cort
Lippe; 2) others trained primarily in Japan, with some international
experiences; and 3) those born in Japan, who have trained and/or worked
extensively in the United States and/or Europe.

The establishment (1991) of the Sonology Department at the Kunitachi
College of Music, one of the earliest computer music research and
composition studios in Japan, has been described as one of two remarkable
events during the 1990s that advanced computer music in Japan (Rai
2004). This facility began with NeXT computers and IRCAM Signal
Processing Workstations – the most powerful digital signal processing
system at that time. Undergraduate students had the rare opportunity to
study real-time signal processing techniques and produce interactive
computer music. Some of these students have since become major figures
in the field, both within and outside Japan.

The founder and director of the Sonology Department was Takayuki Rai. Born in Tokyo in 1954, he studied composition with Yoshiro Irino and Helmut Lachenmann, and computer music with Paul Berg at the Utrecht Institute of Sonology in the Netherlands.[2] Rai, who has won a number of prizes (Bourges, Irino, NEWCOMP, ICMA) for his music, began working in the Netherlands on computer music, especially real-time sound synthesis techniques and interactive computer music, and continued his work at the Kunitachi College of Music in Tokyo for 15 years. Since 1991 he has realized various pieces for instruments and live computer systems using Max/ISPW and later Max/MSP. He has also created interactive multimedia art using a new, specially developed software called 'DIPS' (Digital Image Processing with Sound), serving as project supervisor since 2000.

Labyrinth (2004), a ten-minute work for tape, was realized at the Sonology Department, Kunitachi College of Music in Tokyo and premiered at the SIGMUS Computer Music Symposium in Yokohama. According to the composer, this work concerns a "labyrinth of a mysterious urban soundscape." The music has a number of textures that overlap – many of them contain fast, short pitched figures that repeat in varied permutations, reminiscent of Ligeti's micropolyphony. The repeated figures sometimes are slow enough to hear individual pitches (vibrations), which especially frame the structure at beginning and end of the work

Daichi Ando (b.1978, Japan) studied composition and computer music with Takayuki Rai and Cort Lippe at Kunitachi. Subsequently, he continued his studies in computer music with Palle Dahlstedt and Mats Nordahl in the Art & Technology, International Masters Program at IT-University of Göteborg, Chalmers University of Technology, Göteborg, Sweden. Currently, he is studying applications of numerical optimization methods on art creation in the Iba laboratory, Graduate School of Frontier Sciences, The University of Tokyo, Japan.

Wandering Finger is a piece for 2-track tape. Sound effects and small sequences have been generated by Max with algorithmic composition programmed by the composer, and sequences of the whole piece has been made by ProTools software. The sounds and structure of the four-minute work consist of mostly non-pitched, repetitive figures that are layered.

Shintaro Imai (b.1974, Nagano, Japan) also studied composition and computer music at Kunitachi. After completing his post graduate study in Tokyo, he was invited to attend the Course of Composition and Computer Music at IRCAM (Paris), where he studied composition with Philippe Hurel. Between 2002 and 2003 he was the recipient of a grant from the

Japanese Agency for Cultural Affairs, and worked as a guest composer at ZKM Institute for Music and Acoustics in Karlsruhe, Germany, moving afterwards to the Electronic Music Studio TU Berlin (DAAD). Imai has won a number of awards (Bourges, Musica Nova, Earplay 2001, ZKM International Competition, and Künstlerhaus Lukas in Ahrenshoop, Germany), and his music has been played at several international festivals (International Computer Music Conference 1999 in Beijing, ISCM World Music Days 2002 in Hong-Kong). He is currently a lecturer at Kunitachi, Tamagawa University, and Shobi University in Japan.

Imai's music is related to the organization of microscopic movements of noise inherent in any given natural sound. *Figure in Movement* (2005) was developed for an electroacoustic system, realized at the Electronic Music Studio TU Berlin. The sound materials were processed and organized via a real-time algorithmic sound-generating system based on various granular sampling techniques, using the composer's "Sound Creature" system (a real-time algorithmic sound-generating system by means of extended granular sampling techniques). These materials were originally made from sampled flute sounds, performed by flutist Sabine Vogel. The compositional algorithm and sound synthesis programs were both written in Max/MSP, and for editing and mastering, ProTools was used. The concept of the piece is to "describe an imaginary living sound matter and its surrounding environment," and Imai places his sounds in two and three-layered space (foreground, middleground, background).

Two other composers whose computer works were performed at MOJT 2007 were not solely trained in computer music in Japan. Naotoshi Osaka (b.1953, Nagano) studied electrical engineering at Waseda University, as well as composition with Sesshu Kai and Daishiro Takusari. Between 1978 and 2003 he worked as a researcher at the NTT Communication Science Laboratories and developed prominent computer music software that utilizes various signal processing techniques. As a composer, his works have been performed in Japan and abroad, including Music Today 1995 in Denmark, ICMC, and at the CCRMA Newstage Concert 2006. He currently teaches computer music technology at Tokyo Denki University, and serves as the ICMA Asia/Oceania Regional Director.

Shizuku no Kuzushi (for violin and tape) is modeled on the concept of music concrète. The Japanese word "Shizuku" means "drop of water," which is the basic sound material of the piece. The word "kuzushi" means "variation." The piece is divided into seven sections, and each section is named after syllables in the title: "shi," "zu," "ku," and so on. In order to make variations of the water-drop sound, several digital signal processing techniques, including time variant digital filters, spectrum fold-over distortion, and phase distortion caused by amplitude modulation, were employed on a NeXT computer. As much as possible, variations of the raw water-drop sound were explored throughout the entire piece – a number of these permutations contain pitched sound. The middle section of violin harmonics and overtone spectra that emanate from the tape part, is especially beautiful. This piece was premiered at the Computer Music Independent Concert at the Xebec Hall in Kobe in 1991, and selected for ICMC 1993 in Tokyo.

Hiroyuki Yamamoto (b.1967, Yamagata Prefecture) received his undergraduate and graduate training in music composition from the Tokyo National University of Fine Arts and Music (see bio on p.3). He has won some of Japan's most prestigious awards for his acoustic music. His tape piece *Perspectivae* was composed in the summer of 2002 at INA/GRM Paris. "Materials, recorded by microphone in rooms, streets, churches, airports, etc., each have their own distances and spaces. I edited the recordings, 'zapping' several sounds to make the perspectives unclear."[3] The work contains numerous layers of sounds in different spaces, with many asymmetric repetitions, fast *portamenti*, and interruptions. *Die Passion der Matthaus-Passion* was composed during autumn 2002 in Tokyo. Yamamoto drew materials from the original recorded music of Bach, then re-edited them in the order of Chorus, Aria, Chorale, and Recitativo. The reconstruction also includes re-articulated rhythms, three-tiered spaces, and the addition of noise elements.

A number of composers, though born in Japan, have either trained and/or worked extensively in the United States and/or Europe. Performances of these composers at MOJT 2007 included a violin and tape work of Karen Tanaka, a tape work of Hideko Kawamoto, music for robots by Suguru Goto, and a presentation of a video excerpt of interactive music (performed by *Sensorband*) by Atau Tanaka.

Karen Tanaka (b. 1961) studied composition in Japan with Akira Miyoshi at the Toho Gakuen School of Music in Japan, Tristan Murail at IRCAM, Paris and Luciano Berio in Florence. She has received many prestigious awards and prizes including the Gaudeamus Prize at the International Music Week in Amsterdam, prizes at the Viotti and Trieste competitions, and the Japan Symphony Foundation Award. Tanaka completed a series of important commissions from Japan during the 1990s, and enjoyed increasing performances and broadcasts around the world during this time. She is currently co-artistic director of the Yatsugatake Kogen Music Festival, previously directed by Toru Takemitsu. Tanaka lives now in Santa Barbara, California.

Wave Mechanics II for violin and tape (1994) is in three sections, marked by two extensive cadenzas by the solo violin. Wave mechanics is originally a technical term of physics, used here only as a description of the mathematical relations employed. According to the composer,

> "This piece interprets concepts of wave mechanics in a metaphorical way, rather than deploying them as a system of immutable mathematical rules. The pitches E, B-flat and D which appear at the beginning are used as axis throughout the piece, and harmonics and noise generated by those three notes serve as a foundation of the structure."

Hideko Kawamoto studied composition and piano at the University of North Texas followed by post-doctoral studies at IRCAM in Paris. She has won international awards from the Concorso Internazionale "Luigi Russolo," Pierre Schaeffer International Computer Music Competition, Bourges, Ear '01 (Hungary), and Sonic Circuits International Festival Electronic Music Art (Composition Awards, USA). Currently residing in Southern California, her works have been performed throughout the world.

Night Ascends from the Ear like a Butterfly (1999) was inspired by Haruo Shibuya's poem, *Coliseum in the Desert*. The words Shibuya uses in this poem such as 'night,' 'a time of music,' 'rain,' 'black fountain,' 'piano string,' 'useless choir,' and butterfly provided germinal ideas. These images were developed in the composer's imagination separately from Shibuya's poem, and then transformed into music. To create the butterfly sound, a tremolo passage from Maurice Ravel's piano piece, *Noctuelles* (Night Moths) from *Miroirs* was sampled and processed in the computer using various techniques including filtering, reverberation, and pitch shift. Contrary to the pitched tremolo sound, the composer also used the sound of small pieces of aluminum foil shaking up and down in a metallic bowl, which is non-pitched, to create the surrealistic vision of a butterfly staying in one place, not flying, but moving its wings delicately as it breathes. Several complex textures are often presented simultaneously in different sound spaces. Sections of the work are set off by silences.

Suguru Goto (b.1966) studied composition and piano in Japan, then moved to the United States to continue his studies at New England Conservatory in Boston, with post-graduate studies at the Technical University Berlin and HDK in Berlin, Germany. He studied composition with Lukas Foss, Earl Brown, and Robert Cogan in the US, Dieter Schnebel in Berlin, and Tristan Murail at IRCAM, Paris. Goto has received several prizes and fellowships from the Boston Symphony, Tanglewood, International Rostrum of Composers in UNESCO, Paris, Marzena International Composition Competition (Seattle), and Berliner

Kompositionauftrage 1993. His music has been performed at major festivals throughout the world. Goto has produced computer music and conducted research with the group "Gestural Controller" at IRCAM, Paris since 1995.

RoboticMusic (2003) is performed by robots that play acoustic musical instruments (video of this shown at MOJT 2007) - a snare drum, bass drum, cymbal, gong, and pipe. They were conceived, designed, and created by Suguru Goto, with technical help from Fuminori Yamazaki, iXs Research Corp. in 2003. Goto writes (2006):

"Each robot resembles a part of a human's body, such as an arm, a leg etc. and imitates the gesture of a human's performance. These robots are controlled by a computer in real time with the program Max/MSP/Jitter, through which they can be altered to have various functions that exhibit more advanced intelligence.....the robots in RoboticMusic don't walk on two feet, nor contain eyes, a mouth, etc. The gesture of a human percussionist is modeled in order to create a musical sound and expression. Max, Cycling'74 is utilized as an interface and to generate musical data. With this, one can also send basic parameters to the robots, such as a position of the robot's arm, an offset position, intensity (how hard it hits) and so on. This sends the signals to another computer with Linux via UDP. This has an important role, since it controls the movement of the robot. The computer with Linux is connected to the robots via USB. Each robot has its own interface, which is connected with an actuator and a sensor, and special springs to imitate human muscles."

A number of advantages and disadvantages to robots performing music have been noted by Goto (2006). Modeling the delicate control of the human body, acquired through many years of training by a human performer, is a field of research that has barely begun – an acoustic instrument played by a human has enormous possibilities of musical nuance (2007). "These are not functions of a primitive brain (walking, holding etc.), but for an advanced brain (sensitivity, emotion and very delicate body control)." However, even now, a robot can perform without any rest, more precisely and faster than a human being. Robots also extend the possibilities of ensemble playing – for example, a group of six robots could simultaneously play six different complex rhythms in different tempi. Compared to computer music coming from speakers, the acoustical advantages of robots playing on a stage are obvious – the audience can observe both the sound and gesture of the performance.

Atau Tanaka was born in Tokyo and raised in the U.S. He studied with Ivan Tcherepnin at Harvard, and met John Cage during his time there. While living in the San Francisco area, he was commissioned to compose the first piece for BioMuse, a bioelectrical musical instrument (BioMuse has been used to control real time image processing, creating solo sound/image performances). Tanaka moved to Paris in 1992 to conduct research at IRCAM. In his work with sensor technology, he has been artist in residence at STEIM, Amsterdam, and in 1995 became Artistic Ambassador for Apple France for interactive music technologies. In 1993 Tanaka established *Sensorband* - a sensor instrument trio that has performed widely in network concerts, and projects using large scale architectural and laser instruments. In 1997 Tanaka moved from Paris to Tokyo on a *Sensorband* commission from NTT-ICC. He currently resides in Paris and since 2001, is researcher at Sony Computer Science Laboratories Paris. Tanaka has presented his work at conferences and festivals throughout the world.

Sensorband, formed in 1993 together with Zbigniew Karkowski and Edwin van der Heide, captures gesture and corporeal movement with sensors, translating them into digital data – each member uses his body as an instrument to play music (Bongers 1998). Tanaka plays the BioMuse - a bioelectrical musical instrument that allows the performer to create music with muscular [tension through concentrated movement] and neural [gel electrodes on the performers forearms] activity. Karkowski plays an invisible cage of infrared beams that, when broken, trigger a sample of sounds, and Van der Heide plays a MIDI conductor using joystick-like controls.

One of the goals of *Sensorband* is to make gestural music performances with computers, defeating the long-held belief that musicians of acoustic instruments can perform or interpret gestures, and computers can not. Each of the players has spent time with his instrument to explore it in depth (like the player of an acoustic instrument), unlike many computer musicians who upgrade their instrument each year and must restart a performance practice from the beginning. According to Tanaka, these musical influences and artistic objectives are what is new with Sensorband (Bongers 1998, 23):

> "not necessarily the technology, or the idea of sensor control over computer-generated music, but the aesthetic, structural approaches, and the performance practice we establish."

Notes

1. see biographical information for Atau Tanaka on page 229-30.
2. biographical information and program notes in this chapter taken from information supplied by the composers.

References

Bongers, Bert. An Interview with Sensorband. *Computer Music Journal* 22:1. 13- 24.

Dubost, G. and Tanaka, A. 2002. A Wirelss Network-Based Biosensor Interface for Music. *Proceedings of International Computer Music Conference* (ICMC).

Gaye, L., Holmquist, L-E., Behrendt, F., Tanaka, A. 2006. Mobile Music Technology: Report on an Emerging Community. *Proceedings of New Interfaces for Musical Expression (NIME06)*. IRCAM.

Goto, Suguru. 2007. http://suguru.goto.free.fr/

—. 2006. The Case Study of An Application of the System, "Bodysuit" and "Robotic Music" – Its Introduction and Aesthetics. *Proceedings of New Interfaces for Musical Expression (NIME '06)*. Paris, France.

Loubet, Emmanuelle. 1997. The Beginnings of Electronic Music in Japan, with a Focus on the NHK Studio: The 1950s and 1960s. *Computer Music Journal* 21:4, p. 11-22

—. 1998. The Beginnings of Electronic Music in Japan with a Focus on the NHK Studio: The 1970s. *Computer Music Journal* 22:1, 49-55.

—. 2000. Laptop Performers, Compact Disc Designers, and No-Beat Techno Artists in Japan: Music from Nowhere. *Computer Music Journal* 24:4, 19-32.

Polishook, Mark. 2003. Kobe DSP Off Summer School 2003: Robots and Music. *Computer Music Journal* 27:4, p.86-9.

Rai, Takayuki. 2004. DVD Program Notes. *Computer Music Journal* 28:4, 116-29.

Tanaka, Atau. 2007. Facilitating Musical Creativity: In Collectivity and Mobility. LEA-ACM Multimedia Special Issue, *Leonard Electronic Almanac* 15: 5-6.

—. 2006. Interaction, Experience, and the Future of Music. Springer. Computer Supported Cooperative Work 35: 267-288.

Tanaka, Atau, Tokui, N., and Momeni, A. 2005. Facilitating Collective Musical Creativity. *Proceedings of ACM Multimedia*.

—. 2004. *Malleable Mobile Music. Adjunct Proceedings of the 6th International Conference on Ubiquitous Computing (Ubicomp)*.

Tanaka, Atau and Knapp, R. B. 2002. Multimodal Interaction in Music Using the Electromyogram and Relative Position Sensing. *Proceedings of New Interfaces for Musical Interaction (NIME)*, Medialab Europe.

Tanaka, Atau and Bongers, Bert. 2001. Global String: A Musical Instrument for Hybrid Space. In Fleischmann, M., Strauss, W., editor,

Proceedings: Cast01 // Living in Mixed Realities. 177-181. MARS
Exploratory Media Lab FhG - Institut Medienkommunikation.
—. 2000. Musical Performance Practice on Sensor-based Instruments. In
Wanderley, M. M. and Battier, M., editor, *Trends in Gestural Control
of Music, Science et musique.* 389-405. IRCAM – Centre Pompidou.
Edition electronique - on CD-ROM
—. http://www.xmira.com/atau/

SECTION FIVE

FOUR JAPANESE SOCIETIES AND THEIR CURRENT MUSIC: COMMUNITIES WITHIN JAPAN, AND "OFFSHORE" JAPAN

Among the tremendous variety of music produced by Japanese musicians, particular genres have identified, penetrated, and helped define subgroups of Japanese societies. In this section, relationships of four such subgroups to specific musical genres (influenced by Western music) are discussed: the transculturation of wind band music from America/Europe to Japan; the evolution of sound artists within Tokyo's avant-garde, improvised music scene; strategies of ethnic and artistic self-identification and promotion among Japanese composers in England; and the development of a *chaku-uta* (sampled songs) music market among cell phone users in Japan.

Conductor and music educator David Hebert investigates how the wind band genre has been adopted, radically reinvented, and imbued with new meanings by the Japanese. Wind band music only came to be popularized in Japan during recent generations, but the Tokyo Kosei Wind Orchestra is now widely regarded as the world's leading professional wind ensemble, and the All-Japan Band Association (AJBA) national contest has become the world's largest music competition, with nearly 500,000 participants. Hebert considers the role of spirituality within Japanese wind bands (from grade school through professional levels) in their mission (outreach activities), practices (rehearsal strategies), and repertoire (hybrid repertoire by Japanese composers).

In the late 1990's in Tokyo, a highly minimal improvisatory sound art emerged with a performance approach that pays particular attention to sound texture, gaps and silences. Among the founders of this style was Sachiko Matsubara (who records as Sachiko M). Sachiko M was active as a sampler player from 1994, performing as a member of Yoshihide Otomo's *Ground Zero* from 1994-7. In 1998, she moved in a drastically different direction as a solo artist, by establishing a revolutionary method she has used since this time - manipulating the sampler's internal test tones. Sachiko M does not use a computer (Loubet 2000, 22-3) – rather "a limited set of small digital boxes such as a frequency tester for broadcasters, a small digital mixing console, and a toothbrush and other gadgets for acoustical commentary."

Sachiko M's 2000 release of *Sine Wave Solo* consisted entirely of sine waves. Suddenly, she became the focus of intense interest on the international scene, including European music festivals and Britain's *Wire* magazine (Loubet 2000, 23). "Her world is that of concentration and timing – a captivating, reduced world, which she considers to be the antithesis of the Bubble Economy aesthetic, which is characterized by a blind accumulation of goods, sounds, and memory." Among those who Sachiko M has collaborated with is Toshimaru Nakamura, a sound artist who plays the "no-input mixing board" (a board with the outputs connected to the inputs, thus producing feedback). Another notable figure in this movement in Tokyo is Toshiya Tsunoda, who uses innovative concepts of field recording and collage in his sound art – much of it contains slowly changing sounds of minimal vibration, cut up and re-arranged.

Yann Leblanc, a French anthropologist and ethnomusicologist, writes about links between sound and the body, sound and space in the work of these aforementioned sound artists within Tokyo's avant-garde music community. Leblanc argues that studying the music and performances of these artists requires that one take an interest in all Japanese sound environments, particularly in urban areas like Tokyo where important changes have occurred throughout the years. A very important variety of sounds, signals, and music can be heard there, all of which influence the body's postures and gestures. According to Leblanc, "Directly or indirectly, sound artists invite us to learn to hear all of this differently, showing that listening is indeed a technique of the body in Marcel Mauss's sense."

Yumi Hara Cawkwell is a Japanese composer and performer (solo vocalist of improvised music with electronics) who currently lives and works in London. In addition to a Ph.D. earned in music composition from the City University in London, she studied medicine in Japan and practiced as a psychiatrist for eight years before moving to the UK. Cawkwell examines identity paradoxes concerning Japanese composers and British performers in England. The composers, trained in art-music in Japan and Europe, count their Japanese heritage among their artistic influences – seemingly at odds with their unfamiliarity with Japanese *hogaku* instruments, which comes to light when they are asked to write for

British musicians who play these instruments expertly due to extensive study in Japan.

Keitai culture (mobile phone culture) in Japan has made available astounding capabilities (some as early as four years ahead of the US and Europe) for its consumers. Among the functions available on cell phones are alarm clock, stopwatch, mobile games, email, instant messenger, mp3 and mp4 (video) players, GPS navigation, TV and radio, debit and credit cards, and even use with vending machines.

Noriko Manabe looks at the phenomenon of cell phone *chaku-uta* (sampled songs) in Japan, and how they have grown to comprise 13-percent of total music sales in the first half of 2006. Consumers are downloading *chaku-uta* not for use as ringtones so much as for listening pleasure; they use *chaku-uta* to isolate their favorite parts of songs, usually the chorus. Record companies are releasing *chaku-uta* ahead of the album as a marketing test on the appeal of the album and as a promotional tool. In this update of her continuing project, Manabe uncovers how unique aspects of the Japanese cultural environment affect the development of this market, and tracks the behavior of consumers, record companies, portal operators, and artists to assess how *chaku-uta* are changing what music is heard, and how it is heard.

References

Hebert, David G. 2005. Music Competition, Cooperation, and Community: An Ethnography of a Japanese School Band. Ph.D. diss., University of Washington. Ann Arbor.

Loubet, Emmanuelle. 2000. Laptop Performers, Compact Disc Designers, and No-Beat Techno Artists in Japan: Music from Nowhere. *Computer Music Journal* 24:4. 19-32.

CHAPTER TWENTY

ALCHEMY OF BRASS: SPIRITUALITY
AND WIND MUSIC IN JAPAN

DAVID G. HEBERT

Prelude: Spirituality and Japanese Winds

The process by which East Asian musicians adopted and mastered
European art-music during the twentieth century is still only beginning to
be systematically researched, promising many new insights of global
interest in the coming decades (Everett & Lau 2004; Yang 2007).
Historically, wind bands in Europe and North America were associated
with military, industrial, educational, and religious institutions, yet in
Japan this genre was reinvented and imbued with new meanings while
adopted and firmly entrenched among professional and amateur musicians.
This article provides a succinct overview and interpretation of the
remarkable *status quo* of wind band music in Japan through discussion of
findings from ethnographic fieldwork. As Sherry Ortner has explained
(2007, 43), ethnography produces "understanding through richness,
texture, and detail," but this brief report aims to distill such rich
descriptions in order to convey globally significant developments that will
be unfamiliar to most readers. Broadly, this study also provides a modest
contribution to the question of how music changes – both sonically and
socially – as it crosses cultural boundaries, and the implications this
process may offer toward understanding the perennial role of spirituality in
musical behavior.

Why Spirituality?

The significance of spirituality in wind music is a topic that has
received little scholarly attention. Music education philosopher Anthony

Palmer confronted the issue of spirituality in music (1995, 91) when he questioned,

> "What is that sense of transcendence that arises among people when exceptional musical performance occurs? What are the intangible but very real qualities that tell us we touched something beyond our present perceptions of reality?"

Particularly in the context of Japanese traditional music, the role of spirituality is often perceived as a fundamental yet ineffable feature of authentic artistry. Educational researcher and *shakuhachi* flutist Koji Matsunobu (2007) has identified five key characteristics of Japanese spirituality as embodied in music learning: (a) an insignificance of human existence in contrast with the natural environment; (b) a feeling of awe toward nature; (c) a connectedness with ancestors; (d) a reference to individuals' inner strength; and (e) a sense of absolute power without reference to a particular religion. *Shakuhachi* players born outside Japan have similarly noted the tremendous importance of spirituality in the learning of traditional Japanese wind music, and their work merits careful examination (Blasdel 1988; Keister 2005). Relevant to this inquiry is the extent to which such indigenous beliefs may also be applicable in the context of a tradition imported from Europe and North America.

Music Transculturation and Hybridity

Ethnomusicologists have observed that as established music traditions are newly introduced to another culture, they are typically modified to suit local needs, enabling entrenchment of practices to solidify within various institutional contexts (Flaes 2000). In some cases, new musical fusions and hybrid traditions arise as a result of cross-cultural contact, but in others modifications made to pre-existing traditions are less obvious. Music teaching and learning strategies are one domain in which musicologists and educators have noted considerable diversity that tends to be maintained even as new traditions are introduced (Trimillos 1989; Campbell 1991). In the case of Japan, there are many indications that European art-music has come to be taught with pedagogical approaches that are rather different from that of Europe and North America, with roots that may be traceable to Japanese traditions (Hebert 2005). As I will demonstrate, this is particularly noticeable in the field of Japanese wind bands which have developed into a phenomenon of globally significant proportions.

Institutionalization of Professional Bands

Japan is currently home to the most highly regarded professional wind bands, the world's largest musical instrument company and private music school system, and a vibrant hybrid tradition of original band works forged by a community of prolific Japanese composers. This situation has enabled amateur wind music participation to reach an unprecedented scale, resulting in development of the world's largest music competition, the All-Japan Band Association (AJBA) national contest, which annually includes around 500,000 contestants in more than 14,000 wind bands (Hebert 2005). This section will briefly examine each of the major institutions that contribute to Japan's remarkable wind band scene.

The Tokyo Kosei Wind Orchestra

In recent decades, the Tokyo Kosei Wind Orchestra has come to be widely regarded as the world's leading professional civilian wind band. In terms of ticket sales and recording outputs, this band and its only notable rival, Osaka Municipal Symphonic Band, strongly resemble major symphony orchestras, and are also highly active in the commissioning and performance of new compositions. The Tokyo Kosei Wind Orchestra is patronized by the Rissho Kosei-Kai, a lay Buddhist organization with a unique ideology, and its Fumon Hall headquarters on the religion's main campus in central Tokyo also host the All-Japan Band Association national competition. The ensemble typically makes the premier recordings of required pieces for the AJBA competition and its members serve as contest adjudicators. The Tokyo Kosei Wind Orchestra was founded in 1960, and in 1966 the Rissho Kosei-Kai President Niwano described the role of music as follows (117):

> "Another means of propaganda is music. At the headquarters, we have the Kosei Classical Ceremonial Music Group, the Kosei Brass Band and the Kosei Chorus Group. They present performances at the events of this society and also of the world in general, and at the institutions for the needy with the intention of fostering religious sentiment and establishing better relations with the world through music."

In 1985 the Tokyo Kosei Wind Orchestra's official mission was explained in a concert program as follows (Hebert 2001a, 216):

> "The orchestra's fundamental philosophy is for its musicians to attain ever-higher levels of musical excellence through constant improvement in

personal character. Its permanent objective is to utilize music to cultivate rich human feeling and to make an important contribution to a more positive and progressive society."

Probably the main reason this band came to be widely known outside of Japan is the influence of Frederick Fennell (1914-2004), who served as its director from 1984 to 1994. Widely regarded as the most influential wind conductor of the late twentieth century, Fennell may be credited with steering the ensemble toward performing a higher level of repertoire and releasing numerous recordings through a multimedia publishing company that is also owned by Rissho Kosei-Kai. Eventually their efforts would produce a steady stream of accolades from abroad. In 1989 (McDonald), for example, the international distribution of a mere fraction of the ensemble's recordings was hailed as "one of the major releases of the decade" and "almost an encyclopedic survey of symphonic wind music." Today, posters of the Tokyo Kosei Wind Orchestra hang in the band rooms of many Japanese schools, and students use their definitive recordings as performance models.

The Osaka Municipal Symphonic Band

The oldest surviving western orchestral ensemble in Japan is not an orchestra, but a band. In 1934, the *Osakashi Ongakutai* (Osaka Band Corps), which had been an army-affiliated band since 1923, was brought under the authority of Osaka City, and in 1946, the ensemble changed its name to become the less militaristic sounding *Osakashi Ongakudan*, or Osaka Municipal Symphonic Band (2003, 16). This ensemble and other military bands that regularly performed in Osaka's Tennouji Park during the period of colonial expansion have been credited with inspiring the development of other wind bands throughout Japan prior to the emergence of the Tokyo Kosei Wind Orchestra (Hosokawa 2001). The activities and profile of the Osaka Municipal Symphonic Band gradually developed from the 1950s through 1970s, and in 1981 the ensemble moved into its current office, rehearsal, and performance facilities provided by Osaka city nearby the famous castle at Osakajo Koen. The ensemble began performing numerous high-profile concerts from this location, and in 1996 the band began releasing CDs. Since 2000, Live Performance CDs have been produced, beginning with the ensemble's 80th regular concert.

The Yamaha Corporation

It would be difficult to overstate the influence of the Yamaha Corporation on the development of instrumental music in Japan across the past century, yet its role remains essentially unexamined in most historical accounts (Kobayashi 2000). As early as 1894, the *Eigawa Seisakusho* subsidiary company was providing instruments for *chindonya* (street musicians), military bands, and even musicians of the imperial household (Hiyama 1990, 87). The company began by fixing imported Western instruments, but by 1907 was already producing some of its own. At first, the quality was not good, but craftsmanship rapidly improved. In 1937, the company was redeveloped as *Nippon Kangakki Kabushiki Kaisha*, and in 1970 combined with *Nihon Gakki Seizou Kabushiki Gaisha* to become the wind instrument division of the Yamaha Corporation. The company experienced remarkable growth, and as Hiyama (1990, 293) observed,

> "By 1989 Yamaha had built factories in Michigan capable of producing 100,000 brass instruments per year as well as in Hamamatsu and Toyoka capable of more than 300,000 per year, which produced instruments that circled the globe."

Instrument production had never before occurred on such a large scale, and the Yamaha brand soon became a household name. The Yamaha Corporation has long played an active role in Japan's wind music scene, from sponsoring clinics, workshops, and competitions, to endorsing renowned professional musicians, providing music lessons to hundreds of thousands of students through Genichi Kawakami's Yamaha Music Education system, providing instrumental rental and repair services, and even producing innovative devices such as the Silent Brass System that have changed instrumental rehearsal practices world-wide.

Japanese Wind Band Composers

In recent decades, Japanese composers have produced a unique body of original works for wind band that fuse western art-music with prominent influences from Japanese traditional music and culture. Many of these works were supported by commissions from the aforementioned professional bands or as required pieces for the All-Japan Band Association competition. Two of the most well-known composers active in this movement are Hiroshi Hoshina (b.1936) and Yasuhide Ito (b.1960), both of whom were first interviewed by the author in 2000 (2001b). Others include Toshio Mashima (b.1949), Masamichi Amano (b.1957), and Isao

Matsushita (b.1951).[1] Although each of these artists makes use of rather different compositional techniques, characteristics of Japanese spirituality in music (as outlined by Matsunobu in the first section) are quite noticeable as themes within the band works of each composer.

Hoshina and Ito have written music inspired by infamous historical events from which ghosts are still said to linger, including the annihilation of Hiroshima's civilian population at the conclusion of World War II and the martyrdom of Japanese Christians during the early seventeenth century, respectively. Isao Matsushita's most well known work for band is "Dance of the Flying God," a piece based on Japanese Buddhist principles. The first section of this music takes the notion of "enlightenment from a single tone" as its inspiration, a concept well-known among shakuhachi players. All the wind band musicians play an identical pitch as they gradually enter the performance space in a ritualistic invitation for the *Hiten* (flying angelic beings of Buddhism) to enter the hall for the performance. As the composer explains, the rhythmic motifs and development of the second section are based entirely on *shomyo* chant and mathematical principles derived from a sacred Sanskrit text. Matsushita's other most well known work, "Hi-Ten-Yu", combines *taiko* drumming with Western orchestral instruments.

Composers Hoshina, Ito, and Matsushita are associated with music programs at leading Japanese universities, but there are also some notable wind band composers who arose from outside academia and are able to survive exclusively from their work as composers. Toshio Mashima is a professional jazz trombonist and award-winning composer, and his most well known band work is "Les Trois Notes du Japon", based on three scenes from Kyoto. Each section of this piece features symbols of Japanese spirituality, from the courting of cranes, to scenes in a snowy ravine, and finally the Nebuta purification festival of Aomori. Masamichi Amano is another popular band composer who has produced numerous arrangements and original works for the wind band idiom, but is also widely known for composing soundtracks to animated movies and major feature films. His "GR" (for *Giant Robo: The Day the Earth Stood Still*) is a passionate response to the threat of dehumanizing technology, while "Battle Royale" symbolically protests the horrific effects of an ultra-competitive educational system. Amano's wind symphony "Ohnai" is a powerful homage to the victims of Kobe's Great Hanshin earthquake of 1995. Composer Tetsunosuke Kushida is also widely respected for producing attractive works for young bands based on musical themes from traditional Japanese festivals and *gagaku* court music, as well as "Figuration for *Shakuhachi* and Band", a fascinating piece that artfully combines *shakuhachi* flute with western wind ensemble instrumentation. What should be clear from this overview is that Japanese wind band composers have produced many notable programmatic pieces in a style that fuses local and international traditions, while addressing themes at the heart of Japanese spirituality.

Analysis: Why Professional Bands in Japan?

What caused this unique development of professional wind bands, and why did it occur in Japan rather than other nations? Such questions are not easily answered through traditional historiography, but sociological theory may provide a robust foundation from which to address this matter. Shyon Baumann's theory of artistic legitimation features three essential components: (1) political opportunity structures, (2) resource mobilization, and (3) frames of discourse, each of which are quite evident as one considers the process by which wind bands came to be institutionalized in Japan (2006). As this brief discussion has outlined, Japanese bands began as a feature of militarization. Even the premier of Japan's national anthem "Kimigayo" was offered by a military band in 1870, but wind bands later became integrated into schools with the support of a music industry that was rapidly developing into the largest in world history.[2] Composers responded to this unique market by producing a new genre of original works and contest arrangements that touch at the core of Japanese spirituality during a period of rapid cultural change. The kind of music transculturation and hybridity that ensued arguably entailed an atypically egalitarian view of western music ensembles, in which wind band music was provided the opportunity to prosper as in no other nation before. Professional wind ensembles arose and flourished in this unique environment, supported by the patronage of amateur wind band musicians, who within a system of intense national competition also rose to unprecedented levels of musical achievement and enthusiastic consumption.[3]

Postlude: A Brazen Trope

The thematic framework of this essay, "alchemy of brass," may be interpreted by some readers as an overly-extended metaphor, and (hopefully) will evoke a bit of humor. Still, I would sincerely argue that this notion provides a useful mnemonic to conceptualize fundamental characteristics of the remarkable accomplishments attained by Japanese in the field of wind music. Participants in the wind music scene of Japan –

from young band students through professional composers, conductors, and even instrument makers – have strived and attained the highest levels of achievement in a quest that, like the alchemist's pursuit of gold, often resonates with profoundly spiritual undertones. European musicians may counter in jest that symphony orchestras have always been the "platinum" ensemble at the pinnacle of their art, yet the decision to take wind bands seriously has resulted in some notable successes on the part of Japanese musicians, with ramifications for other forms of art-music, jazz, and even popular music genres within contemporary Japan.

Notes

1. Toshio Mashima was interviewed by the author on December 30, 2006, and both Masamichi Amano and Isao Matsushita were interviewed on January 9, 2007.
2. Although this article is original (and necessarily succinct), much of the data on which it is based was culled from other publications. For more detailed discussion, see David G. Hebert, *Wind Bands and Cultural Identity in Japanese Schools* (Dordrecht and New York: Springer, forthcoming), and David G. Hebert "Kokusaiteki Shitendemiru Nihonno Suisougaku" (Japanese Wind Bands in International Perspective), *Japan Band Directors Association Journal* 13 (2007):35-46.
3. Ibid.

References

Baumann, Shyon. 2006. A General Theory of Artistic Legitimation: How Art Worlds are Like Social Movements. *Poetics: Journal of Empirical Research on Literature, Media and the Arts, 37.*

Blasdel, Christopher Yohmei. 1988. *The Shakuhachi: A Manual for Learning.*Tokyo: Ongakuno Tomosha.

Campbell, Patricia Shehan. 1991. *Lessons from the World: A Cross-Cultural Guide to Music Teaching and Learning.* New York: Schirmer Books.

Everett, Yayoi Uno and Frederick Lau, eds. 2004. *Locating East Asia in Western Art Music.* Middletown: Wesleyan University Press.

Flaes, Rob Boonzajer. 2000. *Brass Unbound: Secret Children of the Colonial Brass Band.* Amsterdam: Royal Tropical Institute.

Hebert, David G. 2001a. The Tokyo Kosei Wind Orchestra: A Case Study of Intercultural Music Transmission. *Journal of Research in Music Education* 49/3.

—. 2001b. Hoshina and Ito: Japanese Wind Band Composers. *Journal of Band Research* 37/1. 61-77.

—. 2005. Music Competition, Cooperation and Community: An Ethnography of a Japanese School Band. PhD diss., University of Washington.

Hiyama, Rikurou. 1990. *Gakki Sangyo: Ongaku Gakki Bijinesu Hayawakari Dokuhon*. Tokyo: Myujikku Turedosha.

Hosokawa, Shuhei. 2001. Seikaino Burasubando, Burasubandono Seikai. Kanichi Abe, Shuhei Hosokawa and Yasuko Tsukahara, eds. *Burasubando no Shakaishi*. Tokyo: Seikyusha. 55-81.

Keister, Jay. 2005. Seeking Authentic Experience: Spirituality in the Western Appropriation of Asian Music. *The World of Music* 47/3. 35-53.

Kobayashi, Tatsuya. 2000. 'It All Began with a Broken Organ': The Role of Yamaha in Japan's Music Development. B. Hans-Joachim (ed.), *'I Sing the Body Electric': Music and Technology in the 20th Century*. Hofheim: Wolke. 59-66.

Matsunobu, Koji. 2007. Japanese Spirituality and Music Practice: Art as Self-Cultivation. *International Handbook of Research in Arts Education*, ed. Liora Bresler. Dordrecht and New York: Springer. 1425-1438.

McDonald, Ron. 1989. East Meets West: The Winds of Change. *Fanfare* 13/1. 91-104.

Ortner, Sherry B. 2007. *Anthropology and Social Theory: Culture, Power, and the Acting Subject*. Durham: Duke University Press.

Osakashi Ongakudan. 2003. *Osakashi Ongakudan Hachiju Shunen Kinenshi*. Osaka: Zaidan Hojin Osakashi Kyoiku Shinko Kosha.

Palmer, Anthony. 1995. Music Education and Spirituality: A Philosophical Exploration," *Philosophy of Music Education Review* 3/2. 91.

Rissho Kosei-kai. 1966. *Rissho Kosei-kai*. Tokyo: Kosei Publishing.

Trimillos, Ricardo. 1989. Halau, Hochschule, Maystro, and Ryu: Cultural Approaches to Music Learning and Teaching. *International Journal of Music Education 14*. 32-43

Yang, Mina. 2007. East Meets West in the Concert Hall: Asians and Classical Music in the Century of Imperialism, Post-Colonialism, and Multiculturalism. *Asian Music* 38. 1-30.

CHAPTER TWENTY-ONE

SONOROUS BODIES

YANN LEBLANC

Painting gives us eyes all over. In the ear, in the stomach, in the lungs [...].

Music traverses our bodies in profound ways, putting an ear in the stomach, in the lungs, and so on. It knows all about waves and nervousness. But it involves our body, and bodies in general, in another element. It strips bodies of their inertia, of the materiality of their presence: it disembodies bodies. We can thus speak with exactitude of a sonorous body [...] (Deleuze 2007, 37-9).[1]

To all the activities mentioned by Marcel Mauss in his article about "body techniques", I wish to add listening. Just as walking or swimming, for example, listening must be considered a technique of the body, resulting from a subconscious learning in a given culture. Of course, this is something ethnomusicology has already sustained. But sounds and noises of our everyday life are also a ground for investigation that shouldn't be ignored.

Usually, our sound environment has become so familiar that we no longer pay too much attention to it. But go abroad, and the surrounding sounds become much more striking.

Visitors to Japan are often surprised by the great variety of sounds they can hear in everyday life. The Australian sound artist Philip Samartzis for example, has recently said in an interview for a French magazine (La Casa 2006, 11) that Japan was a unique place for sound experiences - mostly because of the interaction between noise and silence.[2] It is true that walking in Tokyo, even in Tokyo suburbs, will transport one in a very short time from extremely noisy areas to very peaceful places.

All the sounds, signals, music that surround one in Tokyo tend to organize the itineraries of the body, its movements. They separate or intertwine different spaces. Disorientated by all the unusual sounds that don't function as signals yet, one becomes a little more aware of the conditioning of one's sense of hearing.

Some Japanese sound artists like Sachiko M, Toshimaru Nakamura, Toshiya Tsunoda, Haco and others, seem to pursue a similar goal: as regards listening, we can assert that the will shared by all these artists is precisely to make us unlearn and forget this body technique through their performances or recordings. This is a very important point I would like to insist on - this notion of oblivion, which is present in all kinds of artistic activities.

And why would they want us to unlearn or forget our usual way of listening? To allow us to hear all the sounds without any preconceived ideas; so that our ears are no longer conditioned by dichotomies such as: musical sounds versus noises, or natural sounds versus artificial ones etc. This is why the sound artist Haco, for example, points out in an article that statements such as "a chorus of birds chirping is natural and is therefore a vibrant soundscape, the sound of ocean waves in Jamaica is healing, and the amplification of sine waves is a radical act" are stereotypes which limit our capacity to listen and to hear.[3]

Of course, such proposals are not new: Pierre Schaeffer, with his concept of "reduced listening," John Cage, and many others have tried to conceptualize a new approach to sounds. In fact, it seems this distinction between "pure", "musical" sounds and noises used to not be so important in earlier Japanese culture. Arguments can be found in literature, for example in the Kamono Chômei's essay (2003) Hojoki ("An account of my hut"), and, of course, in some forms of traditional music. I should refer here to Toru Takemitsu's excellent article *On sawari*, in which many examples and reflections on these questions can be found. The difference today is that most artists are influenced by the evolution of technology, which has transformed both the sound environment and the capacities to produce and reproduce sounds in a profound way.[4]

When reading recent Western publications on contemporary electro-acoustic music, one can't help but notice an evolution in the status of sound: terminology has kept stressing the concrete nature of sound ("sound materials," "sound objects," "sound paste"), and has eventually borrowed notions from medicine and biology ("multicellular structure," "atoms," "particules"). Sound takes shape through anatomic conceptions and representations. Does it mean that like surgeons, musicians must learn by cutting, dissecting? We will see if it is the case for the Japanese musicians I will discuss.

I often use the expression "to be all ears" to describe what happens in their performances. It refers to a special relationship to the environment as well as the body, and it should almost be understood literally. The way Toshimaru Nakamura and Sachiko M play their instruments gives a very good illustration of this process.

Toshimaru Nakamura plays with the "no input mixing-board." It is a mixing board whose input is connected to the output: what is heard is the analogical feed-back of the machine. Sachiko M plays an empty memory sampler which is very often called an "amnesic" sampler. After seeing performances of these two artists, I asked them about their background to have a better understanding of their work. Toshimaru Nakamura first played the guitar for several years. Yet he more readily evokes his experience as a sound technician and sound effects engineer. Sachiko M has done similar work for a contemporary theatre company.

When he compares his experience as a guitar player with the way he performs now, with the no-input mixing-board, Toshimaru Nakamura explains that with the guitar he HAS to play it - whereas the no-input mixing-board offers him the possibility to stand aside. Nakamura says "we are two distinct individuals...I just make the connections, I install and prepare or limit the environment and the sound comes by itself. The machine creates the music without me. It is the machine, together with the environment, which play the music."

Does this mean that the real performer is the no input mixing-board, and not Toshimaru Nakamura? In my opinion it is not the case. I think we can apply to this musician, as well as to Sachiko M and others, a remark by Peter Szendi about DJs. For this French musicologist, DJs are listeners who give concerts (Szendi 2001, 91).

Sachiko M goes even one step further - in an interview she repeated to me she was not a musician; she did not play music. She probably meant that she had no references, and was not subjected to any influence. Indeed, if we keep in mind the urban sound environment in Japan, Sachiko M's music is a territory without any codes or signals or affective echoes - far from any kind of musical intention. According to her, the relation she has with her instrument, the sampler, is very different from the one a musician manages to have after years of practice and training. Most of the time, there is some mutual shaping between the musician's body and his instrument, but Sachiko M insists on the distance there is between her equipment and herself.

Here are a few examples. Sachiko M says that she hates music shops, because the sales assistants never understand her. Her sampler is not recent: the sounds she produces with it are usually regarded as a nuisance that engineers try to eliminate. So, contrary to the most frequent method to acquire a music instrument, which means going to a shop and trying several models to see which is most appropriate for oneself, for one's body, Sachiko M has bought her sampler on the web. In addition, we can notice that she does not use the typical vocabulary to describe her activity. When most musicians associate the verb "play" with the name of their instrument ("I play the piano, the clarinet etc."), Sachiko M never says she plays the sampler. Instead of using the word "sampler", she uses a word which describes the sound produced. She says "when I play the sine wave."

Peter Szendi has written a remarkable essay about the transformations that happen to the body of musicians like Glenn Gould or Thelonious Monk when they play their instrument. His book is called Phantom Limbs of Musician Bodies (Szendi 2002). He points out how the body actually develops new connections and new ways of moving through its interaction with the instrument. It ends up giving birth to additional "phantom" limbs.

Throughout the concert, the body is led into a fiction - it is reinvented.[5] At one moment, it is no more Glenn Gould who is on the stage, but "Glenn Steinway", a kind of chimera: Glenn merges with the Steinway. At this moment, the body techniques have been forgotten by the musician, and the audience. This is why I have talked a bit earlier about the idea of oblivion in music and other arts.

With Sachiko M or Toshimaru Nakamura, there is neither such an extension of the body, nor this kind of fusion with the instruments. On the contrary: the body empties itself, so that the sounds can run through it. What is forgotten here is the way our ears function in everyday life. There is a kind of aesthetic linked to disappearance, even though the presence of the musician is still required... unless the artist decides to make a sound installation instead of performing.

Sachiko M's first sound installation was held at *Off Site*, a very small venue in Yoyogi, Tokyo. Her sampler was placed on a small table at the back of an empty room. There, visitors could hear the sounds of prepared Cds. Sachiko M paradoxically called her installation "I'm Here." When I asked her to explain the contradiction between the title and what was heard and seen, she answered: "I thought about the difference between a performance and an installation: mainly, it is the presence or the absence of the artist. I wanted visitors to get the impression I had just left the room."

The body has totally disappeared into sounds, sounds are the only traces left of the body's presence. At this point, then, "being all ears" is similar to "being all sounds".

Notes

1. translated by Daniel W. Smith.
2. I personally would not use these terms: "noise" and "silence", to speak about Japanese sound environment. The anthropologist David Le Breton says about noise that it is a "value judgment made on a stimulus". I believe the notion of silence poses the same problem. See Le Breton 2003, 114.
3. Haco, (View Masters – The Sound Collection and Observation Organization), « A report on the events in 2003: "Sound" as a Mirror (of the viewer) – "Recording", "Finding", "Capturing" Sound. » *Improvised Music from Japan 2004*, Tokyo: 65.
4. Let's remember that Toru Takemitsu considers *sawari*, a polysemious term used to qualify a certain quality of noise (sound) produced by the *biwa* or the *shamisen* and by vocal organs (for example in *"Gidayû-Bushi"*), as one of the main distinctive characters of Japanese traditional music. Talking about the practice of the *shakuhachi* as a demonstration (Takemitsu 2004, 200-1), he points out that "Japanese music poses a huge problem: one note is not enough to make music in the West [...] but in Japanese music, the point is that a single sound has *sawari*. In short, it is noise-like. Compared to western musical sound, it is extremely complex, as it contains many component sounds that are active within it." It is interesting to note that with the arrival of electronic music these "sound components" are more and more highlighted, whereas the dichotomy between "East" and "West" is less and less relevant. Sachiko M too, often creates music with just one sound. It is not a complex sound though, but a very high pitched sound which penetrates and goes through the body.
5. This idea has been developed by Gilles Deleuze and Felix Guattari who, after Antonin Artaud, have elaborated the concept of body without organs (Deleuze 2007, 34): "the body without organs does not lack organs, it simply lacks the organism, that is, this particular organization of organs. [...] In short, the body without organs is not defined by the absence of organs, nor is it defined solely by the existence of indeterminate organ; it is finally defined by the *temporary and provisional presence* of determinate organs." Also see the chapter dedicated to this theme in Deleuze and Guattari 1980, 185-204.

References

Chômei, Kamono. 2003. *La Cabane de Dix Pieds Carrés*. Lyon: Ancre et Encre.

Deleuze, Gilles. 2007. *Francis Bacon: the logic of sensation*. London: Continuum.

Deleuze, Gilles, and Felix Guattari. 1980. *Mille plateaux*. Paris : Editions de Minuit.

Haco, (View Masters – The Sound Collection and Observation Organization). 2004. A report on the events in 2003: "Sound" as a Mirror (of the viewer) – "Recording", "Finding", "Capturing" Sound. in *Improvised Music from Japan 2004*. Tokyo.

La Casa, Eric. 2006. Philip Samartzis. *Revue & Corrigée,* n° 70 (December 2006).

Le Breton, David. 2003. *Anthropologie du corps et modernité*. Paris : Presses Universitaires de France.

Mauss, Marcel. 1993. Les techniques du corps. *Sociologie et anthropologie*. Paris: Presses Universitaires de France.

Schaeffer, Pierre. 1977. *Traité des objets musicaux*. Paris : Editions du Seuil.

Szendi, Peter. 2001. *Écoute – une histoire de nos oreilles*. Paris : Editions de Minuit.

—. 2002. *Membres fantômes des corps musiciens*. Paris : Editions de Minuit.

Takemitsu, Toru. 2004. On Sawari. *Locating East Asia in Western Art Music*, ed. Everett, Yayoi Uno, and Frederick Lau. Middletown: Wesleyan University Press.

CHAPTER TWENTY-TWO

IDENTITY TACTICS OF JAPANESE COMPOSERS IN THE MULTICULTURAL U.K.[1]

YUMI HARA CAWKWELL

I have noticed that sometimes my pieces and I are perceived by British people in a manner different from that which I intend. It seems that this happens to many composers of Oriental origin. For instance, Frederick Lau (2004, 36) writes about the reception by the Western press of Chinese 'new wave' composers:

> "It is not at all clear whether it is the music or the person behind the music that is being heard. However, one thing that is clear is that the reviewers invariably emphasize the composers' ethnicity as a distinguishing feature of their music, as if this essence is readily apparent without the help of musical icons and verbal cues."

This superficial attitude seems to apply to most aspects of life for the Oriental émigré. For example, in the spring and summer of 2003, in London, Orientally-inspired fashion was very much in vogue in women's clothing, from a *kimono*-inspired collar and sleeves to an *obi* belt, from the Chinese dress and hair chopsticks to *ukiyoe* inspired prints: just about everything. But if I, as a Japanese woman, was to wear these clothes, people might think that I was doing so to emphasize my ethnic identity. And if, at the same time, I were to wear non-Japanese influenced items such as a Chinese stand-up collar, they might think that I was Chinese; or else they might believe it to be a Japanese collar. In fact, in 2000, I used a publicity photo in which I was wearing Orientally-inspired clothes designed and made in Britain and Italy, trying to make myself look like an imaginary pan-Asian in order to reflect my music: but it did not work; people thought the costume was a traditional Japanese one! Things are somewhat similar in music; when I use non-European materials people tend to assume that they are of Japanese origin.

Since I moved to London from Japan in 1993, I have encountered comments such as "*gagaku* is excellent" and "I love *Noh* (or *kabuki*) theatre music" from British musicians, scholars and music lovers, as if they expect Japanese musicians to know all about Japanese traditional art-music. When I respond to such comments by saying that we Japanese do not learn much about them at school and they are very inaccessible unless you are born into special families, such people are really surprised.[2] *Gagaku* is imperial court music and has been played exclusively by musicians from only a few families, to which common people have virtually no access.[3] *Kabuki* and *Noh* are in a similar situation. Performers are exclusively male, with very few exceptions. Japanese children may have occasional school outings to see a short production of traditional theatre and may hear some recordings of traditional music, but without much guidance. It is asserted with reason that *Gagaku* is over-promoted amongst non-Japanese. Koizumi (1977, 113-15) says *Gagaku* is regarded as the most suitable music to present to foreigners as a first example of Japanese music, although it is not representative or typical at all; rather, it is exceptional for Japanese music. He argues as follows – 1) it is instrumental music, so there is no need to understand the old Japanese language; 2) it is ensemble music, like Western orchestral music and, ultimately, 3) it is international by nature as it originated abroad (China via Korea) before flourishing in Japan.

Eppstein (1994, 4) argues that the unique case of Western music acceptance in Japan is a result of Westernization without colonization, and by free choice. He also points out that the introduction of Western music in Japan occurred largely via an education system devised to raise the cultural level of the masses, while the diffusion of Western cultural elements in colonized countries was decidedly elitist in character, operating through educational systems that were intended mainly for those select few whom the colonial government chose to favor for its own reasons. On the other hand, Japanese traditional art-music exists in a rarified world, outside that of ordinary Japanese. The training systems and aesthetics of these artistic genres are firmly attached to certain social classes in certain times, so, for ordinary Japanese, they are simply inaccessible. On the other hand, Western-derived musics are very accessible through school education and private instrumental teaching, are available for anyone who wants them, and affordable, compared to Japanese traditional instrumental tuition.[4]

Since the turn of the previous century, Western art-music has been opened up to influences from different musical traditions. For example, Debussy was deeply impressed by the Javanese gamelan, which he heard in the Paris Exposition in 1889, and wrote piano pieces which invoke its sound. Stravinsky incorporated folk songs from Latvia and Russia, as well as American jazz in his compositions. Benjamin Britten used ideas from Japanese traditional theatre in his chamber operas. Some instruments normally associated with jazz and popular music have been included in the orchestra - for example, alto and tenor saxophones in Ravel's *Bolero*. Many composers continued to incorporate such influences into their compositions throughout the twentieth and twenty-first centuries.

However, the use of non-Western traditional instruments has hardly been standard practice. Japanese composer Toru Takemitsu's *November Steps* for orchestra with *shakuhachi* and *Satsuma-biwa* in 1967, and Ravi Shankar's *First Sitar Concerto* in 1971 are relatively well-known experiments from the mid-twentieth century, but these are exceptionally successful cases. Even these successes are often questioned, as Brian Morton (1996, 194), the author of *The Blackwell Guide to Recorded Contemporary Music*, remarked on *November Steps* that "there is no doubt that the popularity of *November Steps* is due in part to a taste for musical exotica." The unfamiliar sound of the instruments themselves has a powerful impact in music and "exotic" sounds can invoke a different world too easily.

Until 2005, I had myself been using musical influences from outside Western art-music, most notably Japanese traditional folk music, which is less known in the West (but far more accessible than Japanese traditional art-music), and British contemporary dance music. But I had used only standard Western instruments in my compositions. I did not have access to Japanese traditional instruments properly until then, and I did not feel that I had enough knowledge to write a piece for them. Also, I felt that it would be very difficult to mix the sound of Japanese instruments successfully with Western orchestral instruments. As Toru Takemitsu (1981, 21), the most internationally known Japanese composer, puts it, "if I write one note for the *biwa*, a world protrudes which I do not want at all."

However, in 2005, I was approached by a British ensemble called OKEANOS to write a piece for *koto*, *sho*, oboe, clarinet and viola. The *koto* and *sho* players spent a considerable time in Japan to learn their instruments. The commission was for a performance in an established annual contemporary classical music concert series called 'The Cutting Edge' organized by the British Music Information Centre. This was the first time I had attempted to write for an ensemble including traditional Japanese instruments. In the process of writing a new piece for them, I had to visit the *sho* player and *koto* player, both British, to learn how to write for the instruments. When I visited the *sho* player, he had invited another

Japanese composer, Akiko Ogawa, who was also asked to write a piece for the same concert. From this time on, I became interested in the phenomenon of British performers of Japanese instruments who ask Japanese composers to write for Japanese instruments, although the composers themselves know nothing about these instruments.

There are a number of Japanese-born composers active in the UK such as Dai Fujikura, Fumiko Miyachi, Keiko Takano and Mai Fukasawa. Most of them were brought up with a Western music background in Japan, educated in UK universities or conservatories, and have established their careers in the UK. With increasing interest in Japanese culture, including more British performers who play Japanese traditional instruments, and the current policy of promoting multicultural arts by the funding bodies such as the Arts Council of England, composers have been asked to write for instruments which they have never seen before. Such an interesting inversion will certainly not continue to be unusual in the future.

Traditionally, Western commentators tend to identify something 'exotic' even if it is not existent. For example, Currid (1996) attempts a detailed analysis of the soundtrack *Merry Christmas Mr. Laurence,* presupposing that Sakamoto was trying to produce "Japanese-ness." However Sakamoto's own explanation (Russel & Young 2000, 178) of his intentions is:

> "I worked hard to get the right music that would make us feel a kind of nostalgia, not for a real place, or country or time, but a nostalgia for nowhere. I wanted to write music that would sound sometimes oriental for Western people and for Eastern people — something in the middle. I wanted to be in-between."

Curiously, most UK-based Japanese composers make a point of promoting their ethnicity as a sales point for their music, although most of them have exclusively studied Western art-music. It is possible that Japanese composers are taking advantage of these imaginary exotic elements. It has been noted how by scholars such as YU (2004) how Oriental composers, Chinese-American in particular, use race politics to promote themselves through. It seems as though, in the UK, Japanese composers have now begun to use exoticism as a form of self-promotion. For example, Fumiko Miyachi, who moved to the UK when she was fourteen years old, introduces herself in the third person in her short biography (bmic 2005, 44):

> "Her music draws inspiration mainly from her multi-cultural background, Japanese and European which are seemingly at odds with each other."

Akiko Ogawa, who was asked to write a piece for OKEANOS at the same time as they approached me also emphasizes her ethnicity to introduce her new piece for them (bmic 2005, 27):

> "As I grew up in Japan as a young child, I have been inherently influenced by the culture of the country musically, which may be particularly apparent in this piece."

Dai Fujikura (2007) comments in the program note for the piece written for OKEANOS that:

> "I did not dwell much on all that clichéd 'crossing-the-border', 'east-meets-west' rubbish that I see in a lot of publicity material for performances using Japanese instruments."

But immediately followed by a comment emphasizing his East-meets-West identity:

> "I was born in Japan but I spent my crucial teenage years in the UK and feel myself to be an equal mix of both cultures."

These are all curiously "self-exoticising" comments. As I mentioned earlier, it is not normally possible to be 'inherently influenced' by Japanese traditional music (although Ogawa was fortunate that her mother played *koto*), and musical cultures of ordinary Japanese and Europeans are not much different. But if we look at these comments from a different angle, they might be saying what they are expected to say: these composers are asked to write pieces including Japanese instruments by British performers after all.

But there is a danger in innocently selling false identity, and ultimately giving the wrong impression of Japanese culture and people, which maintains cultural stereotyping.

Notes

1. Part of this article originally appeared in Chapter 1 of my PhD thesis (Cawkwell 2005, 10-31).
2. Editor note: since 2002, *hogaku* is taught at public junior high schools in Japan. In many local communities outside of Tokyo, traditional Japanese culture (such as tea ceremony, flower arranging, *koto* lessons, etc.) is still quite accessible, and folk and popular musical arts which are connected with religious festivals are still strong in these communities. In fact, finding teachers of traditional arts in these areas could be easier than finding teachers of Western instruments.

3. Editor note: *gagaku* is also the music of Japanese Shinto religion, with shrines throughout Japan.
4. See Pecore (2000, 123) for the cost of Japanese traditional instrumental tuition.

References

British Music Information Centre. 2005. bmic the cutting edge 2005. London: British Music Information Centre.
—. 2007. www.bmic.co.uk
Cawkwell, Yumi H. 2005. Identity, Ethnicity and the International Music Scene: Oriental composers and Western expectations. Unpublished PhD diss., City University. 10-31.
Currid, Brian. 1996. Finally, I Reach to Africa: Ryuichi Sakamoto and Sounding Japan(ese). in John W. Treat (ed.) *Contemporary Japan and Popular Culture*. Richmond: Curzon Press, pp. 69-102.
Eppstein, Ury. 1994. *The Beginnings of Western Music in Meiji Era Japan*. New York: Edwin Mellen.
Fujikura, Dai. 2007. www.daifujikura.com
Koizumi, Fumio (1977). *Nihon no Oto* (Sound of Japan). Tokyo: Seido Sha.
Lau, Frederick. 2004. Fusion or Fission: The Paradox and Politics of Contemporary Chinese Avant-Garde Music. in Yayoi U. Everett and Frederick Lau (ed.) *Locating East Asia in Western Art Music*. Middletown: Wesleyan University Press. 22-39.
Morton, Brian. 1996. *The Blackwell Guide to Recorded Contemporary Music*. Oxford: Blackwell.
Pecore, Joanna T. 2000. Bridging Contexts, Transforming Music: the case of elementary school teacher Chihara Yoshio. *Ethnomusicology* 44 (1). 120-36.
Russell, Mark, and James Young. 2000. *Film Music: Screencraft*. Crans-Près Céligny: RotoVision.
Society of the Promotion of New Music. 2007. www.spnm.org.uk
Takemitsu, Toru. 1981. *Ongaku no Niwa: Takemitsu Toru Taidanshu* (The Garden of Music: Toru Takemitsu in Conversation). Tokyo: Shincho Sha.
Yu, Siu Wah. 2004. Two Practices Confused in One Composition: Tan Dun's Symphony 1997: Heaven, Earth, Man. in Yayoi U. Everett and Frederick Lau (ed.) *Locating East Asia in Western Art Music* Middletown: Wesleyan University Press. 57-71.

CHAPTER TWENTY-THREE

RING MY BELL: CELL PHONES
AND THE JAPANESE MUSIC MARKET[1]

NORIKO MANABE

It was January, 2007. Steve Jobs had just announced the iPhone, and the CNN headline screamed, "The iPhone is so yesterday," with clips showing the Japanese buying soda from vending machines with their cell phones (Yoon 2007). Indeed, Japan has been a leader in mobile consumer applications. It was among the first in the world to offer Internet access through mobile phones, in February 1999. A boom in wallpapers (cell-phone screen backgrounds) and ringtones quickly followed--several years before they would become popular in the United States or Europe. Similarly, consumer acceptance of 3G, or broadband services over cellular phones, was faster in Japan than in Europe or North America. As of October 2007, thanks to more affordable rates and higher speeds, 3G was used by 81% of Japan's mobile phone subscribers, compared with about a third in Italy, a quarter in Britain, and 10% in the United States.[2] Mobile downloads of music were a leading driver of the rapid Japanese adoption of 3G; in the first six months of 2007, mobile downloads comprised 17% of music industry sales and 92% of all music downloads (RIAJ).

This essay examines the consequences of the mobile Internet on the Japanese music industry and its implications for other music markets. First, I recount the history of the mobile internet and ringtones in Japan. Second, I explore the reactions of the Japanese music industry to this opportunity. Third, I describe how Japanese college students use the mobile internet for music, and how their experience differs from that of Americans.

Growth in Japanese internet

Japanese youth have been using mobile technologies since the early 1990s, when the pager was a teenager's must-have item (Okada 2005). In 1994, cell phone carriers began slashing mobile handset prices through subsidies, which led teenagers to replace pagers for phones (Kohiyama 2005). By 1998, there were 1.5 times more mobile phones per person in Japan than in the United States or United Kingdom.[3]

This high rate of ownership provided an excellent setting for the launch of i-mode, an Internet access system through cell phones, by NTT Docomo, Japan's largest carrier, in February 1999. This date coincided with Japan Railways' campaign against talking on cell phones in trains, so that emailing on i-mode provided consumers with a timely alternative (Okabe and Ito, 2005). Given that the average Tokyo resident spent two hours a day commuting on public transportation, mobile phones were more practical internet access devices than PCs. Many Japanese, especially women and children, used mobile phones as their primary internet access device. Conversely, PC ownership was lower in Japan than in the United States (Encyclopaedia Britannica).

Docomo and other carriers also offered user-friendly features, such as the ability to pay for goods through the phone bill rather than a credit card – a prime inhibitor of PC-based purchases. Furthermore, the carriers charged a commission of only 9% to content developers, *vs.* 20-30% for American and European carriers; these lower rates encouraged entrepreneurship among content developers (p.c.).[4]

Japanese carriers also subsidized handsets more heavily, which encouraged consumers to replace their handsets. As of 2006, the cost of acquiring a new customer by subsidizing handsets in Japan was $320 vs. $100 in the United States; hence, the average Japanese replaced their handsets every two years *vs.* three years in the United States and Europe. As a result, they were more up-to-date with mobile capabilities than their Western counterparts (Kazuma, p.c.).

According to J.P. Morgan, the mobile content market in Japan was six times larger in 2005 than that in the US, at about $3 billion (Kazuma, p.c.). Half of these revenues came from music, of which a third was from *chaku-uta* - ringtones sampled from the original recording, or mastertones; or *chaku-uta full* - downloads of an entire song, or full-track downloads (Mobile Contents Forum 2006).

Ringtones in Japan

Ringtones were first popularized in 1996 as users inputted ringtones into keypads with the help of guidebooks. Downloads of ringtones began to be offered by Astel Tokyo (for PHS) in 1997 and by Digital Phone Group in 1998. In 1999, Docomo added polyphonic ringtone suppliers to its official menu, and the polyphonic ringtone rage was on. The Japanese polyphonic ringtone market peaked at 116.7 billion yen ($1.1 billion) in 2004, when the U.S. and German markets were only a fifth of the size, at a little over $200 million.[5]

Chaku-uta was introduced by *au*, the mobile phone service of KDDI, Japan's second-largest carrier, in December 2002 (KDDI). These clips were originally set up as thirty-second ringtones, which users could download for 100 yen each. However, portal operators soon discovered that consumers were not using *chaku-uta* as ringtones, as they were too revealing of one's tastes (p.c.). It took over two years for the majority of Japanese to adopt *chaku-uta* as ringtones. Instead, consumers were using *chaku-uta* to listen to them with earphones while walking around, or with friends, playing them through the phone's speakers. Some consumers were downloading *chaku-uta* to keep up with the latest hits or to try out a song, as CD albums, at $25, were expensive. If they liked the song, they bought the whole song or album (p.c.).

In November 2004, KDDI launched its *chaku-uta* full service, which downloaded a full song directly to handsets for 300 yen a song. It also offered a flat rate for data packet transmission services, without which the total cost of downloading would have been prohibitive. Within thirteen months, the service had already downloaded 30 million songs and was averaging 4 to 5 million songs per month in early 2006 (KDDI). Leadership in *chaku-uta* helped KDDI to increase market share and become the first carrier in Japan - and perhaps in the world - to convert practically all its subscribers to 3G. Growth in mobile download revenues industry-wide has continued at over 40% year after year as market leader NTT Docomo started offering the service in the summer of 2006 (RIAJ).

The Japanese music market

The Japanese music market declined 25% from its peak in 1998 to the mid-2000s (RIAJ). Record company executives blamed aging demographics, as 70 percent of Japanese music buyers in the 1990s were under 30, but more importantly, they blamed the copying of CDs through minidisks and PCs from 1998 onwards, when new PC models facilitated such copying (p.c.).

This trend was helped along by the existence of a large CD rental market, with annual revenues of $3.5 billion *vs*. outright sales of CDs at $6 billion. Numbering over 3,000 stores, these stores were run by reputable nationwide chains, were conveniently located near major train stations, offered a wide selection, and charged only 280 yen to rent an album for a week. Moreover, this CD rental market was completely legal under Japanese copyright law, which invoked the first-sale doctrine for musical recordings (Nihon kompakuto disuku bideo rentaru shōgyō kumiai).

Roadblocks to downloading to PCs

On the other hand, downloading to PCs was relatively small in Japan, at only a tenth of the size of downloads to cell phones, despite high rates of broadband diffusion. One explanation was lower rates of PC ownership; as of 2006, only 58% of Japanese households owned a PC vs. 73% in the United States.[6]

In addition, record company policies inhibited downloading to PCs. They initially priced downloads of a single track on Mora, the online site run by Sony and a consortium of record companies, at 400 yen ($3.64)– an unreasonable price, compared with rental costs. It was only with iTunes' entry in August 2005 that the Japanese sites lowered their prices to 150 to 200 yen a song ($1.36 to $1.82); by that time, mobile downloads had already been firmly established (p.c.). In addition, many young people did not have credit cards necessary to use PC sites; with *chaku-uta full*, the cost was added to the phone bill.

Another major stumbling block was the lack of offerings. Despite the international success of the iPod, major record companies in Japan were at first reluctant to make their music available on iTunes Japan, supplying primarily to Mora. What music they did supply tended to be the latest J-Pop hits, which comprised the majority of Japanese popular music sales, rather than a back catalogue. Even as late as early 2007, only about eight out of the top 20 songs on the best-selling CD charts were available on iTunes Japan, causing many Japanese to consider iTunes as a source for a Western catalogue and Japanese independent releases, rather than the hottest J-Pop hits.

Nonetheless, as the iPod grew to comprise about half of the Japanese digital music player market, iTunes Japan grew in tandem to become the top download site in Japan. Slowly but surely, record companies began to provide product, with BMG Japan and Pony Canyon reaching agreements in late 2006 and Warner in June 2007 (Apple). Nonetheless, as of late 2007, Sony Music Entertainment, Japan's largest music company, was still not offering music on iTunes.

Hence, while downloads to PCs eventually became more accessible, a not-so-user-friendly history of high cost and incomplete catalogue made them less compelling as an alternative for consumers, relative to rental shops. As of 2006, P2P use was also low in Japan, with only 3.5% of PC owners using them actively. However, this number was double that of 2005, and popularity and awareness of sites such as Limewire was growing (Mobile Content Forum).

Reactions of the music industry to *chaku-uta*

Similarly, record companies took a conservative approach to *chaku-uta* at first. They had not benefited much from karaoke or polyphonic ringtones, for which royalties were only paid to the composer. On the other hand, as *chaku-uta* was sampled from recordings, portal companies were obligated to obtain rights and pay royalties to the rights holder of the master recording. Several record companies initially restricted distribution of *chaku-uta* to Label Mobile, a joint venture led by Sony and other record companies (p.c.).

One reason for the record companies' reluctance to an open policy was the fear that *chaku-uta full* would cannibalize CD sales. In fact, *chaku-uta* appeared to be stimulating sales; according to my survey of 100 Japanese college students, two-thirds had bought an album after having downloaded a mastertone or song from that album.

Indeed, total music sales, including downloads but excluding videos, started to climb over last year's sales from April 2005 onwards. In 2006, total music sales were up 1% each year, as a 56% rise in mobile downloads compensated for a 4% drop in CD sales (RIAJ). Both record companies and retailers credited *chaku-uta* for stimulating album sales (p.c.).

The impact was particularly dramatic at Avex, which, unlike other record companies, had embraced downloading early, making its music available on more mobile portals, as well as iTunes and other PC portals (p.c.). The company's focus—pop idols for young women—also corresponded to the biggest market for *chaku-uta*, and sales were helped by the *chaku-uta* boom. In 2006, 21% of Avex's revenues were from cell phone downloads (Avex). The visible success of Avex eventually spurred other record companies to adopt more open policies starting around mid-2005.

Having realized that *chaku-uta* could stimulate CD sales, record companies began using it for promotion. Record companies typically issued a *chaku-uta* a week to two months before the release of an album, using *chaku-uta* sales data to fine-tune their marketing strategy for the CD. The *chaku-uta* for Ayaka's "I Believe," for example, was made available on 128 portals to create buzz at album launch. The song debuted at #3 on the Oricon charts and saw a million downloads in six weeks. Record companies and retailers offered a free *chaku-uta* download for consumers who bought an album (p.c.).

In addition, there were recommendation engines and identification services. Upon hearing a song in a café or on television, a consumer could point the cell phone in the direction of the music, whereupon the phone would identify its name through sound-wave patterns. The consumer could then immediately download it to his/her cell phone or buy the CD on a mobile shopping site. About 30% of chaku-uta users employed these search functions, and 30 to 40% of such searches resulted in a download (KDDI, p.c.).

Impact on music composition

It is easy to postulate that *chaku-uta* had some influence on compositional practices. Downloads of choruses far outnumbered those of introductions, instrumentals, and verses, which were also available. Given this incentive, some songwriters could have been expected to highlight or enlarge choruses while reducing verses and other sections. However, as of mid-2006, Japanese songwriters disclaimed such practices because they considered alternating verses and choruses to be the most effective form for telling a story. Furthermore, as many songs were promoted as commercials, Japanese songwriters were already used to delivering hooks quickly or starting songs with the hook (p.c.). Nonetheless, *chaku-uta* was influencing what songs were developed: a song by Nakama Yukie, which started as a 30-second *chaku-uta* and commercial for KDDI, was expanded into a full-length song only when its appeal became clear through *chaku-uta* sales.

I will now discuss the impact of *chaku-uta* on the behavior of three different populations of college students.

Listening to *chaku-uta*

Between late 2006 and May 2007, surveys were conducted of 100 college students in Sapporo, a city in northern Japan; 30 students in a public university in New York City; and 40 students in a state university in Minneapolis.

These populations exhibited several similarities in their habits of listening to music and the use of ringtones. They tended to acquire music most frequently by copying a CD, either rented or borrowed from a friend, followed by buying a CD. They listened to music most often while at home or commuting, or on the go, such as shopping, waiting, or exercising. Among their favorite genres were R&B, hip-hop, and rock.

A major difference was that Japanese students tended to be heavier users of phones than Americans. Their phones had better capabilities, and more than half had 3G services *vs.* only a quarter of the Americans. While 94% of Japanese had phones with capabilities for mastertones, or sampled *chaku-uta* clips, only 68% of New Yorkers and 35% of Minnesotans did. Hence Japanese acquired more mastertones—mostly through downloads to cell phones--and changed them more frequently than Americans.

Furthermore, they were more likely to use mastertones for listening; they used minidisk players and iPods for long commutes and phones for short waiting periods. A quarter of respondents listened to their phones for more than 15 minutes a day - some as long as two hours. Eighty percent of Japanese users said that *chaku-uta* were handy for listening to just the chorus of a song. As one respondent put it, "It takes too long to listen to the whole song. I just want the hook." Many respondents also played songs for their friends through their phones. They also liked the convenience of buying a song anytime anywhere, often downloading immediately after having heard a song. They were more likely to hear a new song on a *chaku-uta* site or someone else's *chaku-uta* than on the radio.

While American students also said that they listened to music through their phones, they were lighter users of phones as a listening device. As one New Yorker put it, "I use my cell phone to listen to music only if my iPod battery dies. I have a greater selection of music on my iPod."

Americans expressing themselves through ringtones

American students seemed more forthcoming in expressing themselves through their choice of ringtones. Japanese etiquette prohibits the use of cell phones in trains and other public spaces. Hence over half of the Japanese students used vibration mode as their primary ringtone and only used *chaku-uta* at home or when out with friends.

In contrast, only a quarter of Americans used vibration or silent mode. They were also three times more likely than the Japanese to choose songs that had a personal meaning for them as ringtones. The New Yorkers in particular were conscious of projecting images through their ringtones. One student, whose ringtone was a song by the Irish punk band, The Dropkick Murphys, believed the ringtone showed his pride in his Irish heritage, while another, who used the theme from *The Godfather*, showed his love of mobster movies. Students also believed their ringtones portrayed them as "party girls," "sensitive and mellow," or "in control of myself." They also projected negative images onto others based on their ringtones: "My co-worker dresses as if she were 20 years younger. Her ringtone is reggaetón, really loud too, and it makes her look as if she wants to be young and sexy when she is really a sad old woman."

Americans were also more likely to assign ringtones to identify specific callers. As one student put it, "It says a lot when a person has a special ringtone in my phone. I usually pick a song where the lyrics or song reminds me of that person." Hence, they assigned ringtones that showed their feelings toward that person and were not shy about having others hear them; one woman used "Can't Take My Eyes Off of You" for her husband, while another used a love song for her boyfriend and "Girls Just Wanna Have Fun" for her close friends. Conversely, the lack of special ringtones was interpreted negatively; as one student put it, "My boyfriend has the same ringtone for everybody. It tells me that he's not very imaginative or competent."

PC or Phone?

Another difference was the Americans' greater use of PCs. Only a third of the Japanese students had their own PCs, while practically all American students had one. This lack of one's own PC had two impacts: first, only 26% of Japanese owned iPods *vs.* 61% of New Yorkers and 85% of Minnesotans, and the Japanese without iPods used their mobile phones more intensely as music devices. Secondly, Japanese were far less likely to download music or ringtones onto PCs. Not surprisingly, Japanese were more likely to buy CDs containing songs they had already downloaded than Americans (at 68% *vs.* 43% for Minnesotans), while Americans were more likely to have reduced CD purchases due to downloading (at 45% for Minnesotans *vs.* 11% for Japanese).

Conclusion

This study of the consumption of music provided several views on how corporate policies and the availability of technology can affect how music is heard and acquired. The Japanese mobile internet became a viable musical experience largely because the telecommunications industry provided a friendly environment for both users and entrepreneurs through low commissions, subsidized handsets, and an easy settlement system; this was in contrast to the restrictive policy of record companies toward PC downloading, which inhibited growth.

The *chaku-uta* story also demonstrates how unanticipated consumer usage of a service can redefine an industry. Originally meant as a ringtone, *chaku-uta* was detected early on as a product for listening pleasure, thus inspiring the rollout of *chaku-uta full* and a whole new world of mobile promotion.

Comparisons between Japanese and American users revealed remarkable similarities, such as the tendency to listen to music on the go, the use of multiple ringtones, and the prevalence of copying CDs. The differences between Japanese and American users stemmed from the result of the history and infrastructure of the use of technology. American respondents were more likely to own PCs, which made them more likely to own iPods and download music from the Internet. The Japanese were more likely to use mobile phones, the result of a user-friendly business environment for the mobile internet.

Nonetheless, cultural differences appeared to play a role in the social significance of ringtones. While clearly ringtones can have a highly personal meaning for both cultures, American cultural norms of more extroverted behavior likely influenced the high degree with which American students expressed themselves through ringtones (also attaching significance to other people's ringtones). Conversely, many Japanese adopted the norm of non-obtrusiveness by using vibration mode and only used audible ringtones within the confines of their homes and social groups. Further study of such cultural differences in the interpretation of ringtones may prove an interesting line of inquiry.

Acknowledgements

I thank Sumanth Gopinath and Edgar Pope for help in distributing the survey and crunching the data in Minnesota and Japan respectively; Kazuyo Katsuma of J. P. Morgan and Nathan Ramler of Macquarie for help with industry data; the executives, A&R managers, producers, and artists at Avex, Baby Mario Productions, Cultural Convenience Club, Dwango, Faith, File Records, For-side.com, Index, KDDI, MTI, Nippon Crown, Nippon Enterprise, NTT Docomo, Pony Canyon, RIAJ, Rightscale, Softbank, Sony, Sony Music, Solomon I&I Production,

Toshiba EMI, Yahoo Japan, and others who wished not to be named for their time in interviews; and my students at John Jay College and Brooklyn College, for sharing their opinions.

Notes

1. parts of this article have appeared previously in Manabe 2008a and Manabe 2008b.
2. Telecommunications Carriers Association, http://www.tca.or.jp/eng/database/daisu/yymm/0710matu.html; Forrester Research.
3. Calculated by the author from data on "World Data," *Encyclopaedia Britannica,* www.britannica.com, (accessed February 12, 2007). Specifically, there were 47.3 million cell phones for a population of 126.4 million in Japan in 1998, *vs.* 14.9 million phones for 58.3 million people in the United Kingdom and 69.2 million for 276 million people in the United States.
4. p.c. = personal communication
5. Mobile Content Forum; "Jupiter Research Projects Ring Tone Revenues to Reach $724 Million and Mobile Game Revenues to Reach $430 Million in the U.S. by 2009," 15 March, 2005,
http://www.jupitermedia.com/corporate/releases/05.03.15-newjupresearch.html (accessed 27 May, 2007); Informa, quoted in "Introduction to the German Music Market," Peter James and Rosita Kürbis (Berlin: GermanSounds AG –Music Export Germany) 139, accessible at
http://www.musicexport.at/includes/attachment.aspx?type=2&id=133&dl (accessed 27 May, 2007).
6. Internet Association Japan, *Internet Hakusho* (2006); Nielsen Media Research, quoted in ZDNet, December 21, 2006 (accessed November 20, 2007), http://blogs.zdnet.com/ITFacts/?p=12228.

References

Apple, www.apple.com. Accessed November 21, 2007.
Avex, www.avex.co.jp. Accessed February 18, 2007.
Gopinath, Sumanth. 2007. Ringtones, or the auditory logic of globalization. *First Monday* 10 (12, December 2005). http://firstmonday.org/issues/issue1012/gopinath/index.html. Accessed February 18, 2007.
International Federation of the Phonographic Industry, *Digital Music Report* (http://www.ifpi.org/content/section_resources/digital-music-report.html, Accessed January 18, 2007)
Internet Kyōkai. 2006. *Internet Hakusho* (Internet White Paper). Tokyo: Impress.

Itō, Mizuko, Daisuke Okabe, and Misa Matsuda. 2005. *Personal, Portable, Pedestrian: Mobile Phones in Japanese Life.* Cambridge: MIT Press.

KDDI, www.kddi.co.jp.

Kohiyama, Kenji. 2005. The Development of Mobile Communications in Japan. Mizuko Itō, Daisuke Okabe, and Misa Matsuda., *Personal, Portable, Pedestrian: Mobile Phones in Japanese Life.* Cambridge: MIT Press. 61-74.

Manabe, Noriko. 2008a. Going Mobile: Ringtones, the Mobile Internet, and the Music Market in Japan. In *Internationalizing Internet Studies,* ed. Gerard Goggin and Mark McLelland (New York: Routledge, 2008, forthcoming).

——. 2008b. New Technologies, Industrial Structure, and the Consumption of Music in Japan. *Asian Music* 39/1 (2008, forthcoming).

Mobile Contents Forum. 2005. Chaku-uta furu iPod (iTunes Music Store) riyôsha hikaku chôsa hôkokusho (Comparative study of *chaku-uta full* and iPod users). Tokyo: Mobile Content Forum.

——. 2006. *Keitai Hakusho 2007.* Tokyo: Impress.

——. www.mcf.to, accessed November 24, 2006.

Nihon kompakuto disuku bideo rentaru shōgyō kumiai (Japan CD-Video Rental Store Association), http://www.cdvnet.jp/, accessed February 18, 2007.

NTT Docomo, http://www.nttdocomo.co.jp.

Okabe, Daisuke and Mizuko Itō. 2005. Keitai in Public Transportation. Mizuko Itō, Daisuke Okabe, and Misa Matsuda., *Personal, Portable, Pedestrian: Mobile Phones in Japanese Life.* Cambridge: MIT Press.

Okada, Tomoyuki. 2005. Youth Culture and the Shaping of Japanese Mobile Media: Personalization and the *Keitai* Internet as Multimedia. Mizuko Itō, Daisuke Okabe, and Misa Matsuda., *Personal, Portable, Pedestrian: Mobile Phones in Japanese Life.* Cambridge: MIT Press. 41-60.

Record Industry Association of Japan, www.riaj.or.jp. Accessed November 20, 2007.

Telecommunications Carriers Association. http://www.tca.or.jp/eng/database/daisu/yymm/0612matu.html. Accessed November 21, 2007.

"World Data," *Encyclopaedia Britannica,* www.britannica.com, (accessed February 12, 2007).

Yoon, Eunice. "The iPhone is so yesterday in Asia." CNN, www.cnn.com. January 13, 2007.

APPENDIX A

PARTICIPANTS IN MUSIC OF JAPAN TODAY SYMPOSIA

Music of Japan Today 2007
(UMBC; Smithsonian, Washington DC)

Composers: Hiroyuki Itoh, Hiroyuki Yamamoto, Shirotomo Aizawa
Performer: Retsuzan Tanabe (*shakuhachi*)

Lecturers:
Alchemy of Brass: Spirituality and Wind Music in Japan
-David Hebert, Assistant Professor of Music, Boston University
Structural Integration of Television Phenomena in Joji Yuasa's "Observations on Weather Forecasts"
-Colin Holter, University of Illinois, Urbana-Champaign
Time Song II: Howling through Time
-Stacey Fraser, Assistant Professor, Northern State U., SD
Japanese Composers in the Multicultural U.K.: Identity Tactics and Self-Exoticism
-Yumi Hara Cawkwell, Lecturer, University of East London, UK
"Ma" (sense of time and space) as Compositional Tool
-Airi Yoshioka, Assistant Professor of Music, UMBC
Lecture-Recital: Flute Works of Toshio Hosokawa
-Antares Boyle, Sydney Conservatorium
Composing for Shakuhachi and 21-String Koto
-Marty Regan, U. of Hawaii, Manoa
Style and Politics in Kosaku Yamada's Folksong Arrangements, 1917-1950
-David Pacun, Assistant Professor of Music, Ithaca College
A Japanese Zero-Hour? - Postwar Music and the Re-Making of the Past
-Fuyuko Fukunaka, Lecturer, Keio U., Tokyo
"Zenshin kore mimi nari": To be all ears
-Yann Leblanc, Lumiere Lyon 2 University, Lyon, France

Modes of Listening in Tokyo's Avant-Garde Music Community
-Lorraine Plourde, Columbia University, New York, USA
Ring My Bell: Cell Phones and the Japanese Music Market
-Noriko Manabe, CUNY Graduate Center, New York, USA
Forte's Set Complex, My Superset/Subset Network: A Set-Theoretical Excursion into Takemitsu's Japanese Garden
-Hideaki Onishi, Assistant Professor of Music Theory, Yong Siew Toh Conservatory of Music, the National University of Singapore
Music in the Bathtub: Reading Takemitsu's Music Through Western Criticism
-Peter Burt, The Open University, Vienna, Austria
Beyond Tradition: Composer Toru Takemitsu and the Sound of "Sawari"
-Mitsuko Ono, Kunitachi College of Music, Tokyo
Transitions in the Piano Music of Keiko Fujiie
-Margaret Lucia, Associate Professor, Shippensburg University
A Comparison of the works for Flute, Viola, and Harp by Toru Takemitsu and Claude Debussy
-Shuri Okajima, University of Arizona, Tucson, USA
Lecture-Recital: Kongoseki\Kongoseki Variations
-John Welsh, University of Maryland College Park, USA

Works performed (* = premiere):
Aizawa: *Time of Time* for clarinet and percussion* (2007), *Deposition* for *shakuhachi* solo and ensemble* (2007), Itoh: *Salamander 1b* for solo flute (1995-2005), *out of a blaze of light* for clarinet and piano* (2007), Yamamoto: *The Wedge is Struck, the Fog Remains* for clarinet and piano* (2006), *Saxophone The Relay* for solo alto saxophone (1999), *Matsumorphosis* for solo violin (2001), *Perspectivae* for computer tape (2002), *Die Passion der Matthaus-Passion* for computer tape (2002), Shin Kawabe: *Two Etudes from Japanese Folk Tunes* for woodwind quintet (2005), Akira Miyoshi: *Reve Colorie* for 2 clarinets (1982), Yoritsune Matsudaira: *Sonatine for Flute et Clarinette* (1940), Nagako Konishi: *Dawn* for clarinet quintet (2001), Akira Nishimura: *Monologue* for solo violin (1995), Toru Takemitsu: *Rain Tree Sketch* (1982), *Rain Tree Sketch II* (1992) for solo piano, *Herbstlied* for clarinet and string quartet (1993) [Tschaikowsky; arr. by Takemitsu), Toshi Ichiyanagi: *Music for Electric Metronomes* (1962), Karen Tanaka: *Wave Mechanics II* for violin and tape (1994), Hideko Kawamoto: *Night Ascends from the Ear like a Butterfly* for computer tape (1999), Daichi Ando: *Wandering Finger* for computer tape (2001), Shintaro Imai: *Figure in Movement* for computer tape (2005), Takayuki Rai: *Labyrinth* for computer tape (2004), Naotoshi Osaka:

Shizuku no Kuzushi for violin and computer (1991), Suguru Goto: *Robotic Music* (2003), Toshio Hosokawa: *Sen I* for solo flute (1984), *Vertical Song* for solo flute (1995), *Atem-Lied* for solo bass flute (1997), Noboru Tateyama: *Kongoseki* for 2 *kotos* and voice.

Music of Japan Today 2003
(UMBC; Smithsonian, Washington DC)

Composers: Joji Yuasa, Toshi Ichiyanagi, Akira Nishimura, Tokuhide Niimi

Lecturers:
A Japanese Garden?   Western Confluences in Toru Takemitsu's "In an Autumn Garden" for Gagaku
-Ieda Bispo, Joetsu University, Nigata, JAPAN
Overtones of Progress, Undertones of Reaction: Toshiro Mayuzumi and The "Nirvana Symphony"
-Peter Burt, Vienna, AUSTRIA
Childminder of Takeda
-Yumi Hara Cawkwell, City University, London, ENGLAND
Globalism, Fetishization, and the Politics of Japanese Rap
-Fuyuko Fukunaka, New York University, NY, NY
Ichiyanagi as Japanese Composer, and Fluxus
-Luciana Galliano, Universita Foscari di Venezia, ITALY
Cage, Ichiyanagi, Fluxus, Japan: Responses and Resonances
-Rob Haskins, Eastman School of Music, Rochester, NY
Dream, Japanese Gardern and Toru Takemitsu: Large-Scale Structure of Dream/Window through Set-Class Analysis
-Hideaki Onishi, University of Washington, Seattle, WA
Stylistic Counterpoint in the Early Music of Yamada Kosaku
-David Pacun, Ithaca College, Ithaca, NY
Tsugaru Shamisen's Latest Boom: Folk Revival or Pop Sensation?
-Michael Peluse, Wesleyan University, Middletown, CT
Oppositional Dialectics in Joji Yuasa's "The Sea Darkens"
-Kristian Twombly, UMBC, Baltimore, MD

Lecture/Recitalists:

Search for Identity: Postmodern Trends in Japanese Piano Music Since 1985
-Akiko Fukuda, piano (University of Kansas)

Marimba Music of Japanese Composers
-Greg Giannascoli, marimba - Chiu-Tze Lin, piano (Rutgers University)
The Cosmic Metaphor of Toru Takemitsu's "Rain Tree Sketches"
-Tomoko Isshiki, piano (University of Houston)
Harpsichord Music by Japanese Composers
-Calvert Johnson, harpsichord (Agnes Scott College)
Recent Piano Works by Japanese Women Composers
-Margaret Lucia, piano (Shippensburg University)
Piano/Violin Duo Works of Toshi Ichiyanagi
-Yoojin Oh, piano - Olivier Fluchaire, violin (Manhattan School of Music)
"Jiutamai" Dance and Piano
-Chie Sato Roden, piano; Junko Tano, dancer

Masterclasses:

Reiko Manabe, flute (University of California, San Diego) Yuasa *Domains*
Greg Giannascoli, marimba (Rutgers University)
Ichiyanagi *Paginini Personal*; Niimi *For Marimba I*
Akiko Fukuda, piano (University of Kansas) - Nishimura *Tritrope*

Works performed (* = premiere):
Ichiyanagi: *Cloud Atlas X – Cloud in Space* for solo piano (1999),
Cosmic Harmony for cello and piano (1995), *Paganini Personal* for solo
marimba (1982), *The Source* for solo marimba (1989), *Music for Electric
Metronomes* (1968), *Music for Piano No. 7* (1961), *Interrelation* for violin
and piano (1998), Yuasa: *Cosmos Haptic II* for solo piano (1986),
Terms of Temporal Detailing for solo bass flute (1989), *A Winter Day:
Homage to Basho* for fl, cl, hp, perc., and piano (1981), *Icon on the Source
of White Noise* for tape (1967), *The Sea Darkens* for tape (1987), *Eye on
Genesis I* for UPIC (1991), *Calling Together* (1973), *Observations on
Weather Forecasts* for trumpet and baritone voice (1983), *Territory* for fl,
cl, marimba, and bass (1977), *Mutterings* for solo voice and ensemble
(1988), Nishimura: *Madoromi III* for clarinet and piano* (2003),
Organums for vln, fl, cl, vibraphone and piano (1989), *Tritrope* for solo
piano (1978), *Duologue* for timpani and piano (1996), Niimi:
Ohju for solo cello (1987), *The Soul Bird* for flute and piano (1996),
Madrigal II for mixed choir (1981), *Lux Originis* for vln, cl, vcl, and piano
(2002), *For Marimba* (1975), Makiko Asaoka: *Four Pieces for
Harpsichord* (1994), Isaac Nagao: *Ancient Cities* for solo harpsichord
(1986), Karen Tanaka: *Jardin des Herbes* for solo harpsichord (1989),
Asako Hirabayashi: *Sonatina for Harpsichord* (2002), Takayuki Rai: *Pain*

for Two Computers (1983), Mamoru Fujieda: *Patterns of Plants* for tape (1995), Steven Kazuo Takasugi: *Vers une miopie musicale: III. Iridescent Uncertainty* for tape (1999), Yukiko Ito: *two-sides* for tape (2002), Takashi Yoshimatsu: *Pleiades Dances* for solo piano (1986-2001), Toru Takemitsu: *Toward the Sea* for flute and guitar (1981), Junko Mori: *Imagery* for solo piano (1987), Nagako Konishi: *Fantasy for Piano* (1995-6), Keiko Fujiie: *Pas de Deux II, Op. 14* for solo piano (1989)

Asian Music in America (1999)
(Hamilton College; Syracuse Society for New Music)

Composers: Toshimitsu Tanaka, Bun-Ching Lam, P.Q. Phan

Lecturers:
Cross-cultural Syntheses of East Asian and Western Musical Resources in Post-1945 Art Music: Analytical Paradigms and Taxonomy
Yayoi Uno, Assistant Professor of Music, U. of Colorado at Boulder
An Examination of Intercultural Borrowing in Contemporary Southeast Asian Theatre
-Craig Latrell, Visiting Assistant Professor of Theater, Hamilton College
Lecture-Recital: Contrapuntal Harmonic Singing in Original Works
-Stuart Hinds, Houston, Texas
Towards a Global Music: the "Universal Egg" and Toru Takemitsu's "November Steps"
-JoAnn Koh, Assistant Professor of Music, Depauw University
Contemporary Chinese Music and the Harpsichord
-Joyce Lindorff, Associate Professor of Keyboard Studies, Temple U.

Concert: Khac Chi (traditional Vietnamese music)

Works performed:
Tanaka: *Two Movements* for marimba (1980), *Sonate pour Violon et Piano, Op. 1** (1957), Phan: *My Language* for clarinet and piano (1995), *Rough Trax* for oboe and alto saxophone (1995), *Life in Necropolis* for orchestra* (1999), Lam: *Four Beckett Songs* for soprano, violin, clarinet and percussion (1980), *Run* for pipa (1993), Zhou Long: *Wu Ji* for zheng, piano, and percussion (1991), Richard Tsang: *Images of Bells – Improvisations on a Two-Note Theme* for solo harpsichord (1979)

Music of Japan Today: Tradition and Innovation III (1997)
(Hamilton College; Syracuse Society for New Music)

Composers: (Toshiro Mayuzumi), Masao Endo, Harue Kunieda, P.Q. Phan

Lecturers:
Analysis of Takemitsu's Compositions for Piano and Violin or Cello
-Nobuko Amemiya, University of Kansas
Symmetry and Large-Scale Continuity in Toru Takemitsu's "November Steps"
-Hing-yan Chan, Hong Kong
Reconciling Past and Present: Contemporary Art Music of Israel and Japan
-Robert Fleisher, Professor of Music, Northern Illinois University
Innovation Derived from Instrumental Constraints
-Hiroko Ito, Harvard University
Temporal Proportions in Toru Takemitsu's "Requiem for Strings" (1957) and Some Techniques of Film Music Scoring
-JoAnn Hwee Been Koh, Boston University
Cello Technique for Representation of Traditional Japanese Instruments
-Hugh Livingston, University of California, San Diego
Music from the Right: The Politics of Toshiro Mayuzumi's "Essay for String Orchestra"
-Steven Nuss, Assistant Professor of Music, Colby College
Crystallization of East and West ("Poeme Lyrique II" of Chen Qigang)
-Nancy Yunhwa Rao, Assistant Professor of Music, Rutgers University
Film Music of Japan: Godzilla and His Spawn
-Michael Schelle, Professor of Music, Butler University
The Contemporary Symphony in Japan
-Preston Stedman, Professor of Music, California State University, Fullerton
Influence of Western Music from the Meiji Era Through World War II: An Historical Survey through Western-Style Piano Music
-Shuko Watanabe, Lecturer in Music, Washington and Lee University

Lecture-Recitalists:
Transcending Traditional Cultural Concepts in Toru Takemitsu's "Voice" for Solo Flutist
- Asako Arai, Naucalpan, Mexico
Streams of Sound: The Piano Music of Toru Takemitsu

-Junko Ueno Garrett, Rice University
The Marimba Compositions of Keiko Abe
-G.W. Schaefer, Assistant Professor of Music, University of Wisconsin, Oshkosh

Mini Concert Performers:
Takemitsu *Uninterrupted Rests* - piano - Nobuko Amemiya, U. of Kansas
Takemitsu *Rain Tree Sketch II* - piano - Junko Ueno Garrett, Rice U.
Takemitsu *Rain Tree Sketch II* - piano - Mari Kushida, U. of Illinois
Ryo Noda *Mai* - alto saxophone - Claudia Schaetzle, Bowling Green State University
Mayuzumi *Bunraku* - cello - Christopher Stenstrom, Bowling Green State University
Takemitsu *Itinerant in Memory of Isamu Noguchi* - flute - Elda Tate, Northern Michigan U.
Takemitsu *Uninterrupted Rests* - piano - Shuko Watanabe, Roanoke, VA

Works performed (* = premiere):
Mayuzumi: *Pieces for Prepared Piano and Strings* (1961), *Bunraku* for solo cello (1962), Phan: *Enlightenment Concerto* for percussion and mixed ensemble (1994), Kunieda: *Reflection III for Orchestra** (1997), Endo: *Pandora's Box* for solo piano (1995), Toru Takemitsu: *Voice* for solo flute (1971), Yuasa: *Calling Together* (1973)

Music of Japan Today: Tradition and Innovation II (1994) (Hamilton College)

Composers: Masao Honma, Isao Matsushita, Richard Tsang
Performer: Mari Akagi (piano)

Lecturers:
Ithaca College Percussion Ensemble – Time, Space and Texture in the Music of Takemitsu
-Todd Caschetta, Ithaca College
Minoru Miki: Conservative Contemporary or Progressive Traditionalist?
-Edward Smaldone, Queens College, CUNY
The Aesthetic Principals of hana, yugen, and jo-ha-kyu as the apply to the vocal production and rhythmic structures of the music of Noh
-Gerald Large, Hamilton College
Japanese Flute Music: An Extended Tradition
-Elda Tate, Northern Michigan University

Japanese Inspiration and Influences in My Music (1970-93)
-Jackson Hill, Bucknell University
*Solo Piano Works of Masao Honma: Searching for the Japanese
    Sensitivity*
-Shuko Watanabe, Washington and Lee University
*Time in 20-Century Japanese Music: A Zen Approach to Fukushima's
    "Requiem"*
-Kristin Taavola, Eastman School of Music, University of Rochester
Geza Music of Kabuki: Scenic Design Through Music
-Deborah How, University of Southern California

Works performed (* = premiere):
Honma: *Junction III* for clarinet and piano (1990), *Three Movements for
Piano and Orchestra** (1994), Matsushita: *Kochi (East Wind)* for clarinet
and tape (1983), *Go-Un: Five Buddhistic Aphorisms* for chamber
ensemble (1985), Tsang: *Emergence* for vln, vcl, and piano (1983), *Echo
Mime* for clarinet and tape (1992)

Music of Japan Today: Tradition and Innovation (1992)
(Hamilton College)

Guest Composers: Joji Yuasa, Tokuhide Niimi, Masataka Matsuo

Lecturers:
*Japanese and Western Confluences of Large-Scale Pitch Organization in
    Takemitsu's "November Steps" and "Autumn"*
-Edward Smaldone, Queens College, CUNY
*Synthesis of Traditional Elements in Western-style Solo Piano Works by
    Japanese Contemporary Composers*
-Shuko Watanabe, Washington & Lee University
*Looking Forward, Looking Back: Influences of the Togaku Tradition in
    the Music of Toru Takemitsu*
-Steven Nuss, City University of New York
Tradition-Innovation in Japanese Flute Music: Lecture-Recital
-Elda Tate, Northern Michigan University
Nihonjinron
-Gregory Shepherd, Kauai College, Lihue, Hawaii
*Joji Yuasa and the Jikken Kobo: Conceptions of Cosmos Reflected in
    "Cosmos Haptic"*
-Kazuko Tanosaki, Hamilton College, Clinton, NY

Akira Nishimura's "Concerto for 20-String Koto and Strings"
-E. Michael Richards, Hamilton College, Clinton, NY
Japanese and Western Confluence in the Development of Japanese Children's Music in the Meiji Period (1868-1912)
-Takako Matsuura, Ithaca College School of Music
Toru Takemitsu's "Garden Rain" for Brass Ensemble
-Bruce Reiprich, Wilkes University

Works performed (* = premiere):
Yuasa: *Observations on Weather Forecasts* for trumpet and baritone (1983), *My Blue Sky No. 3* for solo violin (1977), *Calling Together* (1973), *Cosmos Haptic* for solo piano (1957), Niimi: *Kazane* for clarinet, violin, and cello (1989), Matsuo: *Hirai* V for Clarinet, Piano and Orchestra* (1992)

DISCOGRAPHY

See http://userpages.umbc.edu/~emrich/mfj2007.htm for updated information and sound clips.

Chapter One

Hiroyuki Itoh – *Salamander - **Living in Fire***, Einstein Records 014 (John Fonville)

Hiroyuki Itoh – *Mirror I for twelve players* – ***Swaying time, Trembling time***, MusicScape MSCD-0019 (Nieuw Ensemble)

Chapter Two

Hiroyuki Itoh – *String Quartet* - ***Swaying time, Trembling time***, MusicScape MSCD-0019 (Arditti String Quartet)

Chapter Three

Hiroyuki Yamamoto – *Noli me tangere* – ***Canticum Tremulum***, Fontec FOCD- 2555 (Ensemble Contemporain Montreal)

See http://sp2.cc.iwate-u.ac.jp/~hiroy/ for score and sound clip downloads of many of Yamamoto's works

Chapter Twelve and Chapter Fourteen

See http://martyregan.com/ for scores and sound files

Chapter Thirteen

See:
http://www.cduniverse.com/productinfo.asp?pid=7222045&style=class ical for sound clip and CD purchase information for Hosokawa's *Atem-Lied*

See:

http://www.cduniverse.com/productinfo.asp?pid=6740617&cart=6837
92774&style=classical - for sound clip and CD purchase information
for Hosokawa's *Vertical Song I*

See http://www.podbean.com/podcast-detail-episode/164890/toru-takemitsu-voice-for-solo-flute - for sound clip and CD purchase information for
Takemitsu's *Voice*

Chapter Seventeen

Joji Yuasa – *Cosmos Haptic II: Transfiguration* for solo piano, Nine
Winds NWCD-0188 (Kazuko Tanosaki)

Chapter Eighteen

Masataka Matsuo – *Distraction* for clarinet and piano, Nine Winds
NWCD-0188 (Tanosaki-Richards Duo)

Akira Nishimura – *Aquatic Aura* for clarinet and piano, Fontec FOCD-2540 (Itakura/Kimura)

Akira Nishimura – *Meditation on the Melody of Gagaku "Kotoriso,"*
Fontec FOCD-2540 (Das Klarinettenduo/Miki)

Tokuhide Niimi – *Fairy Ring* for clarinet and piano, Camerata 28CM-657
(Itakura/Nakagawa)

Chapter Nineteen

Toshiro Mayuzumi - *Campanology* and music of Shintaro Imai:
http://homepage2.nifty.com/paganmusik/omega/foreign.html

Makoto Moroi – *Shosange*, and music of Minao Shibata
http://www.mimaroglumusicsales.com/artists/minao+shibata.html

Atau Tanaka - http://www.xmira.com/atau/

Takayuki Rai
http://www.mimaroglumusicsales.com/artists/takayuki+rai.html

Shintaro Imai http://homepage.mac.com/shintaro_imai/

Naotoshi Osaka http://www.srl.im.dendai.ac.jp/people/osaka/

Hiroyuki Yamamoto – *Perspectivae*, **Tempus Novum XIII on the** Disc,
Tempus Novum Tempus-001 - http://www.netlaputa.ne.jp/~hyama/

—. *Die Passion der Matthaus-Passion* (same CD as above)

Hideko Kawamoto http://homepage.mac.com/hk0008/

Suguru Goto http://suguru.goto.free.fr/

Chapter Twenty

See http://www.timreynish.com/japan.htm and
   http://catalog.bravomusicinc.com/ for information on music and
   recordings by Japanese composers for wind bands

Chapter Twenty-One

See http://www.japanimprov.com/sachikom/ for discography of Sachiko
   M and her work with Toshiya Tsunoda
See http://www.scaruffi.com/avant/tsunoda.html -
   http://sonomu.net/artist/~toshiyatsunoda/ -
   http://www.sirr-ecords.com/cat/012tsunoda.html -
   http://www.hapna.com/H24.html -
   and http://www.forcedexposure.com/artists/tsunoda.toshiya.html
   for recordings of Toshiya Tsunoda
See http://www.last.fm/music/Haco   for recordings and a sound clip of
   Haco

Chapter Twenty-Two

See   http://www.uel.ac.uk/ssmcs/staff/yumicawkwell/research_publ.htm
   for information about the music of Yumi Hara Cawkwell
See http://www.daifujikura.com/ for information about the music of Dai
   Fujikura
See http://www.fumikomiyachi.com/ for information about the music of
   Fumiko Miyachi and
   http://www.spnm.org.uk/?page=shortlist/composer.html&id=211 for a
   score excerpt
See http://www.spnm.org.uk/?id=248&page=shortlist/composer.html for
   information about the music of Keiko Takano, including excerpts of a
   score, and a video interview
See http://www.spnm.org.uk/?page=shortlist/composer.html&id=252 for
   information about the music of Mai Fukasawa, including a score
   excerpt and mp3, and http://www.salon-de-ronsard.com/ for a list of
   her works

CONTRIBUTORS

Shirotomo Aizawa – Composer and Conductor; winner of *Ataka Prize*, and composition prize from National Theater in Japan; undergraduate and graduate degrees from Tokyo National University of Fine Arts and Music.

Antares Boyle – Flutist; M.Mus. from Sydney Conservatorium; prizes at Gisborne International Music Competition (New Zealand), MTNA Young Artist (US); freelance performer in Los Angeles.

Peter Burt – Associate Lecturer for the British Open University, Vienna; author of *The Music of Toru Takemitsu* (Cambridge University Press, 2001), which has been subsequently translated into Italian and Japanese; Guest Editor of Takemitsu Memorial Edition in *Contemporary Music Review* (2002).

Yumi Hara Cawkwell – Composer and Performer (Vocal); Lecturer in Music at University of East London, UK; psychiatrist for 8 years in Japan; Ph.D. in music composition at City University; finalist for British Composer Awards 2006.

Stacey Fraser – Assistant Professor of Music, California State University, San Bernardino; critically acclaimed performances as a soprano with San Diego Opera, Vancouver Symphony, and at Tanglewood.

Fuyuko Fukunaka – Lecturer at Keio University, Tokyo; Ph.D. in musicology from NY University; numerous articles in English, Japanese on 20th and 21st century music including in *Contemporary Opera at the Millennium* (U. of Illinois Press).

David Hebert – Music Educator and Ethnomusicologist; Professor of Music, Sibelius Academy, Finland from Fall 2008; author of *Wind Bands and Cultural Identity in Japanese Schools* (Springer); former faculty at Boston University, Moscow State University, Tokyo Gakugei University, Te Wananga O Aotearoa.

Colin Holter – Composer; Ph.D. student at University of Minnesota; M.Mus. University of Illinois.

Hiroyuki Itoh – Composer; winner of *Akutagawa Award*, first prize at *Nuove Sincronie International Composition Competition*, *Stipendienpreis* at *Darmstadt Ferienkurse*; Ph.D. in music composition from University of California, San Diego; performances by major ensembles and at festivals in Europe and Japan.

Yann Leblanc – Masters 2 "Ingéniere des échanges interculturels," Paris 3 Sorbonne Nouvelle University; Yokohama French Institute; Master 1 in Psychology, Master 1 in Anthropology, Lyon2 University, France.

Hugh Livingston – Cellist, Composer, Sound Installation Artist; extensive research in China on contemporary and historical music (Asian Cultural Council grant); member-director of Mapa Mundi, The Orbis Factor, and The Seven Saties in California.

Noriko Manabe – Ph.D. student in ethnomusicology and music theory, CUNY Graduate Center; articles in *Ethnomusicology*, in edited volume *Interpretare Mozart*, and in *Internationalizing the Internet* (Routledge, 2008).

Hideaki Onishi – Assistant Professor of Music Theory, Yong Siew Toh Conservatory of Music, National University of Singapore; Ph.D. University of Washington, Seattle.

Mitsuko Ono – Musicologist; educated at Kunitachi Conservatory of Music, Tokyo; extensive biographic research of Takemitsu; Editor for *Takemitsu Chosaku-shu*, Complete Takemitsu Edition (*Shogakukan*).

David Pacun – Associate Professor of Music Theory, Ithaca College; article on Kosaku Yamada in *American Music*; other articles in *The American Brahms Society Newsletter*, *Journal of Music Theory Pedagogy*.

Marty Regan – Composer and Ethnomusicologist; Assistant Professor of Music, Texas A&M University; English translator of Minoru Miki's text *Composing for Japanese Instruments* (U. of Rochester Press, 2008); several compositions recorded on commercial labels in Japan.

E. Michael Richards – Clarinetist/Conductor; Associate Professor of Music, UMBC; monograph *The Clarinet of the Twenty-First Century*; most recent article in *Proceedings of 2007 International Woodwind Colloquium*, U. of Edinburgh Press; Japan-US Creative Artist Exchange Fellow; recordings (clarinet) on Nine Winds, CRI, Opus One, New World.

Kazuko Tanosaki – Pianist; Director of Post-Baccalaureate Certificate Program in Music, UMBC; DMA Eastman School of Music; recordings for Nine Winds, CRI, Opus One; articles in *Ongaku Geijutsu, Ongaku no Tomo*; Winner of Young Artist Competition, La Jolla, California.

Hiroyuki Yamamoto – Composer; winner of *Akutagawa Award, Toru Takemitsu Composition Award, JSCM Composition Award*; performances by numerous European, North American and Asian ensembles; faculty at Iwate University, Morioka, Japan.

Airi Yoshioka – Violinist; Assistant Professor of Music, UMBC; DMA from Juilliard School; founding member of *Damocles Trio* and *Modigliani Quartet*; performs with *Continuum, ModernWorks, Son Sonora, Azure*.

INDEX